LONG WAY HOME

CURRENCY PRESS
The performing arts publisher

CURRENCY PLAYS

First published in 2025
by Currency Press Pty Ltd,
Gadigal Land, Suite 310, 46–56 Kippax Street, Surry Hills, NSW 2010, Australia
enquiries@currency.com.au
www.currency.com.au

Copyright: *Introduction: Sowing Sites of Return* © Suzy Wrong; *The Village* © Tasnim Hossain; *Looking for Alibrandi* © Vidya Rajan; *Malacañang Made Us* © Jordan Shea; [all 2025].

COPYING FOR EDUCATIONAL PURPOSES

The Australian *Copyright Act 1968* [Act] allows a maximum of one chapter or 10% of this book, whichever is the greater, to be copied by any educational institution for its educational purposes provided that that educational institution [or the body that administers it] has given a remuneration notice to Copyright Agency [CA] under the Act.

For details of the CA licence for educational institutions contact CA, 12 / 66 Goulburn Street, Sydney, NSW, 2000; tel: within Australia 1800 066 844 toll free; outside Australia 61 2 9394 7600; fax: 61 2 9394 7601; email: memberservices@copyright.com.au

COPYING FOR OTHER PURPOSES

Except as permitted under the Act, for example a fair dealing for the purposes of study, research, criticism or review, no part of this book may be reproduced, stored in a retrieval system, or transmitted in any form or by any means without prior written permission. All enquiries should be made to the publisher at the address above.

No part of this book may be used or reproduced in any manner for the purpose of training artificial intelligence technologies or systems without the express written permission of the author and the publisher.

Any performance or public reading of any play within this collection is forbidden unless a licence has been received from the author or the author's agent. The purchase of this book in no way gives the purchaser the right to perform any of these plays in public, whether by means of a staged production or a reading. All applications for public performance should be addressed to the author/s c/— Currency Press.

Typeset by Brighton Gray for Currency Press.
Cover design by Katherine Zhang for Currency Press.

Currency Press acknowledges the Traditional Owners of the Country on which we live and work. We pay our respects to all Aboriginal and Torres Strait Islander Elders, past and present.

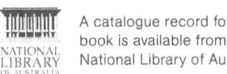

A catalogue record for this book is available from the National Library of Australia

Contents

Introduction: Sowing Sites of Return   v
   Suzy Wrong

LONG WAY HOME

   The Village   1
      Tasnim Hossain

   Looking for Alibrandi   65
      Vidya Rajan based on the book by Melina Marchetta

   Malacañang Made Us   177
      Jordan Shea

Introduction:
Sowing Sites of Return

For as long as these lands have been called Australia, we were persuaded to fear our own difference. Assimilation was cast as a fragile raft, the only vessel by which we might float upon hostile waters. The white man enthroned himself as sovereign, demanding we surrender our memories, our tongues, our ways of seeing. To mimic him was to survive; to vanish into his singular vision was to find protection.

But decades eroded this façade. The white man's vision was never sanctuary, only mirage. That monolith of performative uniformity was nothing more than a prison—one that could not silence the hum of histories refusing to die. Our forced submission built his machine, pushed his project forward, yet left us always outside, forever the labour, never the inheritors. The truth is plain now: the promise of belonging was a weapon, not a gift.

We began to assert authorship of our own narratives, peeling back layers of artifice like old skin, searching for shards of truth to stitch into something that might resemble authenticity. To live under colonisation is to walk in muddled waters, where the currents of past, present, and future swirl without mercy. Yet modernity calls on us to respect every tide, to honour the ancestors behind us, to confront the turbulence of now, and to imagine shores not yet reached.

The endeavour of reconstructing 'post'-colonial identity is never simple, often messy, sometimes uncertain. Yet it has emerged as a crucial methodology of artistic practice, one that interrogates our position within inherited structures while simultaneously reshaping the cultural field in which we operate, bending the world so that it might, finally, begin to bend toward us. The work of reimagination is both a rebellion and a remembrance. It demands that we hold history close enough to feel its pulse, but not so tight that we cannot breathe into something new.

To create from such a place is to stand in contradiction, and yet that is precisely where vitality lives. Art born of migration and displacement holds within it the ache of two worlds—one left behind, one never fully attained. In that liminal space between departure and arrival, between loss and renewal, a new language of being begins to form. We learn to speak in multiplicity, to hold conflicting truths at once, to claim beauty from fracture. Each act of creation becomes a small reclamation, a way of saying that we are still here, and that presence itself can be an act of resistance.

Tasnim Hossain, Vidya Rajan, and Jordan Shea step into the work of reconstitution with courage and clarity, not only reshaping our sense of theatre but reimagining how we walk and speak upon these lands as guests striving for belonging while honouring the unbroken custodianship of First Nations peoples. Their work sits within a continuum of stories that challenge colonial frameworks of representation, reclaiming theatre as a space where our languages, gestures, and truths can stand unmediated.

Their stories are rooted in Dharug, Gadigal, and Meanjin Country, where young protagonists listen to the echoes of ancestry to make sense of their own unsettled present. From those reckonings emerge visions of tomorrow, futures that shed the weight of colonial falsehoods and turn instead toward what is honest and just, equitable and true. Through these works, the stage becomes a site of return—not to a singular homeland, but to a diasporic sense of self that is, by nature, both dispersed and deeply rooted. For us, 'belonging' relates to notions of place that are simultaneously physical and metaphysical.

Like their playwrights, the characters in this triptych of tales belong to a generation newly stirred by purpose. They reach toward callings in music, medicine, law, and politics, giving form to the hopes once carried across seas by their parents and forebears. Those first journeys were acts of survival, yet beneath every crossing lingered a quiet wish that life might unfold more gently for the ones who followed. The young inherit not only memory but the unfinished labour of liberation. They build upon foundations laid by those who could only dream, carrying forward a longing that is both weight and inheritance.

In these three works, a curious symmetry emerges, each tracing the lineage between father and child. In Hossain's *The Village*, Jay walks the same road as Dr Sharma, learning to heal as his father once did. In Rajan's rendering of *Looking for Alibrandi*, Melina Marchetta's seminal 1992 novel, Josie moves toward the world of law, guided by Michael's steady presence and the quiet reconciliation of their intertwined identities. And in Shea's *Malacañang Made Us*, Leo rises, almost unwittingly, to lead a protest, as though his father's silenced fervour and hidden past in activism has found a new voice within him.

Together, these stories sing of lineage and longing, of how dreams travel quietly through blood and memory until they find, in the next generation, their chance to live again. It is natural that we begin to ask what legacy means in these stories and in our own shared lives. We inherit the legacies of those who journeyed before us, of parents who planted hope in foreign soil, and we watch as a new generation begins to forge its own. Their task is both beautiful and heavy, to shape a world that no longer excludes, to claim spaces where voices like ours can be heard with dignity and force.

Ours is a history of resilience turned into vision. Though the daily grind may swallow thought of legacy, though survival often feels like the only goal, the truth remains that every act of endurance becomes a seed for tomorrow. Even in an economy that romanticises struggle, we keep building. And in doing so, we honour all who came before, transforming their dreams into our living proof. What began as persistence has become continuity—a quiet inheritance of will and imagination passed down through generations, carried in our gestures, our choices, our art.

It is this intergenerational current that animates each of these plays. The contrasts between elders and youth are striking yet tender, revealing how resilience evolves into renewal. Elders bear the bruised sweetness of survival, fruit ripened and rotted by the same sun, while the young reach for untested meanings, yearning to plant something untethered, something that might grow more dignified. Their stories unfold not in opposition but in continuation, revealing the delicate balance between gratitude and revolt that defines every act of becoming.

These are dramas born of friction but not of enmity. In these homes, there are no villains. The white man, once omnipresent, is now spectral, an echo outside the door, a faint vibration in the walls. Inside, new visions are conjured, unbound and luminous, free to shape their own horizon. The conceptual absence of the coloniser does not erase his shadow, but it allows the stage to breathe again. It allows our people to exist in fullness, to love, to falter, to argue, to dream without explanation.

The theatre, in this sense, becomes a mirror and a map. It reflects who we have been, but also points toward who we might yet become. Every gesture, every word spoken under the lights, carries the charge of centuries. It is a conversation between ghosts and descendants, between silence and expression, between the colonial archive and the living, breathing body. To perform is to reclaim the right to visibility; to write is to refuse erasure.

It has taken us many years to arrive. The long road home can feel endless, as though the horizon keeps receding, as though struggle itself is a story without a final page. Yet within the linearity of time lies infinite circularity. To embrace this notion of temporality is to understand that what once bound us in chains of subjugation, exclusion and injustice can begin to loosen its grip. The present can therefore be seen differently, not as a pause before completion but as a day already whole. We learn to stand in our fullness, no longer haunted by lack.

And perhaps this is the quiet triumph of these plays—their ability to remind us that belonging is not a destination but a practice. It is built slowly, through art, through memory, through love that persists even when the world remains unkind. It lives in the rhythms of language reclaimed, in the gestures of care passed between generations, in the courage to speak truth without apology.

These playwrights show us that the work of decolonisation is not solely about dismantling the old, but about imagining what might take its place. Their characters do not merely resist; they create. They take the fragments of displacement and make from them a new kind of wholeness, one that honours where they come from while daring to dream beyond it.

In witnessing their art, we are reminded that identity is not fixed, that culture is not static, that history itself is porous. The act of storytelling becomes a sacred ritual through which we recover what was almost lost, and make visible what was once denied. It is both mourning and celebration, both reckoning and renewal.

We stand now at a threshold, aware of the distance still to travel, but also of the ground already reclaimed. The journey toward a decolonised imagination continues, not in grand declarations, but in the quiet persistence of creation. In every stage lit with truth, in every line that dares to speak what once could not be said, there is freedom.

And so, the stories of Hossain, Rajan, and Shea do more than entertain. They form a constellation of voices mapping a future where the descendants of migrants and the custodians of this land might dream together. They remind us that art, at its most powerful, is not a mirror held to the past, but a light cast forward, illuminating paths we have yet to walk.

To create, to write, to perform—all of it is an act of faith. It is a way of saying that the story is not over, that we have not disappeared, that our voices still carry across the waters. The horizon, once a line of exile, becomes a promise. And on these lands, long renamed yet never forgotten, we continue to speak, to build, to belong.

Suzy Wrong

Suzy Wrong is a radio broadcaster, podcaster, and actor, but she's best known for her incisive theatre criticism on her iconic website Suzy Goes See.

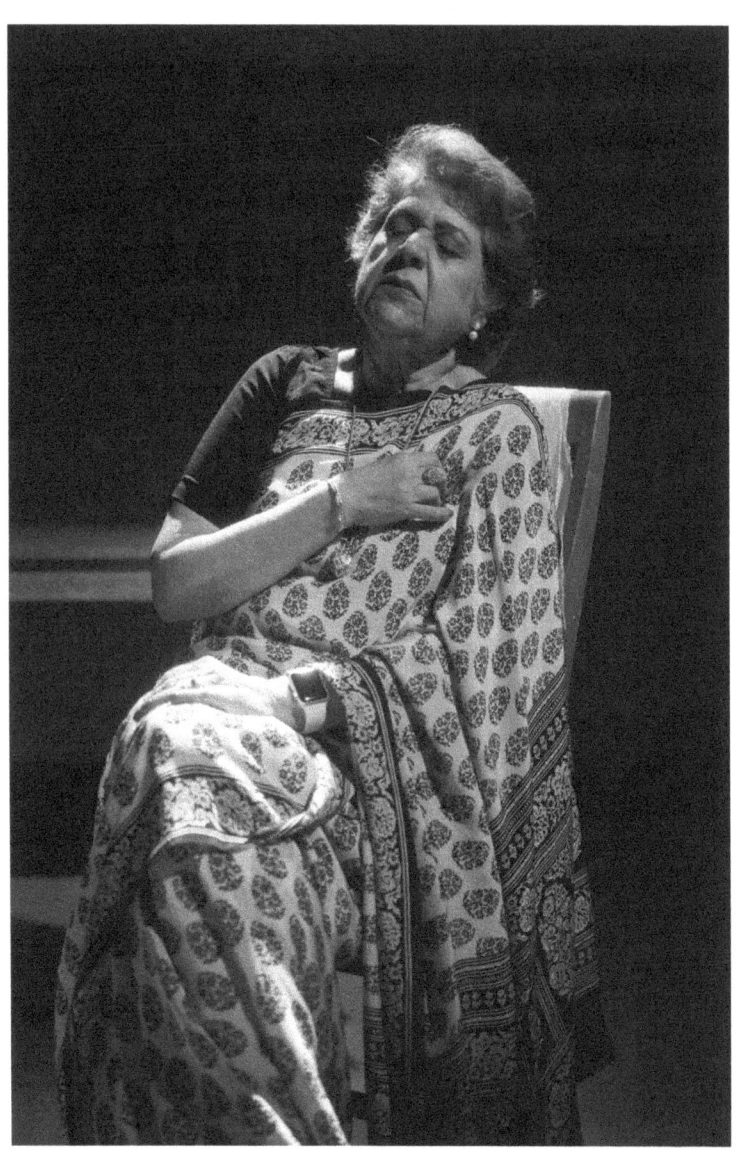

Kumud Merani as Aparna in Q Theatre's production of The Village, *2023 (Photo: Eddy Summers)*

THE VILLAGE
by Tasnim Hossain

TASNIM HOSSAIN is a playwright, director and screenwriter.

The Village premiered at Q Theatre at the Joan Sutherland Performing Arts Centre in 2023. She has been shortlisted for the 2022 Griffin Award for her script *Bombay Takeaway*. She wrote and toured the solo works, *Boys Light Up*, *Letters to John* and *Zak and Reefa's Bollywood Funeral*, to festivals around Australia. She has written work for ATYP, Shopfront Youth Arts and Canberra Youth Theatre.

From 2022 to 2025, she was Resident Director, followed by Associate Artist, at Melbourne Theatre Company, where she directed the Australian premieres of *Never Have I Ever* and *English*, which transferred to Canberra Theatre Centre after an extended season and was nominated for two Green Room Awards. She also directed *I Wanna Be Yours* for Melbourne Theatre Company's Education program, which toured regional Victoria. She developed and led Future Creatives, a development program for early career theatre designers from culturally diverse backgrounds.

Tasnim has been an Artistic Associate at the National Institute of Dramatic Art, Griffin Theatre Company's Studio Artist, and ATYP Resident Playwright. She was selected to be a part of Sydney Theatre Company-CAAP Directors' Initiative, as well as Melbourne Theatre Company's Women in Theatre program. She received the Women's Agenda 2022 Emerging Leader in Arts and Entertainment Award. She was a Theatre Network Australia's Leadershift program participant, as well as a Creative Australia Future Leader.

Thank You

Nick Atkins for instigating this project
Penrith City Council's City Activation Community and Place Team
The Joan's Team
The people of Kingswood, without who this work would not exist

The Village was first produced by Q Theatre at Joan Sutherland Performing Arts Centre, Dharug Country, Penrith, on 21 September 2023, with the following cast and creatives:

CHRISTINE	Wendy Strehlow
APARNA	Kumud Merani
TAYLAH	Olivia Bourne
JAY	Darren Kumar

Director, Bali Padda
Stage Manager, Sophie Jones
Musical Director, Sound Designer and Composer, Christine Pan
Set and Costume Designer, Soham Apte
Lighting Designer, Tim Hope
Original Music, Divinia Jean
Creative Directors, Q Theatre, Rowan Bate and Shy Magsalin
Project Officers, Q Theatre, Kate Bobis and Brianna McCarthy
Marketing and Communications, Fleur Wells
Public Relations, Lisa Finn Powell

CHARACTERS

TAYLAH, seventeen, recently moved in with her grandmother, plays guitar. Of Anglo or European heritage.

CHRISTINE, early sixties, Taylah's grandmother, a long-time Kingswood resident. Of Anglo or European heritage.

APARNA, late sixties, Jay's grandmother, or Dadi, who is currently visiting from India. Of Indian heritage.

JAY, eighteen, Taylah's next door neighbour, current uni student. Of Indian heritage.

NOTES

The action is set between two neighbouring houses in Kingswood, in Western Sydney.

The play should feel familiar, but a little heightened, maybe a little bit magical.

The actor playing Taylah might score scenes by playing her guitar. She might also provide translations to English for Jay and Aparna's characters if they speak in Hindi.

N.B. The current draft is monolingual.

SCENE 1

Two houses, side by side. Raised garden beds in front of each. On one side, struggling marigolds. On the other, roses, rhododendrons, a riot of colour.

TAYLAH *sits on a step or a camp chair beside the marigolds, strumming a guitar.*

TAYLAH: So, I'm going to tell you a story. It's a story about neighbours. It about my nan and her new friend and … a boy.

CHRISTINE *enters, wielding secateurs.*

CHRISTINE: Tell it right, girl. I think it's about you as much as it is about me.

TAYLAH: Fine, it's a story about *me*, my nan, my nan's new friend and her grandson. The boy.

CHRISTINE: Much better. Always best to tell it like it is.

TAYLAH: Nan, I'm trying to tell the story. Do you mind?

CHRISTINE: Alright, alright. I'll just pop in and put the kettle on for all these people here. Can't have them just hanging around like a dog's ba—

TAYLAH: Alright, Nan. Just let me get on with it.

CHRISTINE *exits.*

I've been writing this song. It sounds a bit like this …

TAYLAH *plays a sequence of chords; there's potential but it's very disjointed.*

JAY *enters to speak directly to the audience.*

JAY: So Taylah hasn't introduced me yet, has she?

TAYLAH: I was getting to it.

JAY: No, you weren't. I'm the 'nan's new friend's grandson'.

TAYLAH: I was just about to introduce you.

JAY: No, you weren't. And I know why. [*To audience*] It's because she's in love with me.

TAYLAH: I am *not*.

JAY: Yeah. You are.

TAYLAH: I am not. This isn't a love story.
JAY: Yes, it is.
TAYLAH: It isn't. We haven't even met yet.
JAY: Umm. We definitely have.
TAYLAH: I mean, in the story. Which isn't a love story, by the way. We haven't met yet in the story. We haven't even met your grandma.
JAY: Handful, isn't she?
TAYLAH: You could say that again.
JAY: Handful, isn't she?
TAYLAH: You are so lame.
JAY: You love it.
TAYLAH: Actually hate it. Like, a *lot*.
JAY: Not even close. Although, I don't really like you when we first meet.
TAYLAH: Well, I don't like you either. Are you gonna let me tell the story or not?
JAY: Sorry, *ma'am*, would you like me to enter again? Do it properly this time?
TAYLAH: If it means I don't have to look at your face for another few seconds.

    JAY *bows with a flourish.*

JAY: As you wish.

    JAY *exits.* TAYLAH *sighs and begins playing once more.*

SCENE 2

CHRISTINE'*s kitchen.* TAYLAH *sits and strums a guitar.*
TAYLAH *begins to sing 'The Parting Glass'.*

TAYLAH: Of all the money that e'er I had
    I spent it in good company
    And all the harm I've ever done
    Alas it was to none but me
    And all I've done for want of wit
    To mem'ry now I can't recall
    So fill to me the parting glass
    Good night and joy be to you all

So fill to me the parting glass
And drink a health whate'er befall,
And gently rise and softly call—

Jangle of keys. TAYLAH *stops, tries to hide the guitar and looks for something else to do. Grabs an apple from a bowl. Takes a bite.*

CHRISTINE *enters, carrying the mail.*

CHRISTINE: What were you playing just now?
TAYLAH: Nothing.
CHRISTINE: It sounded like—
TAYLAH: It's nothing.
CHRISTINE: You should have played that a few months ago.
TAYLAH: Who plays Ed Sheeran at a funeral?
CHRISTINE: It's not Ed Sheeran. It's an old folk—
TAYLAH: It *is* Ed Sheeran. It's on one of his albums.
CHRISTINE: Right.

Beat.

You know, it would be nice to hear you play again sometime.
TAYLAH: I play all the time.
CHRISTINE: I meant here, at home, when I'm around. Maybe you could play for me one night.
TAYLAH: You could just come to one of my gigs.
CHRISTINE: I'm at the hospital all the time.
TAYLAH: I've got a gig later tonight.
CHRISTINE: I would but I just can't tonight. I'm knackered.

TAYLAH *shrugs. A moment of connection lost.*

Beat.

Have you just been at home all day?
TAYLAH: Not like I had anywhere else to be.
CHRISTINE: Didn't you go to the Plaza like I—
TAYLAH: It's not the Plaza. Not anymore. It's Westfield. And I told you, Nan. No-one actually walks into a shop with a résumé anymore and hands it over. That's not how they do it.
CHRISTINE: I took your mum to the Plaza when she was your age with a stack of résumés. She got a job at Grace Brothers the same day.

TAYLAH: Yeah, well, it's not like that anymore. You have to know people to get anywhere.
CHRISTINE: That's not new, Taylah. It's always been like that. Doesn't mean you shouldn't try.
TAYLAH: I do work hard but it's all group interviews and psycho … psycho … aptitude tests even for jobs at places like Maccas, and clothes shops and stuff.
CHRISTINE: Psychometric testing?
TAYLAH: Yeah. That. And it makes me feel stupid and dumb and I hate it.

Beat.

So how was work?
CHRISTINE: Long.
TAYLAH: And how were the patients?
CHRISTINE: Ill.
TAYLAH: You should retire.
CHRISTINE: I'm too young to retire.
TAYLAH: I don't know, Nan. Seventy is pretty old.
CHRISTINE: I'm sixty-two!

Beat.

TAYLAH: Like I said, old.
CHRISTINE: You need to do something, Taylah.
TAYLAH: I am doing something.

TAYLAH waves the apple around, takes a big, obnoxious bite.

Mmmm, so delicious!
CHRISTINE: I mean, like a career. Or at least a job. What do you want to do?
TAYLAH: I dunno.
CHRISTINE: You must have thought of something.
TAYLAH: Play music.
CHRISTINE: It's fine to have a hobby but I meant, like, a job.
TAYLAH: I have a job. I write my own music and I perform.
CHRISTINE: You write music?
TAYLAH: Yeah.
CHRISTINE: Really?

TAYLAH: Uhh, yeah.
CHRISTINE: I didn't know you wrote your own music. I thought you played covers. Of that Billie Irish girl.

    TAYLAH *shrugs.*

So, how's that pay?
TAYLAH: It's fine. I pay for all my own stuff, don't I?
CHRISTINE: That's not—
TAYLAH: It's not like I need you to buy me things.
CHRISTINE: That's not what I'm saying. It's all well and good to do something you enjoy but what about when your rent is due or you've got children?
TAYLAH: Nan. I'm not planning on having kids anytime soon. I'm planning on doing exactly what I'm doing right now: playing gigs and saving money. And then I'm going to go to Queensland to live with Dad and Marina and then you won't have to worry about me anymore.
CHRISTINE: I'm a grandmother, it's my job to worry.
TAYLAH: I mean, it isn't though, is it? That's a mum's job and you're not exactly—

    Silence.

CHRISTINE: Have you thought more about talking to—
TAYLAH: No, Nan. I don't want to.
CHRISTINE: It might help you—
TAYLAH: I don't need to. I've got friends. I don't need to talk to anyone else.
CHRISTINE: Okay. If you change your mind, I can help you—
TAYLAH: I won't.

    CHRISTINE *sighs and looks through the mail.*

CHRISTINE: This isn't us. [*Reading*] 'Aparna Sharma.' Must be next door. Can you run it over? It looks important.
TAYLAH: In a minute.
CHRISTINE: Now, please, Taylah.
TAYLAH: I will. Later.
CHRISTINE: You'll forget later.
TAYLAH: You do it then.

CHRISTINE: Taylah, I have been *at work* all day, run off my feet. It looks like you've been sitting right here, at this table, since I left you eating breakfast.

TAYLAH: I changed my top.

CHRISTINE: Into another pyjama top.

TAYLAH: I'm … writing a song.

CHRISTINE: You're eating an apple. And unless you count the sounds you're making while you chew with your mouth open as music, I really don't think that's true.

TAYLAH: I've got a gig tonight.

CHRISTINE: At the pub? Even after your disaster of a trial shift?

TAYLAH: No. At the RSL.

CHRISTINE: Did the pub ever call you back?

TAYLAH: …

CHRISTINE: Taylah, you really should try harder to—

TAYLAH: Have you ever thought about the fact that maybe I have been trying and nobody wants me?

CHRISTINE: Have you been trying?

TAYLAH: You know what? Doesn't matter. Where's that letter?

> TAYLAH *rifles through the mail.*

CHRISTINE: I really think you—

TAYLAH: Can we please talk about this later?

CHRISTINE: You can always come / to me when—

TAYLAH: Nan! You asked me to take the letter next door. That's what I'm doing, okay?

CHRISTINE: Okay.

> TAYLAH *leaves her apple core on the table, takes the letter and exits.*
>
> CHRISTINE *sighs.*

SCENE 3

APARNA*'s kitchen.*
A doorbell rings.
APARNA *enters with* TAYLAH.

TAYLAH: It's fine, really. I was just going to drop this off and go.
APARNA: Nonsense. Come in. Sit down.

>APARNA *herds* TAYLAH *into a seat.*

I have seen you with your grandmother, helping her with so many bags of shopping. You are very nice young girl. What is your name?
TAYLAH: Er, Taylah.
APARNA: Tailor?
TAYLAH: That's right.
APARNA: Tailor is somebody who makes clothing, no?
TAYLAH: I mean, sure. That's probably where it came from, you know, like … ages ago.
APARNA: In India, we name our girl children nice things, like flowers or good virtues or goddesses, not jobs for low-class men.
TAYLAH: I don't think my mum was thinking about it like that.
APARNA: No, of course not. Different people, different customs. Also, in Australia, you have a very good cricketer. Mark Taylor. Maybe your parents name you after good cricketer. *Excellent* cricketer. Many girls have boy's names here. So many Sams. So many Daniels.
TAYLAH: If it's a girl, it's *Danielle*.
APARNA: That is what I said. Daniel.

>*Beat.*

TAYLAH: Anyway, I'll just leave you with this and go …

>TAYLAH *holds up the envelope.*

APARNA: I am making tea. I will make you tea also.

>APARNA *steers* TAYLAH *to a seat.*

TAYLAH: I'm a coffee—Great. Tea sounds great.

APARNA *exits, humming 'Ye Banks and Braes'.* TAYLAH *listens intently.*

What is that?
APARNA: Hmm?
TAYLAH: What are you humming?
APARNA: It is a song. In Bengali.
TAYLAH: Is it? I feel like I've heard I before.
APARNA: It is called *'Phule phule'*.
TAYLAH: What does that mean?
APARNA: It is about flowers in a wind. Not wind. A breeze. A very beautiful song.
TAYLAH: Where are you from?
APARNA: India. From Kolkata.
TAYLAH: So you speak another language?
APARNA: I speak three. Well, four, if you include English. But I am not very good at it.
TAYLAH: You sound okay to me.
APARNA: No. It is very bad. In India, I do not need to speak English so much. Only to watch *Dallas* and *Knight Rider*.
TAYLAH: …
APARNA: You know? KITT? David Hasselhoff? So famous.

TAYLAH *shrugs.*

TAYLAH: Do you miss it? India?
APARNA: Sometimes. But my son and his family are here.
TAYLAH: No other family?
APARNA: I have two more sons, in America. But nobody left in India. But when I am here in Australia, I miss it. I miss my home. So I sing to remember.

APARNA *hums as she exits.*

TAYLAH: I swear I've heard that song.

APARNA *re-enters with a plate of samosas.*

APARNA: Please, take.

TAYLAH *takes a bite of samosa.*

TAYLAH: Oh my god.
APARNA: You don't like it?

TAYLAH: No, they're *amazing*!
APARNA: Please. Take more.

    TAYLAH *eats.* APARNA *drinks her tea.*

TAYLAH: These are delicious.
APARNA: Please eat.
TAYLAH: Thanks.
APARNA: My grandson, he is never at home to eat my cooking. Almost one year I have been here and he is always so busy. Always study, study, study.
TAYLAH: His loss. These samosas are amazing.
APARNA: He will not eat samosas. Chicken only and the white part of eggs and rice—brown rice, not even basmati rice. 'Too oily, Dadi,' he tells me.

    And the white part of egg? Me and my brothers would fight each other to eat the egg yolk and this grandson of mine washes it down the sink.

    He is trying to ... what do you say? Swole. He is trying to become 'swole'.

    TAYLAH *laughs.*

    You know my grandson?
TAYLAH: I don't think so. He sounds ...
APARNA: Boring. I know. Life needs a bit of masala, just like food.
TAYLAH: Sure.
APARNA: But he is very smart.
TAYLAH: Yeah?
APARNA: He is going to be a surgeon, like his father. Cardiothoracic surgeon.

    APARNA *places a hand on her heart to show* TAYLAH *what she means.*

TAYLAH: Right.
APARNA: So, Taylah, now tell me. This letter. What is it?
TAYLAH: It looks official. [*Reads*] 'Department of Home Affairs.'
APARNA: Immigration. Can you read it for me?

    TAYLAH *hesitates.*

    Please. I don't know where my reading glasses are and my English ...

TAYLAH: I think your English is great.
APARNA: Please.

    TAYLAH *opens the envelope and reads.*

TAYLAH: 'We're writing to inform you … ' Oh god.
APARNA: What is it?
TAYLAH: It says your new visa was denied.
APARNA: Oh. That is all?
TAYLAH: 'You must leave Australia as per the original date'. Friday the fourteenth … that's next month.
APARNA: I see.
TAYLAH: Is there … is there anything I can … ?
APARNA: Have another samosa.
TAYLAH: Look, I should let you—I should go.
APARNA: Stay with me until my grandson gets home.
TAYLAH: What about your son or daughter, or whatever?
APARNA: My daughter-in-law is working late. My son is … away.

    Beat.

Please.

TAYLAH: I guess I can stay for a bit.

    Silence.

So … how long have you been in Australia?
APARNA: Almost one year. Minus one month.
TAYLAH: That was a stupid question.

    APARNA *smiles.*

Are you sure I can't help?
APARNA: I sent application for extension, but it was not good enough reason, so I must leave.
TAYLAH: Surely there's something you can do.
APARNA: Share samosas with my neighbour. Enjoy my last month in Kingswood.
TAYLAH: That's it?
APARNA: I have had … nice time in Sydney.
TAYLAH: Your first time?
APARNA: Yes. My first time. I think maybe my last.
TAYLAH: I'm sure that's not—

APARNA: For parent visa, must have someone sponsor—
TAYLAH: Your son could sponsor you again.
   Beat.
APARNA: Maybe.
TAYLAH: Look, I really better go. I've got a gig tonight.
APARNA: What is a gig?
TAYLAH: A performance. Music.
APARNA: What kind of music?
TAYLAH: Top-forties stuff. Usually. Pop. Popular music. Oldies stuff sometimes, when it's in the afternoons.
APARNA: It is you I sometimes hear playing guitar?
TAYLAH: Probably.
APARNA: You sing very nicely.
TAYLAH: Thanks …
APARNA: I heard you singing earlier. A sad song, maybe? It reminded me of songs in my language.
TAYLAH: Yeah, it is a sad song. I was meant to sing it at a funeral.
APARNA: So, like a prayer?
TAYLAH: Not quite.
APARNA: You should come and visit me more. In my last month here. My grandson is every day at uni.
TAYLAH: I'll see what—
APARNA: And please, call me Dadi.
TAYLAH: Daddy?
APARNA: Dadi. It means grandmother.
TAYLAH: I've already got a grandmother.
APARNA: Now you will have two.

SCENE 4

CHRISTINE *at the kitchen table going through a box of papers.*
TAYLAH *enters.*

TAYLAH: You're still awake?
CHRISTINE: Just going through Dinah's things.
TAYLAH: Why?
CHRISTINE: There's boxes and boxes of it in the garage.
TAYLAH: It's our stuff.
CHRISTINE: Most of this seems to be paperwork. Junk.
TAYLAH: It's still our stuff. Mine and Mum's.
CHRISTINE: Do you want to go through it with me?
TAYLAH: Not really.
CHRISTINE: Taylah. Are you happy here?
TAYLAH: Uhh, I guess.
CHRISTINE: I've been wanting to ask you. Because I think … Do you want to stay here? More permanently, I mean.
TAYLAH: I think I'm pretty done with Sydney, actually.
CHRISTINE: I meant here. With me.
TAYLAH: In Kingswood?
CHRSTINE: Yes.
TAYLAH: No way! I mean … Not like that. I don't really—I wanna spend time with Dad and Marina and meet the baby.
CHRISTINE: You could always visit them and come back.
TAYLAH: Yeah, but I could also move to Queensland and come visit you here. It's not like Sydney's going anywhere. I wanna go live somewhere that's actually close to the beach. Somewhere you can swim in winter. Gympie sounds nice. Dad said he likes it there.
CHRISTINE: You should check it out first. You might hate it.
TAYLAH: Yeah but I already hate it here so what's the difference?
CHRISTINE: Your friends are here.
TAYLAH: I'll make new friends.
CHRISTINE: What about your music?
TAYLAH: What about it?
CHRISTINE: There'd be fewer opportunities in a place like that.

TAYLAH: You said it was a hobby so what does it matter?
CHRISTINE: It matters to you.
TAYLAH: I can take a guitar anywhere. And I'm sure they have pubs in Gympie.
CHRISTINE: So why aren't you there with your dad right now?
TAYLAH: He's been busy.
CHRISTINE: Taylah, I—
TAYLAH: I called Dad last night. He said they're just moving into a better place now. He told me. There'll be a room for me and maybe even another one that I can turn into a recording studio.
CHRISTINE: Your father—
TAYLAH: Stop it.
CHRISTINE: Stop what?
TAYLAH: Hating on Dad. You never liked him.
CHRISTINE: That's not it.
TAYLAH: Yes, it is.
CHRISTINE: Whatever *he* told you—
TAYLAH: *Mum* used to tell me how much you hated him. How much you hated her going out with him.
CHRISTINE: She was a kid with a boyfriend who was just as starry-eyed as her. A kid who had you.
TAYLAH: She was twenty-two when she had me.
CHRISTINE: She was still so young.
TAYLAH: Yeah. And she died at thirty-nine. So clearly she had no time to waste.

Beat.

CHRISTINE: What do you want to do with your life, Taylah?
TAYLAH: Write music and hang out.
CHRISTINE: 'Hang out?' What does that even mean? Tell me. What does that look like, on a practical level? And you haven't written a thing, have you?
TAYLAH: Of course I have. How would you even know?
CHRISTINE: What are you—
TAYLAH: Why are you asking me all these questions? Why now?

Beat.

Do you—Do you want me to go or something? Do you not want me here?

CHRISTINE: Taylah, I just asked you if you wanted to stay here with me. Properly. Long-term.

TAYLAH: No, I don't want to be some loser living with her grandma. Like some kinda orphan.

CHRISTINE: That is not what I said.

TAYLAH: What do you want from me?

CHRISTINE: I don't want anything *from* you. I want things *for* you. Study, work, whatever. Find something that's actually worthwhile doing.

TAYLAH: …

CHRISTINE: What did you want to be when you grew up, hey?

TAYLAH: I don't remember.

CHRISTINE: I remember—You once wanted to be a nurse, right? So go do that.

TAYLAH: I don't want to be you.

CHRISTINE: It's not about being me. You've always loved helping people. Think of something outside yourself. It'll help …

TAYLAH: Help with what?

CHRISTINE: The loss. The grief.

TAYLAH: I'm not grieving. I'm done with that. And I'm not some little girl. And I don't want to be a nurse. Who would want to waste their life working that hard for nothing?

Beat as it hits CHRISTINE.

CHRISTINE: It's hard but everything good in life is.

TAYLAH: It doesn't have to be.

CHRISTINE: I just want you to stop …

CHRISTINE *sighs*.

TAYLAH: Stop what?

CHRISTINE: Waiting. Waiting for something to happen.

TAYLAH *goes to exit again. She stops and sighs. Defeated.*

TAYLAH: Nan?

CHRISTINE: Yes, Taylah?

TAYLAH: Could I have twenty bucks?

CHRISTINE: What for?
TAYLAH: Petrol.
CHRISTINE: What about the money from the gig?
TAYLAH: The guy told me to invoice him.

> CHRISTINE *sighs. She finds her wallet under the piles of papers. Pulls out a twenty.*

CHRISTINE: Is this enough?
TAYLAH: Yeah …

> CHRISTINE *pulls out another twenty and hands both to* TAYLAH.

Thanks.
CHRISTINE: But I want you to pay me back, Taylah. It's important to learn the value of money. I want you to learn at least something from me while you're living here.

> *Beat.*

TAYLAH: Right. Thanks.
CHRISTINE: Taylah …
TAYLAH: What, Nan?
CHRISTINE: Whatever you think is going to happen, with your dad, with your music … Music is a hobby. It's great for you to be able to share what you're thinking and feeling, to have some sort of outlet. I get that, you need that.

But if this is something you think you could do professionally, then you'll need much more than just talent.

Things like this are all about timing and luck and you're not—
TAYLAH: Not what, Nan? Lucky? I know. Trust me, I know.

> TAYLAH *exits.*

SCENE 5

APARNA*'s front garden. As she works,* APARNA *sings 'Phule Phule'.*

APARNA: Phule phule dhole dhole
    Bohe kiba mridu baye
    Totini hillol tule
    Kollole choliya jaye

    TAYLAH *enters carrying her guitar.*

TAYLAH: That song! I *swear* I know it.

APARNA: It is a very famous song in Kolkata. Rabindranath Tagore wrote it. He was very famous. Nobel Prize winner. He was even offered to be knighted but he refused the British!

TAYLAH: … Right.

APARNA: How are you today, Taylor?

TAYLAH: I'm good. How are you … ? What was it again? The word for grandmother?

APARNA: Dadi.

TAYLAH: How are you, Dadi?

APARNA: Not too good. Bad knees. Getting old. My heart is weak.

    Beat.

TAYLAH: Er … right.

APARNA: Is that your guitar?

TAYLAH: Umm, yeah?

APARNA: Where are you going with it?

TAYLAH: Thought I'd take it to Triangle Park. Do some busking.

APARNA: What's that?

TAYLAH: Where you play on the street? And people give you money.

APARNA: Like … beggar?

TAYLAH: No, like buskers.

APARNA: In Kolkata, only beggars sing in the street.

TAYLAH: Well, in Penrith, buskers do.

    Beat.

APARNA: That's nice. You sing this popular music?

TAYLAH: Yeah. I do.
APARNA: My husband, he used to like Beatles songs.
TAYLAH: Really?
APARNA: He liked George Harrison.
TAYLAH: My nan liked Paul. *Likes* Paul. Still does. Hated that Heather woman.
APARNA: George Harrison was very good to Bengali people.
TAYLAH: Cool.
APARNA: My husband liked the song … uhh, 'coo coo, ca-choo' … ?
TAYLAH: Uhhh, I don't know that many Beatles songs. I really only know 'Hey Jude' and 'Imagine'.
APARNA: 'Imagine'.

    APARNA *tsks.*

Silly song. Imagine if no colour, no religion, all the people same. Boring. Of course, there are no wars or fighting if everyone is same. Better that people are different and then we must learn to be friends.
TAYLAH: I hadn't thought about it like that.
APARNA: I am very wise.
TAYLAH: I can see that.
APARNA: I like 'she loves you, yeah, yeah yeah!'

    APARNA *shimmies.*

It is very 'cool' that you play guitar. I always liked music as a little girl.
TAYLAH: Yeah?
APARNA: But not so many opportunities. It's so good that you can make money singing and playing guitar on the streets in this country and nobody thinks you are a beggar.
TAYLAH: I mean—
APARNA: It is very good to have interest in arts. I loved dance and music very much.
TAYLAH: Did any of your kids go into the arts?
APARNA: Oh no, no, no, no. Definitely not. They were all very good, *well-behaved* sons.
TAYLAH: Oh.
APARNA: No, it was me. I wanted to learn dancing and singing when I was young.
TAYLAH: You still can.

APARNA: Me? No, I am old. Singing and dancing is for children your age.

TAYLAH: I'm not a child. I'm seventeen.

APARNA: If you're not a child, you're old enough to get married. Are you getting married?

TAYLAH: If those are the only two options, I wanna pick child. For now.

APARNA: So will you sing a song for me?

TAYLAH: Now?

APARNA: Why not? Oh, I can give you money, for this busking business if you …

TAYLAH: No, it's not that, just … You know what? Umm, okay. I'll play for you.

Beat.

What do you want me to play?

APARNA: Sing one of your traditional songs.

TAYLAH: Like what?

APARNA: Like 'Phule Phule'. Traditional *Australian* songs.

TAYLAH: I don't think Australia really has traditional songs. I mean, I learnt some Cold Chisel. And Acca Dacca. For my dad. But 'Thunderstruck' does not sound good on acoustic guitar.

APARNA: Does your dad watch your busking too?

TAYLAH: Nah, he's in Queensland. I'm going to go up and live with him and his girlfriend.

APARNA: Girlfriend?? Hmm.

TAYLAH: They have a new baby. A little half-brother. I've never had any siblings before.

APARNA: Who does he look like? Your brother? Your dad or your … dad's girlfriend?

TAYLAH: I don't know. Can't tell from the photos. He's only four months old. I haven't met him yet.

APARNA: …

TAYLAH: My dad's girlfriend was having a tough time while she was pregnant. That's why I'm living with my nan. Just till the baby's a bit older and then I'll move up and live in Queensland with them.

APARNA: It is nice to have brothers. I had three sons. They were so close when they were little and now they live on different sides of the world.

TAYLAH: Do you visit them?
APARNA: It is difficult. With visas and everything. Very expensive. And my health, you know? I am old.
Beat.
Will you sing a song for me?
TAYLAH: Oh. Maybe 'Waltzing Matilda'? I played it at school once. I think I still remember the chords.
APARNA: That one! Waltzing, like the dancing?
TAYLAH: I guess so?
APARNA: Play that one! I want to remember an Aussie song for when I can no longer listen to this language, these voices, like my grandson's.
TAYLAH pulls her guitar out, tunes it, strums.
TAYLAH: Alright. Here goes.
TAYLAH takes a breath and plays.
Once a jolly swagman camped by a billabong,
Under the shade of a Coolabah tree,
And he sang as he watched and waited till his billy boiled,
'You'll come a-Waltzing Matilda with me.'
… Are you sure this is the one you want to hear?
APARNA: Yes!
TAYLAH: Okay …
Waltzing Matilda, Waltzing Matilda,
You'll come a-Waltzing Matilda with me,
And he sang as he watched and waited till his billy boiled,
'You'll come a-Waltzing Matilda with me.'
… I forget this next bit.
APARNA: Keep singing.
CHRISTINE enters, unseen, and watches.
TAYLAH: I don't remember the middle. But the last bit goes:
Up jumped the swagman and sprang into the billabong
'You'll never catch me alive' said he,
And his ghost may be heard as you pass by that billabong
'Who'll come a-Waltzing Matilda with me?'
Waltzing Matilda, Waltzing Matilda

You'll come a-Waltzing Matilda with me
And his ghost may be heard as you pass by that billabong
'You'll come a-Waltzing Matilda with me.'
APARNA: Beautiful!

Beat.

What does it mean?
TAYLAH: I think it's about someone killing a sheep or something? Or they get killed? Actually, I think they kill themselves.
APARNA: Oh.

Beat.

Interesting. This traditional Australian song is very ... different. Our traditional songs are mostly about rivers and flowers.
TAYLAH: Yeah, ours are about bushrangers and convicts.
APARNA: Convicts?
TAYLAH: Criminals.
CHRISTINE: A different kind of history then, I think.

TAYLAH and APARNA both jump.

TAYLAH begins to put away her guitar.

APARNA: Oh, I did not see you. Good morning. I am Aparna.
CHRISTINE: Christine. I see you've met my granddaughter, Taylah.
APARNA: Yes. She is a very nice young lady. Good manners.
CHRISTINE: Really? Taylah, weren't you going in to—
TAYLAH: I am. I'm going.
CHRISTINE: Make sure you hand out those résumés. I didn't print them out at the nurses' station for nothing.
TAYLAH: *I will*, Nan.
CHRISTINE: Don't forget.
TAYLAH: Bye, Aparna. I mean, Dadi.

TAYLAH exits.

APARNA: Very nice girl.
CHRISTINE: If you say so.

Awkward pause.

APARNA gestures at CHRISTINE's drooping flower bed.

APARNA: I like your ... marigolds. We use them in our wedding jewellery.

CHRISTINE: It's nice that she sang for you.
APARNA: I love music. Very much.
CHRISTINE: Have you got your own grandchildren?
APARNA: Yes. Many. Mostly in America. But here I have my grandson. Jay. I am his father's mother. Are you Taylor's father's mother or her mother's mother?
CHRISTINE: I am her grandmother on her mother's side.
APARNA: And your daughter lives with you too?
CHRISTINE: She died last year. Ovarian cancer. Taylah lives with me now.
APARNA: My condolences.
CHRISTINE: Thank you.
APARNA: My eldest son, in America, is an oncologist. It did not stop his wife getting cancer. Stage Two. Breast cancer. But they found it and they operated and she is okay.
CHRISTINE: That's lucky.
APARNA: All my sons are doctors. My grandson, Jay, is studying to be a doctor. He will be a cardiothoracic surgeon. Like his father.
CHRISTINE: Your son? Cardiothoracic surgeon? Is your—Is Dr Shaan Sharma your son?

Beat.

APARNA: Yes.
CHRISTINE: I work at the hospital.
APARNA: Oh. You work at the Nepean Hospital? The same one?
CHRISTINE: Yes.
APARNA: I see. Well, my son, he has taken a position in Darwin. Temporary.
CHRISTINE: Right.
APARNA: And what do you do, at the hospital? What is your specialisation?
CHRISTINE: I'm a nurse.

Beat.

APARNA: A *nurse*.
CHRISTINE: Yes. I've been a nurse in my community for more than forty years.
APARNA: ... Very good.

CHRISTINE: And what do you do?

APARNA: Me? Oh, I am a housewife. I *was* a housewife. My late husband was a doctor, and all my sons are now doctors, and many of my grandchildren also.

One of them is an interior designer in Sacramento—sometimes in these other countries, they choose different things, you know—but at least his brother, he is a radiologist.

But no, I did not need to work.

CHRISTINE: That must be nice.

APARNA: Very nice.

Beat.

You should come to our house and have dinner with us. You and your granddaughter.

CHRISTINE: Oh. Umm. I really don't—I wouldn't want to—

APARNA: Very nice. I will prepare dinner for tonight.

CHRISTINE: Tonight?

APARNA: I am not busy. My daughter-in-law is working and my grandson is always at university.

CHRISTINE: And your son? He's returning soon? From …

APARNA: Darwin. Yes. Soon.

CHRISTINE: It's very nice of you but I don't think we could tonight. Maybe some other time.

Beat.

APARNA: Okay. You just tell me and I will cook dinner.

CHRISTINE: Right. Well, I better be heading in and getting some sleep. I covered a night shift. At the hospital. As a *nurse*.

APARNA: Have a good sleep. Very nice to meet you.

CHRISTINE: Likewise.

CHRISTINE *exits.*

APARNA *returns to gardening, singing 'Walzing Matilda'.*

SCENE 6

Late night. Outside APARNA'*s house.*

TAYLAH *is drunk, rummaging through her bag for her phone and keys. She drops the keys with a loud jangle.*

TAYLAH: Oh shit.

> *Lights come on.*

Shit, shit, shit.

> *The door opens.* JAY *stands there barefoot in shorts and a T-shirt.*

TAYLAH: Shit.
JAY: Who the hell are you?
TAYLAH: Who the hell are *you*? What are you doing in my house?
JAY: This is *my* house and you're trespassing.
TAYLAH: What are you talking about?

> TAYLAH *looks around. Realises that she's in front of the wrong house.*

JAY: Why are you breaking into our house?
TAYLAH: I am not breaking into your house. I'm breaking into mine. I mean, I'm trying to *get* into my house.
JAY: Which is clearly not this house, so please get off our property. Or I'm calling the cops.
TAYLAH: The cops? That's a bit unnecessary.
JAY: You're standing in my grandma's flowerbeds and if she sees you trampling them, I'll have to call an ambulance instead. For you.
TAYLAH: Okay, fine! I'm going, I'm going!

> TAYLAH *goes to exit.*

Wait!
JAY: What now?
TAYLAH: I think I dropped my phone in your garden somewhere.
JAY: So?
TAYLAH: Can you help me look?

> *A moment.* JAY *heaves a sigh and steps outside.*

> JAY *and* TAYLAH *search on their hands and knees in the semi-darkness.*

I've never seen you before.

JAY: What?

TAYLAH: You know, never seen you around?

JAY: You stalk your neighbours, do you?

TAYLAH: Only the hot ones.

> JAY *pauses for a moment, continues searching.*

Not that there are any. I mean, I went to school with pretty much everyone around here. Gross. But you didn't go to my school. Where did you come from?

JAY: Are you asking where I'm from?

TAYLAH: … Yeah?

JAY: I'm *Australian.*

TAYLAH: What?

> *Beat.* TAYLAH *realises her mistake.*

No, no. I got that. I wasn't being racist, I—I meant your *school*. What school did you go to?

JAY: James Ruse.

TAYLAH: Gross.

JAY: … Thanks?

> *Beat.*

TAYLAH: You're the grandson.

JAY: The what?

TAYLAH: Yeah, that's right! The famous cardiothoracic surgeon. What a mouthful.

JAY: I'm not a surgeon.

TAYLAH: Not yet.

JAY: I'm a med student.

TAYLAH: Close enough. *Son* of the cardiothoracic surgeon. Cardiothoracic surgeon junior. From a long line of cardiothoracic surgeons.

JAY: Can you stop saying that?

TAYLAH: *Cardiothoracic surgeon?*

JAY: Yes.

TAYLAH: Why? Don't you like it?
JAY: No.
TAYLAH: Me neither. Doctors suck. Didn't do anything for my mum. And nobody would want *you* operating on them anyway.
JAY: What's that supposed to mean?
TAYLAH: I mean, you're not dressed very professionally, are you?
JAY: 'Cause I totally asked for the opinion of some drunk girl in the middle of the night?
TAYLAH: I'm not drunk. And *that* doesn't really scream 'trustworthy doctor', does it?
JAY: I'm dressed for *bed*. Which is where I was until *you* woke *me*.
TAYLAH: My pleasure!
JAY: I wasn't thanking you.
TAYLAH: You should be. We're having an adventure.

    JAY *scratches himself on a rosebush.*

JAY: Ow! We're looking for your phone in my grandmother's rosebushes at one in the morning. I don't think anyone would count that as an adventure.
TAYLAH: Yeah, it is.

    Beat.

You know, my mum used to take me looking for fairies at the bottom of the garden.
JAY: Fairies?
TAYLAH: Yeah. When I was little.
    Our backyard used to be all overgrown—Dad never mowed it, I mean, back when he was around—and there were these dandelions up to my knee and all these spiderwebs and they'd catch dew in them and Mum would say that the fairies made dresses out of them.
    Out of spiderwebs and dandelion fluff.

    A lovely moment of connection.

JAY: Wait. You're the neighbour girl, the one who made friends with my Dadi, the one whose mum …
TAYLAH: That's me. You're the one with the cute Indian grandma. I'm the one with the dead mum.
JAY: I'm sorry, I didn't—

TAYLAH: What are *you* sorry for? You didn't kill her. Unless you invented cancer.
JAY: No, but—
TAYLAH: But what?
JAY: I just—
TAYLAH: What?
JAY: …
TAYLAH: Don't. Don't look at me like that.
JAY: How can you even tell how I'm looking at you? It's pitch black!
TAYLAH: I can feel it. It feels like—you feel sorry for me but you don't even know anything about me.
JAY: I wasn't—
TAYLAH: Stop it.
JAY: I swear I wasn't—
TAYLAH: I don't want you to feel sorry for me.
JAY: I don't feel—
TAYLAH: Yes, you do. Everyone feels sorry for me. Everyone looks at me like that. Even my nan.
JAY: I'm not—
TAYLAH: Just—just fuck off and leave me alone.

TAYLAH *exits, leaving* JAY *on the ground.*

SCENE 7

CHRISTINE'S *house.* CHRISTINE *at the table, dressed for work, on her phone.*

TAYLAH *enters, worse for the wear, with toast.*

CHRISTINE: How was your night?
TAYLAH: Fine.
CHRISTINE: What time did you come in?

TAYLAH *bristles.*

TAYLAH: One o'clock.

CHRISTINE *doesn't rise to the challenge.*

CHRISTINE: The kettle's just boiled. I put out a mug for you.
TAYLAH: I'll just grab a coffee on my way …

CHRISTINE: On your way *where*? Since when are you awake at eight a.m.?
TAYLAH: What's it matter?
>	*Beat.*
> I've been doing some … trial shifts.

CHRISTINE: Where?
TAYLAH: Maccas.
CHRISTINE: That's great.
TAYLAH: Don't get too excited. It's only been a week.
CHRISTINE: I told you résumés would work.
TAYLAH: The store manager and I used to play netball together. I DM'ed her. I didn't give her my résumé. I told you they don't do that anymore. It's all about who you know. It was that thing, what's it called when you know someone and they give you stuff because of it.
CHRISTINE: Nepotism.
TAYLAH: Yeah, it was that. It definitely wasn't a résumé.
CHRISTINE: Well, as long as you've got something, then that's good.
TAYLAH: I do have something. My music.
CHRISTINE: That's not what I meant.
TAYLAH: Course not.

> TAYLAH *leaves her half-eaten toast on the counter.* CHRISTINE *clocks it.*

CHRISTINE: I think it would be good if you started contributing to rent.
TAYLAH: What?
CHRISTINE: Since you have a job now.
TAYLAH: It's just a trial.
CHRISTINE: Still. I can put it into a savings account for you. For later.
TAYLAH: So, you don't trust me to save it?
CHRISTINE: That's not what I'm saying, Taylah. I just want you to be smarter than Dinah because when your dad left—
TAYLAH: What, Nan? Coz you keep saying the same things about Mum and Dad and I'm just so—

> *Doorbell rings.*

CHRISTINE: Are you expecting someone?
TAYLAH: Why would I—

CHRISTINE: A package? One of your Iconics or something?
TAYLAH: No.

Doorbell rings again.

CHRISTINE: Don't rush or anything.

CHRISTINE sighs and exits.

Some moments pass before CHRISTINE *returns with* JAY.

TAYLAH: What are you doing here?
CHRISTINE: So you do know him?
TAYLAH: Yeah.
CHRISTINE: He says he's the 'grandson of the elderly Indian lady next door'.
TAYLAH: She's probably the same age as you.
CHRISTINE: I'm not elderly. I'm still working.
TAYLAH: Whatever.
CHRISTINE: So you're friends?
TAYLAH: No, I met him last night when I—
JAY: Dropped your phone. And here it is.

JAY hands TAYLAH *her phone.*

It wasn't in the rosebushes after all. I got all those scratches for no reason.
TAYLAH: Where was it?
JAY: In the rhododendrons—
CHRISTINE: Your grandmother has lovely rhododendrons.
JAY: I'll … Thanks. I'll let her know.
CHRISTINE: Please do.

Awkward silence.

Right then. I'm heading into work. Make sure you pack a lunch, Taylah. Don't waste your money when we've got food at home. And don't be late for your shift.
TAYLAH: I won't.

Beat as CHRISTINE *waits for something more but nothing.*

CHRISTINE exits.

Want some breakfast?
JAY: Nah, I'm good.

TAYLAH: Suit yourself.

 TAYLAH *turns back to her breakfast, in dismissal.*

 JAY *hovers.*

JAY: What are you eating?
TAYLAH: Toast.

 TAYLAH *holds it up.*

JAY: Cool.
TAYLAH: Heaps cool.
JAY: So …
TAYLAH: … want a coffee?
JAY: Sure!
TAYLAH: Help yourself.
JAY: Oh. Never mind.

 Beat.

So you were really drunk last night.

 Silence.

You're lucky I managed to find your phone.

 Beat.

It was, like, right in there and—
TAYLAH: What are you trying to say?
JAY: What?
TAYLAH: Why are you here?
JAY: To bring you your phone?
TAYLAH: And you did, so …
JAY: Glad you got home safe.
TAYLAH: Okay.
JAY: And that I could find your phone for you.
TAYLAH: I already said thank you.

 Beat.

JAY: You didn't, actually.
TAYLAH: I did.
JAY: I mean, you didn't but I didn't bring it around for thanks or / anything …

TAYLAH: Thank you.
JAY: Oh. Pleasure.
TAYLAH: What was your name again?
JAY: Jay.
TAYLAH: Taylah.
JAY: You were kind of a dick to me last night.
TAYLAH: I'm kind of a dick to a lot of people.
JAY: But only the ones you think are hot.
TAYLAH: Is that what I said?
JAY: Yeah.

   Beat.

Looked like you had a good night.
TAYLAH: I was out with friends.
JAY: Yeah?
TAYLAH: Played a gig. Stayed out.
JAY: You're in a band?
TAYLAH: Solo. I play guitar and sing.
JAY: That's you?
TAYLAH: What's me?
JAY: The girl who sings. I could never work out which house it was. All old songs.
TAYLAH: No, I sing top-forties stuff. I do covers of pop songs and that.
JAY: I dunno, I just hear … sad songs, I guess.
TAYLAH: Nah. Not me.
JAY: If you say so.

   Beat.

You know, I don't know if you remember this, but you also said that I was the most good-looking guy you've ever met and that you now believe in love at first sight.
TAYLAH: Wait. I didn't say any of that.
JAY: You didn't. But you thought it.
TAYLAH: You're really cocky. It's kind of a dick move.
JAY: I'm a dick to a lot of people. They get used to it. It's part of my charm.

   A smile. A silence.

You look … familiar. Like I've seen you before.

TAYLAH: Yeah, last night. On your front lawn.
JAY: No, before that. I couldn't tell in the dark but …
TAYLAH: I have one of those faces.
JAY: Nah, I've seen you before.
TAYLAH: Sometimes I busk outside Penrith Station.
JAY: Nahhh …
TAYLAH: I played a gig at the bowlo.
JAY: What would *I* be doing at the bowlo?
TAYLAH: I don't know.
JAY: Got it! Maccas drive-thru.

Beat.

TAYLAH: That's me.
JAY: You look … heaps younger.
TAYLAH: Thanks?
JAY: Nah, I mean, I thought you were, like, thirty-five the other night but you're, like, my age.
TAYLAH: Wow. You know, I think I remember you too.
JAY: Yeah. From last night.
TAYLAH: No, from the drive-thru.
JAY: What? No.
TAYLAH: Yeah, I *do* remember you. It was Friday—no, Thursday— my first shift. And you were by yourself and you bought like, forty chicken nuggets and then asked if you could get a Happy Meal toy.
JAY: Umm … no.
TAYLAH: Yeah, it was you!
JAY: No.
TAYLAH: Yeah, and you were even driving that piece of crap that was in your driveway last night. It's more dent than car.
JAY: I wasn't going to eat all the nuggets by myself.
TAYLAH: Yeah, sure.
JAY: I wasn't. And my mum likes Happy Meal toys.
TAYLAH: Sure she does.
JAY: She … collects them.

   TAYLAH *smirks. She has clearly won the point.*

  Hey …
TAYLAH: What?

JAY: I just wanted to say ... I'm sorry about the way I was looking at you last night.

TAYLAH: What? Like a creeper?

JAY: I wasn't creeping on you. *You* were creeping on *me*. I just meant I was looking at you like I ... like I felt sorry for you, I guess.

Beat.

TAYLAH: Right. That.

JAY: But I don't. I don't feel sorry for you.

Actually, I get it. I mean, no, I don't. My parents are both alive, not—Anyway. What I meant to say is that I hate it when people feel sorry for me. It sucks.

And I don't feel sorry for you. I think you're kinda rude. Which is funny. Because my grandma calls you the 'nice Aussie neighbour girl'.

TAYLAH: Yeah, well, she's nice.

JAY: She's okay.

TAYLAH: She's very friendly. Very ... extroverted.

JAY: She's an Indian grandma. They're all extroverted.

TAYLAH: It just seems like she doesn't get the chance to get out much, which is a shame.

JAY: She's fine.

TAYLAH: Must be hard somewhere like here. So far away from everyone. And with all of her health issues too.

JAY: Health issues? Pfft, she's a tank. She'll outlive us all.

TAYLAH: Still. It must get lonely.

JAY: She's not lonely.

TAYLAH: I feel like she might be.

JAY: No, she isn't. She's got me.

TAYLAH: She told me you spent all your time at uni and getting 'swole'.

JAY: Getting—Right, well ... you can't become a doctor without studying and that's what she wants. That's what she keeps saying. 'Cardiothoracic surgeon, beta. Just like your father. So proud!'

Silence.

So, are *you* going to say sorry?

TAYLAH: What for?

JAY: You told me to fuck off. On my own lawn. At one in the morning.

TAYLAH: Yeah, well, you deserved it.

    JAY *scoffs*.

JAY: My dad always used to say that I was a pain.

TAYLAH: Mine moved to Queensland.

    TAYLAH *holds up a water glass in a mock toast*.

Cheers. At least I've got Nan, even though she's basically a grumpy old man inside a grumpy old lady body. And you've got your Dadi. Even if she does have to go back in a month.

JAY: Back where?

TAYLAH: Back to India … ?

JAY: She's not going back. She's got a visa.

TAYLAH: I don't think so. Or at least, I'm pretty sure it's finished.

JAY: That's not true.

TAYLAH: It is. She literally got a letter. From the Immigration Department. Said her appeal had been rejected or something and that she had to leave.

JAY: When?

TAYLAH: Next month. By the fourteenth.

JAY: When did she get this letter?

TAYLAH: Last week.

JAY: Oh my god.

TAYLAH: Oh …

JAY: Why would she tell *you*?

TAYLAH: I don't know. I was just there. The letter must have been delivered here accidentally and when I took it over, she asked me to read it for her.

JAY: Why wouldn't she tell me?

TAYLAH: Look, I'm sorry. I didn't know it was, like, sensitive or whatever. She gave it to me and asked me to read it for her, so I read it. I wasn't—

JAY: I gotta go.

TAYLAH: Wait—

    JAY *exits*.

Shit.

SCENE 8

APARNA*'s house.* APARNA *washes breakfast dishes.* JAY *enters.*

APARNA: Did you forget something?
JAY: Why didn't you tell me?
APARNA: Tell you what?
JAY: You're going back to India.
APARNA: You knew I would have to go back.
JAY: But why now?
APARNA: My visa is finished.
JAY: But you can get it renewed. Can't you?
APARNA: …
JAY: Just write a letter. I can help you.
APARNA: You have more important things to do.
JAY: Like what?
APARNA: Your studies.
JAY: This is more important.
APARNA: No. You should focus on your studies. Study is the most important thing. Always.
JAY: Not more important than family.
APARNA: You must study so you can help your family. That is the biggest help.
JAY: I could help in lots of ways.
APARNA: I don't want you to worry.
JAY: Why didn't you tell me?
APARNA: It is fine, Jay.

    Beat.

JAY: You could … You could ask Paapa.

    Beat.

APARNA: Yes. Of course.
JAY: Because I reckon he would …
APARNA: It will be fine. Go now. Or you will be late to university.
JAY: You're gonna call him?
APARNA: I will. Don't worry. I will call him and we will fix this.

JAY: Okay.
APARNA: Trust your Dadi.
JAY: I do, I just—I don't …
APARNA: What, Jay?
JAY: Nothing.

> *Beat.*

APARNA: How was Taylor and her nani?
JAY: Fine.
APARNA: Good. I like that girl. She is like a little chilli.
JAY: A what?
APARNA: A little chilli. Sharp. Bright.
JAY: … A firecracker?
APARNA: A what?
JAY: That's what we call people like that.
APARNA: Yes, a firecracker. We must have her come with her grandmother for dinner.

> I always worry about what they serve, these Aussies. So few items and no rice.
>
> Will you do that? Will you go over and ask them to come one night this week?

JAY: I mean, I can but …
APARNA: Please. Please don't worry. Go to university. Go. Everything will be okay.
JAY: Okay.

> *Beat.*
>
> Love you, Dadi.

APARNA: Make sure you eat lunch. You can't study on an empty stomach. And don't be home too late.

> *JAY exits.*
>
> *APARNA pulls out a piece of paper and dials it into her phone. APARNA waits but it goes to voicemail.*

Shaan, it is your mother. Please call me back. Whatever happened, I am sure that it can all be forgiven and forgotten. Your son needs you. Your mother needs you. Please come home.

> *APARNA hangs up.*

SCENE 9

Night outside the two houses.
TAYLAH *outside her house, in a rumpled Maccas uniform, on the phone.*
JAY, *who has returned from a run, watches on.*

TAYLAH: I could still come. But, what if I—No, I'm sure it'll—
Okay …
No, I heard you. Fine. Okay. I'll—
It's fine. Yeah. Okay, fine, I don't—I—
Doesn't matter. I don't …
Yeah. Next time. Sure.
Bye … *Bye.*

JAY approaches.

JAY: That sounded …
TAYLAH: You know you shouldn't creep around like—
JAY: Like what?
TAYLAH: Doesn't matter.
JAY: Are you … okay?
TAYLAH: Why?
JAY: I dunno. You just seemed …
TAYLAH: What?
JAY: Nothing.
TAYLAH: *What?*
JAY: Sad.

Beat—not what TAYLAH *was expecting.*

TAYLAH: I was … annoyed. If you must know.
JAY: Look, I just—Never mind. My Dadi told me to ask you and your nan for dinner.
TAYLAH: Why?
JAY: Because being neighbourly is important to her? Because she likes force-feeding people? I don't know.
TAYLAH: When?
JAY: I dunno, sometime this week. Tomorrow?
TAYLAH: Tomorrow? Okay, sure. I'll let Nan know.

JAY *goes to leave.*

On the phone? It was ... You know, it doesn't matter.
JAY: Your boyfriend?
TAYLAH: That wasn't my boyfriend. I don't have one.
JAY: Ah.
TAYLAH: I *don't*.
JAY: Hey, I didn't say anything.
TAYLAH: You know, you're really ...
JAY: Attractive? Intuitive?
TAYLAH: Sweaty, actually. But annoying, is what I was going for.
JAY: Good. Being annoyed at me is better than whatever you were just ...

    JAY *gestures instead of finishing the thought.*

TAYLAH: So I'm meant to thank you?
JAY: Only if you want.
TAYLAH: You are super annoying.
JAY: It's a speciality. That's what my dad used to say.
TAYLAH: I thought you said he called you a pain.
JAY: Annoying, a pain, he used to say a lot of things.
TAYLAH: *Used* to say?

    Beat—JAY*'s said too much.*

JAY: I grew out of it.

    JAY *goes to leave once more.*

TAYLAH: Oh, I almost forgot. I have something for you.
JAY: Can it wait? I'm really tired and I've got an early—
TAYLAH: It'll only take a minute. Promise!

    TAYLAH *exits inside the house.*

    JAY *sighs and waits.*

    TAYLAH *re-enters and runs over to* JAY, *maybe a bit puffed.*

TAYLAH: Close your eyes.
JAY: Taylah, I—
TAYLAH: Close your eyes.

    JAY *sighs and does so.*

TAYLAH *puts something in his hand.*

JAY *opens his eyes and looks at it.*

JAY: A Happy Meal toy.

TAYLAH: Yeah, for your mum.

JAY: Why did you get me this?

TAYLAH: Because you looked really sad that day. When I couldn't give you one.

JAY: I wasn't.

TAYLAH: Okay.

Silence.

JAY: I'm gonna go.

TAYLAH: Okay.

JAY: Thanks. For the ... I should go. Get some sleep.

TAYLAH: Why are you even out so late?

JAY: Only got home from uni at nine. Didn't have time for a run till now.

TAYLAH: And how is that going for you? Uni?

JAY *hesitates.*

Wanna sit?

JAY *sits.*

JAY: Hate it. Hate uni. It sucks donkey's balls.

TAYLAH: That's very ... graphic. And everyone hates uni, right? Why do you think I didn't go?

JAY: It's not uni. Not specifically. Uni would be fine if I were doing something else. It's not that. It's ...

TAYLAH: It's what?

JAY: Medicine. I hate ... medicine. So much.

TAYLAH: Then why are you doing it?

JAY: Coz I'm smart.

TAYLAH: Wow, up yourself much?

JAY: It's just ... a fact. Like being right-handed.

TAYLAH: Okay.

JAY: I'm not being arrogant about it. I don't think I'm better than other people because I got a good ATAR. I kinda wish I got a shit one.

TAYLAH: No, you don't.

JAY: Maybe. At least nobody would be making me do med or something.
TAYLAH: People make other people do things they don't want to all the time. Doesn't matter if you're smart or not.
JAY: I guess it could be worse. If I'm a doctor, I'll be making heaps of money.
TAYLAH: Money doesn't necessarily make you happy.
JAY: Yeah? How do you know?
TAYLAH: I don't. I mean, that's just what people say, right? I figured I should too.
JAY: My dad's a doctor and my uncles are doctors and my cousins are doctors. All my friends from school are studying to be doctors and all we do is try to one-up each other all the time. That's it, they're all I've got.
TAYLAH: You've got your Dadi.
JAY: Who wants me to be a doctor. What else am I supposed to do? You tell me.
TAYLAH: Whatever you want.
JAY: Is that what you're doing?

JAY looks pointedly at her uniform.

TAYLAH: Yes, I am.
JAY: Never met anyone who thought serving McFlurries was an actual career.

Icy silence.

Taylah …
TAYLAH: What?
JAY: That was a shitty thing to say.
TAYLAH: Yeah, well …
JAY: It was.

Beat.

Everything's all just a bit …
TAYLAH: A bit what? Suffocating? Hard to deal with the nagging and the pressure and the expectations?

It's clear that TAYLAH is talking about them both.

Beat.

JAY: Do you ever think about what it would be like if you could just … get up and go? Anywhere you wanted.
TAYLAH: Always. I think about it all the time. Why do you think I love music?
JAY: What do you mean?
TAYLAH: When I play, I go away. I disappear.
JAY: Yeah?
TAYLAH: Yeah.
JAY: I'd like to see you play sometime.
TAYLAH: I've got a gig tomorrow night?
JAY: Didn't you just say you'd come to dinner at ours?
TAYLAH: Oh shit, of course. Sorry, I forgot it was tomorrow night.
JAY: That's okay.
TAYLAH: Yeah, but your grandmother is going soon and … There's gotta be something we can do about that.
JAY: Not really. Dadi is stubborn and my dad's a dick. It's not like he's gonna help.

Beat.

It feels like Dadi has just given up and I just feel so useless and—I dunno. Doesn't matter. Ignore me.
TAYLAH: I get it.

Beat.

How about we do dinner and then we can all go to the gig? My nan took tomorrow night off and your Dadi wants to see me perform and … you could come too.
JAY: A double date? Cute.
TAYLAH: It's at the bowlo.
JAY: That's not really my scene.
TAYLAH: Guess you'll miss out then.
JAY: Guess I will.
TAYLAH: Shame.
JAY: But maybe I can fit you into my mad busy schedule.
TAYLAH: Yeah, slot me in with your cardiothoracic studies.

Beat.

JAY: So where do you go? When you play?

TAYLAH: Someplace else. This? This is all boring. This house is boring. Cancer is boring. It's better in movies. Living someplace else. Parents being killed off-screen, by an evil queen or a botched mugging.
JAY: Like Batman.
TAYLAH: My parents were millionaires too.
JAY: Wow. I had no idea.
TAYLAH: Yeah. I don't think I've told you this yet but … I'm basically a superhero.
JAY: Really?
TAYLAH: Christine isn't my grandmother. She's actually my butler. Her real name's Alfred. She's a man.

>JAY *laughs.*

JAY: Just casually saving the world, are you?
TAYLAH: Yep, slinging McFlurries and taking on Immigration at the same time.
JAY: Sounds dangerous.
TAYLAH: Oh, it is.
JAY: Taking down the bad guys, one gig at a time. The Dark Knight: The Musical.
TAYLAH: The Caped Crusader.

>TAYLAH *improvises a cape.*

JAY: The Caped … Guitarplayer.

>JAY *tries the same thing with a cape, miming playing a power chord on a guitar.*

>*Beat.*

TAYLAH: You killed it.
JAY: Sorry, I tried.
TAYLAH: Nup, killed it dead. I'm outta here. That was embarrassing.
JAY: Wait! So tomorrow night—
TAYLAH: Bye!!

>TAYLAH *exits.* JAY *watches for a moment. He grins.*

SCENE 10

APARNA's *kitchen.*

APARNA *ladling food into dishes.* JAY *setting the table.*

JAY: You know you didn't have to cook all afternoon only for the next-door neighbours to tell us it was too spicy.

APARNA: I wanted to. We should be good neighbours.

JAY: Why do we always have to do what we *should* do?

APARNA: That is how society works. Because we are all responsible for what we should do.

JAY: It's all just pretend though. It's lying.

APARNA: What is the other option? You can't just do whatever you want. How will you take responsibility? What will people say?

JAY: Wow, Dadi, you—

APARNA: Also, it means that you must now sit down and have dinner with me too.

JAY: I'm only going to eat some chicken and rice. No dessert.

APARNA: But I made your favourite.

JAY: Dadi, I am not going to eat any gulab jamun.

APARNA: Really? But who did I work so hard to make them for?

JAY: The neighbours.

APARNA: But you are my beloved grandson. You will break my heart if you do not try.

JAY: I'll break your heart if I don't eat the gulab jamun. I'll break your heart if I don't become a doctor. It's a wonder—

A knock at the door.

APARNA *nods at* JAY *to get the door.*

Fine. I'll go get it.

APARNA *puts the finishing touches to the meal. Nods, satisfied.*

JAY *returns with* TAYLAH *and* CHRISTINE.

CHRISTINE *offers a box of Jatz biscuits, already open.*

CHRISTINE: Taylah forgot to tell me that we had a dinner invite. I'm afraid I didn't have much at home …

APARNA *takes the box.*
APARNA: Thank you.
> JAY *takes the box from* APARNA.
> CHRISTINE *holds out her hand.*
> APARNA *holds up hands, palms together, offering namaskar.*
> *They both switch.*
> *Finally, an awkward handshake.*

JAY: I'll just put them on a plate.
> JAY *pours the Jatz onto a plate. There aren't very many.*
> *The others watch him in silence. It's excruciating.*

CHRISTINE: Right, then.
> APARNA *spoons some chutney into a bowl, offering it to* CHRISTINE *and* TAYLAH.
> *Beat.*
> *They each dip a biscuit and eat.*

TAYLAH: That's really good. What is it?
APARNA: It is … [*To* JAY] *chaatni ko Angrezi mein kya kehte hai?* (*In Hindi: What do you call chutney in English?*)
JAY: Chutney.
APARNA: Made from … *isko kya bolte hai?* (*In Hindi: What do you call it?*)
JAY: Apricots.
APARNA: Apricots!
CHRISTINE: I'd never thought of apricots as an Indian fruit. I always think of mangoes and …
> *Silence.*

APARNA: The fruit I want is not available here. Our other neighbour gave me apricots last year. Raw apricot.
JAY: Green apricots.
APARNA: Green apricots. I made it into chutney.
CHRISTINE: Which neighbour was that?
APARNA: Annie. House number fifty-two. We were friends.

CHRISTINE: Oh, I haven't seen Annie in a while. What's she up to?
APARNA: Stroke. She is expired.
CHRISTINE: Oh. I'm sorry to hear that.
APARNA: We are all old now. My husband is expired. My parents are expired. My sister is expired. Everyone left is old.

Beat.

CHRISTINE: Well, I don't think so. I think it's all a matter of perspective.

APARNA *nods politely.*

CHRISTINE: I'm still working and going strong, aren't I, Taylah?
TAYLAH: Uhh, sure.
JAY: Dope. Let's eat.

They sit. APARNA *serves rice. She starts with* CHRISTINE, *heaping her plate high.*

CHRISTINE: Oh, umm, there's no need to—Ooh, that's a bit much, could we—Taylah, do you want some of mine?

CHRISTINE *pulls her plate out from under* APARNA*'s ministrations and shares some rice with* TAYLAH. APARNA *is defeated. She uncovers dishes instead.*

TAYLAH: Oooh, that looks good. What is it?
APARNA: Chana masala.
TAYLAH: And what's that?
JAY: Spicy lentils. Well, chickpeas.
TAYLAH: Oh. Yum.

APARNA *urges* JAY *to serve.*

JAY: I'll do it.

JAY *takes* TAYLAH*'s plate and dollops on a spoonful of chana masala, hands it back.*

CHRISTINE: So, Aparna, how long have you been in Australia?
APARNA: Almost one year.
CHRISTINE: That's a long time away from your friends and family in India.
APARNA: My husband has expired. My sons are overseas. Sydney. California. Philadelphia.
CHRISTINE: What about friends?
APARNA: Difficult to make friends in Sydney. Very big. Very quiet.

CHRISTINE: It's not that quiet.
APARNA: No shops on the streets. No children playing. It is just houses, houses and houses. Everyone is in a house or car or in office.
TAYLAH: This is nice.
CHRISTINE: It's a bit spicy.
APARNA: You don't like it?
CHRISTINE: No, it's not that.
APARNA: Huh?
CHRISTINE: I can't really—I can't really eat a lot of this stuff. I don't do well with spices and dairy.
APARNA: I tried to make it less spicy.

Beat.

CHRISTINE: Right.
TAYLAH: Did you know, Dadi's sons are all doctors. Jay's dad too.
CHRISTINE: *Dadi?*
TAYLAH: It means grandmother, remember?

Beat.

CHRISTINE: Oh yeah. That's right.

A phone buzzes, JAY*'s.*

JAY: [*to* APARNA] It's Paapa.
APARNA: Answer it.
JAY: But …
APARNA: Pick it up.
CHRISTINE: We don't usually have our phones at the dinner table.
TAYLAH: Nan …

JAY *gets up from the table, taking the call.*

JAY: [*on the phone*] Hello, Paapa.

JAY *exits.*

CHRISTINE: Well then.

Silence.

Perhaps the muffled sound of JAY*'s conversation.*

APARNA: Please. Take some more. The daal is not too spicy.
CHRISTINE: No, thank you. I've had plenty.

APARNA: Taylah? Please take some more.
TAYLAH: I'm good, thanks, Dadi.
APARNA: You do not like it?
CHRISTINE: That's not what she said. She's just full.
APARNA: Oh. Okay.
CHRISTINE: It seems Taylah's taken a shine to you, Aparna.
APARNA: A shine?
CHRISTINE: She likes you. If only she was as chatty with her own grandmother.
APARNA: Taylah is very nice girl. She is like my own granddaughter.
CHRISTINE: She's not though, is she?
TAYLAH: Nan!
CHRISTINE: Because you're going to go away, right? Soon.
APARNA: Jay has made a Facebook for me. And I can call her.
CHRISTINE: Like everyone else who's promised to call.
TAYLAH: Please, Nan—

   JAY *reenters*.

JAY: So, my dad just called me—
TAYLAH: Oh …
JAY: —asking how some 'friend of mine' found his number and called him at work about sponsoring his mum's visa again.
   He said it was especially stupid when he'd told his wife and son to give him space.
CHRISTINE: Taylah, what did you do?
TAYLAH: I … I just wanted to help.
JAY: By calling my dad?
TAYLAH: Dadi wanted to stay and I wanted to help her.
JAY: She is not your Dadi.
TAYLAH: No, but—
JAY: You don't get to call her that.
TAYLAH: I'm sorry, I—
JAY: He doesn't answer my calls for months but you—you go right ahead and get in touch with him and that's when he calls me?
TAYLAH: I thought I could help.
JAY: How, Taylah? How exactly did you think you could help? That's so stupid!

CHRISTINE: Jay, maybe you should—
TAYLAH: I'm not.
JAY: He knew the visa was ending. He'd been thinking about it but this call from some random girl made him realise that it was all just drama.
TAYLAH: Jay, I …
JAY: Do you know what he said?
TAYLAH: What?
JAY: That he had his second chance now. That Dadi wasn't his problem anymore. That I wasn't his problem anymore.
CHRISTINE: Jay—
JAY: What?
CHRISTINE: Perhaps your mother could support the visa?
JAY: She doesn't have the money. She was a stay-at-home mum for twenty years because my dad always told her she wouldn't have to work. And it's not like my grandmother was even nice to Mum anyway, were you, Dadi?
APARNA: *Mujhe sharam aati thi.*
JAY: Why would *you* be ashamed?
APARNA: Because *my* son abandoned his wife and son. *My* son left his family for another woman. *My* son left his widowed mother like a burden on her daughter-in-law.
JAY: You're not—you're not a burden.
APARNA: All widowed women are. We have nowhere to go.
JAY: You do. I can … I'll sign the documents.
APARNA: You *can't*. You are a student. You have no income.
JAY: I just—I don't know how to fix this. Any of this. Why would you call him, Taylah? Why would you do that?
TAYLAH: I thought I could explain it to him. Make him understand. I was trying to help.
JAY: Why do you care? Why do you actually care what happens to my Dadi? It's *my* family.
TAYLAH: Because …
JAY: Because what?!
TAYLAH: Because I'm sick of people leaving.
CHRISTINE: I think that's enough.
JAY: Join the fucking club.

APARNA: Jay, *bas*!

JAY: Why, Dadi? He left. Dad left. And we don't talk about it. We don't talk about anything.

APARNA: Why should we talk about all of that? You focus on your studies.

JAY: Fuck studies! You need me more. Mum needs me more.

APARNA: Studying is the biggest help. Graduating and becoming a doctor, that is the biggest help.

JAY: You don't get to tell me what to do, Dadi. I heard Paapa say …

Before he left, he said he never wanted this life, his parents made him. You made him do it. He never wanted to be a doctor or marry Mum or have me.

APARNA: I made many mistakes.

JAY: I don't want to be like him.

CHRISTINE: Come on, Taylah. Thank Aparna for the meal.

APARNA: My heart …

APARNA breathes shallowly.

CHRISTINE: Are you okay?

APARNA: I …

CHRISTINE: Sit down. Does anything else hurt?

CHRISTINE sits APARNA down and checks her vitals.

APARNA: My arms. And my neck.

CHRISTINE: Right. Taylah, call Triple Zero. Now.

SCENE 11

A hospital room. APARNA *lies in a hospital bed asleep, monitors beeping.*

CHRISTINE, *in her scrubs, enters to take obs.*

APARNA *begins to wake.*

APARNA: What time is it?

CHRISTINE: It's four-thirty in the afternoon.

APARNA: How long …

CHRISTINE: Just overnight.

APARNA: I am in the hospital?

CHRISTINE: Nepean. Yes.
APARNA: This is where my son worked.
CHRISTINE: You're even in the cardio ward. Everyone here would have been his patients.
APARNA: Yours too.
CHRISTINE: Sometimes.

Silence.

APARNA: Is Jay okay? Is everyone okay?
CHRISTINE: Are *they* … ?

Laughing.

They're *fine*, Aparna. He went to get a coffee. Your daughter-in-law just went home to sleep. She's been here all night. Stop worrying about them. Think about yourself. Get some rest.
APARNA: And my … ?
CHRISTINE: He should be flying in this evening.
APARNA: All of our family dramas here in this hospital. What will people think?

Silence.

CHRISTINE: Should I go find Jay?

CHRISTINE *turns to exit.*

APARNA: Christine, wait. I have something to ask you. Will you look after my grandson? Like he is yours? Once I am gone.
CHRISTINE: Aparna, you're not going to die. It was serious but you're going to recover.
APARNA: No, not that. I still have to go back to India.

APARNA *tries to get out of bed.*

CHRISTINE: Aparna, you can't—Please get back into bed.
You can't travel like this. I'll speak to Dr Sharma when he gets in. We'll see what we can do about keeping you here. I mean, not the hospital. At home. In Sydney.
APARNA: I do not want to stay where they do not want me.
CHRISTINE: You know, teenagers have a funny way of saying the things we fear but never actually meaning it. They're very frustrating like that.
APARNA: Maybe I should go back to India. Not be a burden.

CHRISTINE: I think your grandson would argue otherwise.
APARNA: I do not have energy to argue.
CHRISTINE: Good. I'll send him in.

SCENE 12

A hospital corridor. JAY *drinks a coffee.*
TAYLAH *enters with a Maccas bag, watches for a moment.*

TAYLAH: How is she?
JAY: Hasn't woken up yet. Your nan's with her now.
TAYLAH: I'm sure she'll be fine. Nan's very good at her job. And how are you?

Silence.

Stupid question.

Silence.

JAY *spots the bag in* TAYLAH*'s hand.*

JAY: Is that …

TAYLAH *holds it out.*

TAYLAH: I figured you might not have eaten and the hospital café is *awful*. Even though my mum had cancer, that was definitely the worst bit.

JAY *takes it and looks inside.*

JAY: A Happy Meal.
TAYLAH: Yeah. I wasn't sure what else you liked.

Beat.

JAY: I lied to you.
TAYLAH: About?
JAY: The Happy Meal toy.
TAYLAH: Yeah?
JAY: It wasn't for my mum.
TAYLAH: Yeah, that was pretty obvious.
JAY: Maccas was a thing that my dad and I used to do. Mum was a KFC person—weirdo—but Dad would always get a McChicken and a Happy Meal for me. So … cheers.

TAYLAH: Is your dad coming?
JAY: Yeah, tonight. My mum called him.
TAYLAH: When did you last see him?
JAY: Months ago.
TAYLAH: Do you want to?
JAY: I don't know. But maybe he'll help Dadi stay.
Pause.
Are you still heading up to … where was it? I don't think you ever mentioned where your dad was other than just 'Queensland'.
TAYLAH: Gympie.
JAY: *Gympie*? Is that even a real place? It sounds wrong.
TAYLAH: Yep, and I'm not going.
JAY: Why not?
TAYLAH: Gympie's scene seems kinda country music. Not really my thing. I do not do flannel.
JAY: Hey, thanks for hanging out with Dadi the last few weeks. I think she really appreciated it.
TAYLAH: It was nice hanging out with Da—your grandma.
JAY: It's okay. You should call her Dadi.
She's so far away from everything she knows. I don't think she ever expected a life like this, you know?
TAYLAH: I don't think my nan did either. Your children are meant to bury you, not the other way around.
Beat.
JAY: So what are you going to do? Now that you're not going to … Gympie. Nah. Still sounds so wrong.
TAYLAH: I finished the song I've been writing. I was going to play it last night. After dinner, at the gig.
JAY: I'm sorry you missed it.
TAYLAH: That's okay.
TAYLAH: You should follow me.
JAY: Should I?
TAYLAH: You should. I posted the song this morning. You'll be able to tell everyone that you knew me before I was famous.
JAY: I wanna hear it.
TAYLAH: Now?

JAY: Why not?

> *Beat.*

TAYLAH: Okay. My guitar's in the car—

> CHRISTINE *enters.*

CHRISTINE: Your grandmother is awake.

JAY: Is she going to ...

CHRISTINE: She's going to be fine, she's just tired. And asking after you.

TAYLAH: See?

> JAY *hesitates.*

CHRISTINE: I'm sure it's fine.

JAY: But I said—I was an arsehole last night.

CHRISTINE: She just wants to see you.

> *Beat.*

> I promise. It's fine. If we stayed angry every time our grandchildren said or did something thoughtless, we wouldn't have enough hours in the day for anything else. Just go in and see her.

> JAY *goes to exit.*

> Oh, and Jay, try to get her to lie down and actually stay in bed.

> JAY *exits.*

> CHRISTINE *sits in* JAY*'s chair, exhausted.*

> *Silence.*

TAYLAH: I'm sorry I've been so, y'know, thoughtless.

CHRISTINE: That's alright, Taylah.

TAYLAH: It isn't though.

CHRISTINE: No, it isn't. But I get it. You're tired. I'm tired. God, I'm so tired.

TAYLAH: When's it going to stop feeling like this?

CHRISTINE: Couldn't tell you, love.

> *Beat.*

TAYLAH: I really miss her.

CHRISTINE: Me too.

TAYLAH: Sometimes it feels like ... none of this matters, you know what I mean?

Music doesn't matter. Getting a job doesn't matter. It's not going to make Mum come back or Dad suddenly want me to go and live with him.

Like, what's the point?

CHRISTINE: Of course it matters. It all matters.

I have seen so many people come and go from this hospital, from so many walks of life. Sometimes, they get better and they walk out of those doors. Sometimes, they don't.

But in forty years, I have never met someone who doesn't matter.

TAYLAH *hugs* CHRISTINE. *It catches them both offguard.*

TAYLAH: Thanks, Nan.

CHRISTINE *breaks the hug.*

CHRISTINE: I'll ruin my mascara.

TAYLAH: Nan, you've never worn mascara in your life.

CHRISTINE: Go get your guitar. I heard you, a little concert in the hospital? Live Aid, is it? The Aparna Telethon?

TAYLAH: Alright, alright. I'm going!

TAYLAH *exits.*

SCENE 13

A hospital room. APARNA *sits up in bed,* JAY *on the edge of her bed.*

JAY: So you'll stay?

APARNA: We will see.

JAY: When Mum called Paapa to tell him, it sounded like he would try to help.

APARNA: Stubborn, my son. Just like his son.

JAY: So are you. Christine told me you keep trying to get out of bed.

Silence.

JAY: Do you miss it? Home?

APARNA: There is nobody there. Nothing but my house.

But the neem tree is there, in our courtyard.

The Hooghly River is there and the Princep Ghat is there.

That has been home for all these years but what does that mean when all the people are gone?

JAY: I want you to stay.
APARNA: I want to stay too.

> TAYLAH *enters, guitar in hand.*
> CHRISTINE *trails behind her.*

TAYLAH: Hi, Dadi. How are you feeling?
APARNA: A bit tired, but okay.
TAYLAH: Sorry, I—
JAY: Dadi, Taylah wants to play her new song for us.
TAYLAH: Nan said I could come in and …
APARNA: I am very glad. You know I am very fond of music.
TAYLAH: Okay, do you want to—Nan, are you sure this is okay? It is a hospital and …
CHRISTINE: It's fine. It's just one song.
TAYLAH: Okay …

> TAYLAH *takes a deep breath. She sings.*
> *The song is full and rich and beautiful.*
> TAYLAH *finishes the song.*
> *There is silence.*

JAY: Wow.

> *Beat.*

APARNA: Very beautiful.
TAYLAH: Thank you.
APARNA: Very nice.
CHRISTINE: Oh, my girl. You sing like your mother used to.
TAYLAH: Thanks, I—
JAY: Shit. Taylah …
APARNA: Jay!
JAY: Sorry, Dadi. [*To* TAYLAH] You just … wow.
TAYLAH: Thanks.

> *Silence.*

Dadi, what was that song you sang?
APARNA: Which one?

> TAYLAH *hums 'Ye Banks and Braes'.*

Ohhhh.

APARNA *sings the first few lines of 'Phule Phule'.*

Phule phule dhole dhole … that one?

CHRISTINE: That's … That sounds like 'Ye Banks and Braes'.

TAYLAH: What?

CHRISTINE: It's an old Scottish song. I used to sing it to your mother when she was little.

TAYLAH: You did?

CHRISTINE: I'm sure she would have sung it to you.

CHRISTINE *sings the beginning of 'Ye Banks and Braes', and after a line,* APARNA *joins in in Bangla.*

TAYLAH: But how would Dadi know it? [*To* APARNA] How do you know the same song?

APARNA: These things, they are all connected. Like us now.

SCENE 14

CHRISTINE *and* TAYLAH*'s garden.*

Tayla stands with her guitar. Perhaps she strums it to the tune of 'Ye Banks and Braes'.

CHRISTINE *and* APARNA *work together in the garden,* APARNA *a little more stiffly than before. They do not hear* TAYLAH.

TAYLAH: Jay was right. His dad is a total dick.

But the famous cardiothoracic surgeon, Dr Sharma, does fly in and visit Dadi and then support her visa renewal. Finally.

And the Immigration Department says yes.

Jay transfers out of medicine to study business. He doesn't really love that either but it's not med and he'll finish heaps quicker and start with a decent salary. He can help his mum take care of Dadi.

His dad still sucks. My dad also still sucks.

Nan's finally retired. Hung up the scrubs and dusted off her secateurs. What a cliché!

She gets really into building flatpack garden furniture from IKEA. And she takes up baking scones and knitting socks for babies.

Beat.

Nah! No way, she'd suck at that. But she does volunteer with this program that runs a drop-in at local parks to help people get access to healthcare and stuff like that.

I quit working at Maccas and get a receptionist job at a recording studio. It has nothing to do with music, really, but I get to see other people doing the thing that I want to be doing and, I dunno, it helps. I guess.

I start singing around Penrith. I get some gigs in the city. Nothing too fancy, but I get to meet new people and some of them want me in their bands. I dunno yet. We'll see.

And then …

JAY *enters, carrying a Maccas bag.*

JAY: Hey, I wanted to talk to you about something.
TAYLAH: Go on.
JAY: Here?
TAYLAH: …
JAY: Okay, so …

TAYLAH *gestures to the bag.*

TAYLAH: That for me?
JAY: Uhh, yeah, I—
TAYLAH: You know I worked there for six months, right? I've seen things I can't unsee. And I don't go all mushy about Happy Meal toys the way that you do.
JAY: Low blow.
TAYLAH: What did you want to talk to me about?
JAY: We should hang out. Like, properly.
TAYLAH: We're hanging out right now.
JAY: You know what I mean.
TAYLAH: Remember what I said?
JAY: What did you say?
TAYLAH: 'This is not / a love story.'
JAY: 'Not a love story.' No. Definitely not.
TAYLAH: But I think I was wrong. I think it might have been a love story all along. Just not us two.
JAY: Yeah, nah, gross.
TAYLAH: Definitely. It was theirs.

TAYLAH *gestures to* CHRISTINE *and* APARNA *side-by-side in the garden.*
TAYLAH: All of ours.
JAY: I like that.
TAYLAH: Me too.
TAYLAH *and* JAY *share a smile.*

THE END

LOOKING FOR ALIBRANDI

by Vidya Rajan based on the book by Melina Marchetta

An award-winning multidisciplinary artist, VIDYA RAJAN works in writing for stage and screen, contemporary performance, comedy and interactive media. She is a graduate of the VCA and a former writer-in-residence at the Malthouse. Vidya's practice is deeply interested in play, speculative fiction, colonial legacies and emergent technology; and her work is often described as contemporary, inventive and sharply hilarious. Her work has been programmed by spaces like Arts House, Now or Never, Sydney Festival, Darwin Festival, the Blue Room, Griffin, Malthouse and Belvoir; and she has acted in and written for shows on ABC, Netflix and SBS, amongst others. Recently, her projects have been shortlisted for the International New Media Prize, the Freeplay game awards, and acquired by ACMI, while her scriptwriting both won (*The Feed SBS*—Comedy Writing) and was nominated for (*Looking for Alibrandi*—Best Stage Adaptation) awards at the AWGIEs.

Chanella Macri as Josephine Alibrandi (Josie) and Lucia Mastrantone as Christina in Malthouse Theatre and Belvoir Street Theatre's co-production of Looking for Alibrandi, *2022 (Photo: Daniel Boud)*

Looking for Alibrandi was first co-produced by Malthouse Theatre and Belvoir Street Theatre at Merlyn Theatre, The Malthouse, on the lands of the Wurundjeri Woi-Wurrung and Boon Wurrung peoples of the Kulin Nation, Melbourne, on 9 July 2022 with the following cast and creatives:

JACOB COOTE	John Marc Desengano
MICHAEL ANDRETTI	Ashley Lyons
JOSEPHINE ALIBRANDI (JOSIE)	Chanella Macri
CHRISTINA & SERA	Lucia Mastrantone
IVY & JOHN BARTON	Hannah Monson
NONNA, SISTER BERNADETTE & MARGARET THROSBY	Jennifer Vuletic

Director, Stephen Nicolazzo
Set and Costume Designer, Kate Davis
Lighting Designer, Katie Sfetkidis
Composer and Sound Designer, Daniel Nixon
Choreographer and Musician, Rosa Voto
Musician, Renato Vacirca
Vocal Coach, Matt Furlani
Dialect Coach, Paulo Bongiovanni
Cultural and Language Consultant, Lucia Mastrantone
Stage Manager, Cecily Rabey
Assistant Stage Manager, Harry Dowling
Understudy, Clarisse Bonello

Adapted from the 1992 novel by Melina Marchetta. This script was commissioned and developed by Malthouse Theatre, in partnership with Belvoir, and premiered at both theatres in their 2022 seasons. This is the consolidated 2025 script for National Tour with Brink Productions.

CHARACTERS

NONNA ALIBRANDI [KATIA]. An Italian woman in her sixties.

SISTER BERNADETTE. An older Anglo-Australian nun at Josie's school: St Martha's College.

MARGARET THROSBY. The Australian ABC radio broadcaster Margaret Throsby.

CHRISTINA ALIBRANDI. Mid-thirties, a first generation Italian-Australian woman. Daughter of Katia; mother of Josie.

SERA RUSSO. Eighteen, Josie's best friend at school, a fellow Italian-Aussie teen, fake-blonde hair.

MICHAEL ANDRETTI. Mid-thirties, a first generation Italian-Australian man. Josie's father.

JACOB COOTE. A seventeen-year-old teenager from a working-class Sydney suburb.

JOHN BARTON. A seventeen-year-old Anglo-Aussie teenager.

POISON IVY [IVY]. A seventeen-year-old Anglo-Aussie teenager. Rich, naturally blonde.

JOSEPHINE ALIBRANDI [JOSIE]. Seventeen going on eighteen. A second-generation Italian-Australian schoolgirl.

CASTING NOTES

This is a play for six actors.

The actor playing Nonna also plays Sister Bernadette and Margaret Throsby.

The actor playing Christina also plays Sera.

The actor playing John Barton doubles as Ivy.

The actor playing Josie does not/must not double.

The ensemble takes on roles of passing students, reporters, the Wog ASIO, etc.

ADAPTATION/STAGING NOTES

The play takes place in 1996, the year John Howard came into power, and the more positive assertions of the Labor government towards 'New Australians' became tenuous again. This adaptation seeks to emphasise the intergenerational relationship between the three Alibrandi women—a coming-of-age for one requires a coming-of-age for all. Josie's journey, in this reworking, is one of understanding the flimsy foundations of the 'Australian dream'; finding solidarity across generational healing, and seeing her own Otherness.

The production's choices/visual language should reflect these understandings if possible. The script here is written to reflect a fluid space: all action takes place in the Alibrandi kitchen—with passata-making stations in the original production. This space morphs into other places, times, imaginings and moments. The body and voice of Josie Alibrandi anchors the space and its point of view. The show has a feeling of sifting memory and time.

DIALOGUE NOTES

An interrupted line of dialogue is indicated by a dash, such as—.

Overlapping dialogue over two lines is indicated by a / in the lines.

At various times, Josie moves from addressing the audience to other characters. This is indicated in brackets [ ] as required.

When characters switch between Italian and English, this is indicated square brackets [ ] as required.

LANGUAGE & CULTURAL NOTES

The rhythms of interchanging Italian and English, as well as the syntax of Katia Alibrandi's English were developed in consultation with the director, cast and Italian language experts.

This is an un-translated version for reading purposes, with an invitation to performers to find their own colloquial expression and ownership of language through their own consultation.

The casting in this premier production supported this approach, with the cast members' differing dialects and ethnicities influencing their physical and linguistic performance choices, and the meaning these roles, and this 'Australian migrant story' might hold for them and an audience.

ACT ONE

1. BEFORE EVERYTHING

A moment in the space.
We are in a distant memory coming into being.
At first, the stage is in darkness. There is the feeling of being near the ocean, on the deck of a ship at night.
We hear faint sounds of a woman singing. An old Italian war-time song.
In glimmers of light, we start to make out the figure of this woman. We see she is dancing: an arm above her hand; a hand hitching up a skirt; feet en pointe.
Her song gains momentum. She starts to spin, to laugh—free and giddy.
The deck of the ship grows crowded with voices.
The woman grows disoriented.
Her laugh turns into a cry. She loses her balance.
Lights snap on.

2. THE YEAR BEGINS

Nonna's kitchen (present day).
We see the woman plainly now—it's NONNA. *Her cry morphs into an irritated scold as she realises she has stepped on a tomato. We see she is in a very domestic setting, her kitchen—the kitchen of an Italian nonna in the nineties.* NONNA *examines her foot, and yells out—*

NONNA: Josie!

> *Tomatoes roll into the space, as if tumbling out of clumsy arms ... and sure enough, here comes* JOSIE ALIBRANDI, *arriving like a storm, chasing after the fallen tomatoes and holding an empty carton in her arms.*
>
> JOSIE *stops short and looks at* NONNA—*oops! Then, she snaps to look right at the audience.*

JOSIE: [*to us*] Here we bloody go.

NONNA: [*Italian*] These are San Marzano tomatoes— [*English*] you think we can just go pick them in the field—

> CHRISTINA ALIBRANDI *enters, with her own crate of tomatoes. She kisses her mother.*

CHRISTINA: [*Italian*] Hi Mamma.

NONNA: [*Italian*] Look at this mess— [*English*] Why are you both so late, huh?

CHRISTINA: Someone had trouble waking up this morning.

JOSIE: It's literally six o'clock! [*To us*] National Bloody Wog Day— starts at the crack of dawn. Why? Nobody knows.

> CHRISTINA *and* NONNA *have already begun cutting the tomatoes.* JOSIE *joins in.*

NONNA: [*Italian*] I have been working since five in the morning, at my age, [*English*] at my age no help around here— [*Italian*] look at all of this— [*To* JOSIE, *English*] What are you doing? [*to* CHRISTINA] What is she doing?

CHRISTINA: She's cutting off the bad bits.

NONNA: Is horrible.

JOSIE: Hey!

NONNA: You do like that we have no tomatoes left.

> CHRISTINA *looks closer at* JOSIE'*s work.*

CHRISTINA: She's not completely wrong, Josie.

JOSIE: Alibrandi, you're the one who showed me.

CHRISTINA: Alibrandi, I thought you were ready—

> NONNA *grabs* JOSIE'*s knife off her.*

NONNA: She no ready— [*Italian*] You stick to sorting the bad tomatoes, okay? *Vabene.*

JOSIE: Ridiculous.

NONNA: [*Italian*] This your fault Christina, you have spoilt her. By the time I was her age I could— [*English*] Josie, I say I learn this when I was very young, by time I was your age—

JOSIE: I understand what you're saying!

NONNA: You no understand.

JOSIE: Yes I do! [*Italian, not a great accent*] By the time you were my age, you could make the sauce in your sleep, with your eyes closed!
CHRISTINA: *A capido?*

> NONNA *and* CHRISTINA *stare at* JOSIE *for a beat and burst out laughing. They imitate her bad Italian.*

JOSIE: Hey, I'm first in Italian class at St Martha's!
CHRISTINA: Come on, Josie—it's St Martha's. That's not saying much.

> JOSIE *rolls her eyes at us. She abandons her tomatoes and reaches into a backpack for some books—she's got more important things to do.*

> NONNA *and* CHRISTINA *continue with the tomatoes.*

[*To* NONNA] Ma, you alright for Josie to come over next Wednesday?
NONNA: Wednesday?
CHRISTINA: I'm working those nights now. If it's not alright, that's—
NONNA: [*Italian*] I am always alright! I tell you [*English*] come to live here and you say no. [*Italian*] Christina. Instead you send your daughter over while you go parading all over town.
CHRISTINA: I don't think doing the reception at Leichhardt Medical Centre is parading around town, Ma! I just don't want to leave Josie at home on a weeknight.

> JOSIE *looks at us, annoyed. Then, to* CHRISTINA *and* NONNA—

JOSIE: I'm perfectly capable of staying on my own, you know.

> *They ignore her.*

NONNA: Of course you not leave her at home alone, Christina! You not so crazy— [*Italian, to* CHRISTINA*, about the tomatoes*] Are you crazy? You're putting it in too quickly!
CHRISTINA: [*Italian*] My god, Ma!
JOSIE: Did you two hear what I just said?

> *Clearly not.* NONNA *and* CHRISTINA *have started to bicker.*

CHRISTINA: [*Italian*] I am putting it in fine, the water's boiling.
NONNA: [*Italian*] This isn't boiling. How can you say this is boiling?

> *As* NONNA *and* CHRISTINA *start squabbling over the pot in Italian,* JOSIE *turns to us.*

JOSIE: [*to us*] We usually come to Nonna's every weekend but now Ma's picked up an evening shift at the clinic and gotten it into her head that I can't be left alone. Like I don't have enough to deal with this year. Only the most important year of my life! But apparently, Nonna breathing down my neck every Wednesday after school is just what I need to ace the HSC. Thanks, Ma.

    NONNA *and* CHRISTINA*'s bickering rises.*

NONNA: [*Italian*] You're as bad as your daughter. These have been cut badly!

CHRISTINA: [*Italian*] They're fine. [*English*] I was in this house for seventeen years, I think I know how to make—

NONNA: [*Italian*] You learnt nothing and you are teaching her nothing—

    But JOSIE*'s had enough ...*

JOSIE: You know if it's so much trouble, why don't we just go down to Woolies and get some Leggo's? It tastes the same.

    CHRISTINA *and* NONNA *immediately freeze. The silence is murderous.*

    JOSIE *grins at us. She knows what she's just done ...*

    NONNA *begins to mutter in disbelief.*

NONNA: Leggo's ... Leggo's ...

CHRISTINA: Okay, Josie. [*Italian*] Have some respect. [*English*] You're not too old to be slapped.

NONNA: [*Italian*] See? See, Christina. Leggo's. You don't listen to me and look at her, [*English*] no understanding of tradition— [*Italian*] sits there laughing like a gypsy. *Leggo's*. [*English, to* JOSIE] Close your legs!

JOSIE: Can't, sorry. Didn't inherit the Alibrandi elegance like you and Ma. So, it's legs out for me, Nonna!

CHRISTINA: Josie!

JOSIE: What? I've got work to do, Ma. I can't be worrying about my bloody legs.

    JOSIE *returns very deliberately to her book.* CHRISTINA *sighs and goes over to her daughter, as* NONNA *stirs the passata, violently.*

    CHRISTINA *gently takes the book out of* JOSIE*'s hands.*

CHRISTINA: [*softly*] You're beautiful, okay, Josie? Now, come on—

> *She gestures for* JOSIE *to return to the passata-making.* JOSIE *sighs and gets up. As they return,* CHRISTINA *glances at the book.*

Romantic poets! I studied this at school you know—

> JOSIE *grumpily pummels some tomatoes, an echo of* NONNA's *own violent handling.*

JOSIE: Yeah, well. I was trying to get a head start 'cause some of us are trying to, you know, have a future. Don't see how you expect me to be first in my year if I'm always being interrupted.

CHRISTINA: Oh no, I don't. My wish for you has always been to be second. Third, even.

JOSIE: Uh-huh.

CHRISTINA: Do you think you can manage that?

JOSIE: I'll try my best.

> NONNA's *had enough of their camaraderie. She catches* JOSIE's *arm—*

NONNA: [*Italian*] You have to be careful! [*English*] Look at where she's putting this!

CHRISTINA: [*to* JOSIE] Where were you putting it?

NONNA: [*before* JOSIE *can say anything*] She is eighteen this year, Christina! And I try not to tell you, I keep my mouth shut, have I said even one word, but I can feel it, the curse—

JOSIE: [*to us*] Ooh a little early in the schedule, wondered when the curse would pop up.

CHRISTINA: Ma, not the bloody curse.

JOSIE: [*to us*] Nonna thinks all the Alibrandi women are cursed. Because bad things happen to us. Except the only bad thing she ever talks about is Mama giving birth to me, so ... yeah. Also, the devil is involved somehow.

> JOSIE *does the sign of the cross.*

NONNA: [*Italian*] Where is your belief? [*English*] Is real. The curse, you laugh at me but I know [*Italian*] is real. [*English*] But you never come to church. She never come to church, Christina.

JOSIE: I go to mass at school!

NONNA: [*Italian*] Please! Australians don't know how to do mass. [*English*] Australians don't know how to do mass.
JOSIE: It's the same thing, Nonna. Tell her, Ma.
CHRISTINA: Well ...
JOSIE: Ma!
CHRISTINA: They don't even drink the wine, Josie.
NONNA: [*Italian*] Anyway, doesn't matter, [*English*] you two never listen to me, you'll be lost to the devil forever.

> JOSIE *looks at us as if to say—told ya, here comes the mention of the devil.*

CHRISTINA: [*jokingly*] Ah but Ma, I thought I was already lost to the devil so long ago.

> *Everyone freezes.* NONNA'S *face goes stony, as* CHRISTINA *realises she's overstepped ...*

NONNA: [*Italian, to* CHRISTINA, *quietly*] You joke about this?

> *A panicked* JOSIE *rushes to speak over her, to save* CHRISTINA.

JOSIE: Hey—hey Nonna, do you have my uniform?
NONNA: What?
JOSIE: My uniform, you know how you said you'd alter it. But if you weren't able to, that's okay, we can go to a tailor or—
NONNA: [*English*] Of course, I able! Don't be silly—

> *She starts to look for it.*

—*Figamila*, yes I keep it here for you—let me see. I had to make big—you grow a lot these month.
JOSIE: Not that much!
NONNA: Yes. Very much. So big. So fast.
CHRISTINA: Ma. It's that age.
NONNA: [*Italian*] You. Shut up. [*English*] Make me coffee.

> CHRISTINA *squeezes* JOSIE'S *arm—don't take* NONNA'S *comments to heart, and heads to a spot in the kitchen to look for the coffee.*

> NONNA *retrieves her tailoring and flourishes the uniform at* JOSIE, *but becomes distracted by* CHRISTINA'S *search. She snaps—*

NONNA: [*English*] I not say espresso! Did I say I want espresso?

CHRISTINA: You just did.
NONNA: No, I say Nes-coffee.
CHRISTINA: [*Italian*] You didn't say Nescoffee!
NONNA: You know no how make to dress, now you know how to make Nescoffee?

> NONNA *shoves the uniform at* JOSIE *and goes over to* CHRISTINA.

CHRISTINA: For god's sake, of course I know how to—

> NONNA *pushes* CHRISTINA *aside, talks over her.*

NONNA: How you can pass on her anything, Christina, when you yourself cannot make a simple cup of Nescoffee—
CHRISTINA: I wasn't aware Nescoffee was a great tradition, Ma—

> *As* CHRISTINA *and* NONNA *start to bicker again,* JOSIE *sighs and looks at us, moving back to the passata area as she speaks.*

JOSIE: [*to us*] It's always the same old bloody thing. 'Tradition'. And I'm just here in the middle of it. I'm not sure how much more of this I can take, honestly— [*To* NONNA *and* CHRISTINA*, loudly*] Hey, you know I've really been wondering lately what it would be like, to be free, to be truly emancipated.

> NONNA *and* CHRISTINA *immediately stop talking.*

NONNA: What—what is she say—what is emancipey?
JOSIE: It's what the child stars do in Hollywood, Nonna, you know, to be separated from their awful families. I think I'd really love that.

> JOSIE *grins at us, and absentmindedly throws some basil in the passata pot.*

NONNA: [*English*] The way you speak! [*To* CHRISTINA] Christina, what will people say when they hear her speak like this?
CHRISTINA: Probably nothing they haven't already said before, Ma. Josie, stop teasing your Nonna—
JOSIE: I would never joke about emancipation. I love emancipation. *Emancipation*, Nonna.
NONNA: [*Italian*] See, the devil is at our door. The devil—

> *But* CHRISTINA *is staring at the basil in* JOSIE*'s hands.*

CHRISTINA: Oh god, Josie.

JOSIE: What?

> *She looks down at her hands.*

Shit.

> *As* JOSIE *hastily puts down the basil,* NONNA *and* CHRISTINA *launch into trying to save the passata. They push* JOSIE *out of the way and hover over the pot, as a cacophony of yelling in Italian at each other begins.*
>
> JOSIE *stares at them. The sight is comical at first, but then ... it's painful too ... these two women, sniping away, hunched over the pot, nothing ever changing ...*
>
> *Beat, then* JOSIE *turns to us.*

[*To us*] You ever just feel like you wanna take off? Away from everything in your life? Because if you don't, I dunno—

> *She looks at her mother and grandmother.*

—sometimes I feel I just wanna run, run so fast I'm already in tomorrow …

> *As she trails off, the scene morphs into ...*

3. *RADIO NATIONAL INTERVIEW*

ABC studios (the future).

... a radio show. We're on air, in the midst of an interview on ABC Radio National. This is a fantasy, though we shouldn't be quite sure of that yet ...

NONNA *is now* MARGARET THROSBY [THROSBY]. *And* JOSIE *has transformed too, into an 'older' version of herself.*

THROSBY: And if you're just joining us, our guest today is Josephine Alibrandi.

JOSIE: Thank you. Thank you so much for having me, Margaret. Throsby. I can never just say Margaret. Throsby.

THROSBY: Josie—you're a lawyer.

JOSIE: A barrister.

THROSBY: A barrister, a two-time Order of Australia medalist—didn't know they gave it out twice—

JOSIE: They made an exception.
THROSBY: And a mother. And a wife. To of course, my dear family friend's son—
JOSIE: Oh, are you friends with the Bartons?
THROSBY: Yes, I watched John grow from a little boy into the man he is today.
JOSIE: Oh, how wonderful. Yes, John and I have been soulmates since we met at school—
THROSBY: Yes, but Josie, you must tell me—
JOSIE: Yes?
THROSBY: You must tell me, / how you do it?
JOSIE: / How I do it? I get that question a lot, especially from young girls who look up to me, and I do take that responsibility seriously, Margaret. Throsby.
THROSBY: Mmmm, the girls. Yes. Yes.
JOSIE: Honestly, I owe it all to my mother—a saint—you know she had me at sixteen? She fell pregnant and was cast out of the family by my Nonno. And my Nonna said nothing and didn't see her until Nonno died.
THROSBY: Oh, Non-*NO*! Non—*NA*! How awful. How … *ethnic*.
JOSIE: Oh it was deeply ethnic, Margaret Throbsy. Deeply so. But that's how it was back then.
THROSBY: And your father?
JOSIE: Out of the picture. My mother did it all alone, never even told anyone who he was, except me.
THROSBY: And you never tried to find him?
JOSIE: No. We didn't need to. Especially after my scholarship to St Martha's, I was set.
THROSBY: Scholarship! Could you *be* any more of an inspiration?
JOSIE: Well—
THROSBY: Josephine.
JOSIE: Yes?
THROSBY: Josephine.
JOSIE: Yes, Margaret. [*Whispering*] Throsby.
THROSBY: Josephine Alibrandi!
JOSIE: Yes.

A school bell starts ringing and doesn't stop, as THROSBY *rises to transform into a nun—*SISTER BERNADETTE.

SISTER BERNADETTE *thrusts a rolled-up* Dolly *magazine into* JOSIE*'s hands.*

SISTER BERNADETTE: Josephine Alibrandi, just what do you think you're doing?

At this intrusion from real-life, a school-bell rings out and the scene snaps into ...

4. SCHOOL BEGINS

A classroom, St Martha's.

JOSIE *sits at a classroom desk, as* SISTER BERNADETTE *towers over her.* IVY *and* SERA *start to file in.*

JOSIE: Me, sister? What am I doing? Just my education, like always. I mean, we all need to know more about sinful urges, right? To be wary. It's a Catholic's quest in life. And sin is all around us. It's in here, for sure—

She taps the Dolly *magazine.*

—and it's definitely in the world. I mean, look at John Howard—sorry, Ivy, I know you love him.

IVY: What?

SISTER BERNADETTE: [*sighing*] You're a bright girl, Josephine. I'm not sure brushing up on *Dolly* magazine's 'Are you good-girl hot or bad-girl hot?' quiz is the best use of your time . Let's not start this year with detentions, again. This is study period. So, study.

JOSIE: Yes, Sister.

SISTER BERANDETTE: I'm ... going to take this away now.

SISTER BERNADETTE *tucks the* Dolly *magazine under an arm, and glides off.*

JOSIE: [*to* SERA] I reckon she's totally gone off to read it, hey.

SERA: You think she's gonna look for tips? Like, ten ways to please your man, except you can't because your man is God? Oh my god, Josie—nuns don't have sex! Imagine never having sex.

IVY: [*under her breath*] I don't think she needs to imagine …

JOSIE flinches. SERA notices.

SERA: *Vaffanculo.* Don't let her upset you, *bellezz.*

JOSIE: As if.

SERA: Good. 'Cause I'm having a breakdown thinking bout Sister Bernadette and I need some support. Like she's gonna go her whole life with no-one touching. Then she'll turn to dust and die. I can't even think about it!

JOSIE: Yeah, but nuns are Brides of Christ, right? So, Jesus probably pays her a visit from time to time.

SERA: [*laughing*] Oh my god, like when she prays? Maybe he makes her do stuff on her knees. Like a holy orgy. The father, the son and the holy ghost!

JOSIE: [*laughing*] That's fucked.

They collapse into loud giggles. IVY *looks over at them, and raises her voice.*

IVY: What is it with you wogs? Even if you're not going to work, respect that others are.

JOSIE: 'Scuse me?

IVY *stares at her and just looks back at her books.* JOSIE *starts to lose her cool.*

[*To us*] Fucken Ivy Lloyd! Always on my case like poison. Her father owns all of the North Shore obviously. Look at her. Mosman, obviously. Heard a rumour he's gonna buy her a breakfast show for her eighteenth. Classic. [*To* SERA] Oi, what are you doing??

SERA *has jumped up, rummaging through her bag in a panic.*

SERA: Oh my god, oh my god, oh my god.

JOSIE: What?

SERA *retrieves a tube of cream from her bag and stares at in dismay.*

SERA: I forgot! You cannot miss a day or you lose all your progress! Hold!

She shoves the tube at JOSIE *to hold, and starts to undo the buttons on her school shirt.*

JOSIE: Sera, what the fuck?
SERA: Cover me, *bella*!
JOSIE: I—what—
SERA: Quick!

> JOSIE *gives up trying to reason and jumps up to cover* SERA, *noticing as she does that* IVY *is staring at them with horrified disgust.*

JOSIE: What are you looking at? [*To* SERA, *in a loud whisper*] Sera, why does this smell like toothpaste?
SERA: [*loudly*] 'Cause it's got toothpaste in it! It's my own mixture. It's to firm up the collagen in your boobs. You should try it sometime, Josie. You too, Poison Ivy.
IVY: What did you just call me?
SERA: Oh my god, sorry—she just says Poison Ivy all the time, so now I say it.
JOSIE: I don't say it all the time! [*To* IVY] Only when you're being awful. [*To us*] So I say it all the time.
SERA: [*to* IVY, *holding out the mixture*] You sure you don't wanna try it?
IVY: I would rather die.
JOSIE: That can be arranged.
IVY: I'm sure it could. That's sort of your people's specialty, isn't it?

> *She smiles smugly at them.*

JOSIE: Our people?
SERA: What people?
IVY: Um … oh—maybe I wasn't being clear. I can speak slower, if that would help? English is a very complex language—
JOSIE: Do you wanna get your face smashed in?
IVY: Threats? Really, Josephine? I'm captain, Alibrandi, and though it's hard to believe, you're deputy captain. And you may not be used to this, but that comes with an expectation of—

> *Small beat.*

—class.
JOSIE: How could I forget … [*To* SERA] You done yet?
SERA: You got to be thorough, *bellezz*. You don't want them lopsided.
IVY: Fucking disgusting.

JOSIE *glares at* IVY *then looks at* SERA *and cringes. She sighs and looks at us.*

JOSIE: [*to us*] Sera Russo and I became friends because we're the only two wogs at St Martha's Our Lady of Anglo Conception—

JOSIE *does the sign of the cross.*

—she's not here on a scholarship though, obviously. Her dad's one of those new rich wog builders whose house has a bloody Trevi Fountain out the front. The Russos secretly look down on us sinful Alibrandis but they've gotta be nice to me 'cause Sera doesn't have many friends 'cause, well …

She looks at SERA.

Sera, is Sergio making you do this? [*To us, quickly*] Sera's boyfriend. Total parking-lot wog. Works for her dad actually. Dad still thinks she's the Virgin Mary.

SERA: No way, *bellezz*. It's for me and for him. You'll get it someday.

JOSIE: Doubt it.

An irate IVY *slams her book shut, tired of their chat.*

IVY: Honestly—did the two of you literally come off the *boat* this morning?

JOSIE *stares at her, a bit too shocked to respond.*

JOSIE: What did you say?

The school bell starts to ring as a smug IVY *glides off her desk.*

IVY: I … think she's done with her tits.

IVY *exits as* JOSIE *spins to face* SERA, *embarrassed.*

JOSIE: [*to* SERA, *fiercely*] I don't know why you had to do this right now!

SERA: You can't get beauty results without discipline, Josie. Didn't your mother teach you nothing?

JOSIE: No.

They look at each other and burst into laughter, traipsing off together …

5. WOG ASIO

A moment in the space.

JOSIE *and* SERA *sneak off to the beach after school, ducking and weaving, trying to avoid ... Wog ASIO! We see Wog ASIO—a bunch of nonnas in scarves and sunglasses—follow the girls like bloodhounds.*

SERA *blows a kiss at someone. Wog ASIO clutch each other in horror.*

JOSIE *smokes a cigarette. Wog ASIO freak out further.*

SERA *takes out a bikini. Wog ASIO reach their horrified peak and scatter immediately to report this terrible news to their network.*

The girls part. The scene morphs into ...

6. AFTERNOON AT NONNA'S

NONNA*'s living room.*

JOSIE *collapses onto a classic Italian nonna's house-style carpet. Next to her,* NONNA *is already on the floor, surrounded by photo albums.*

NONNA *thrusts an open album at* JOSIE, *tapping a photo.*

NONNA: Here it is, Josie—this is the one! You see this one?

> JOSIE *glances at it. She looks for a surface to put her homework down.*

JOSIE: Yeah, Nonna, you've showed me like a thousand times.

NONNA: Look at my hair, here. All the girls in my village, always jealous of me.

JOSIE: We know. You're good-looking, Nonna.

NONNA: No! All gone now. But then, yes, so many men after me.

> JOSIE *mouths along as* NONNA *speaks.*

Five proposals, Josie. On boat to Australia, five men ask me to marry but I say no to all. I am engage to Nonno. He waiting for me in Australia. Five.

JOSIE: Any hot ones though?

NONNA: [*Italian*] Be quiet. [*English*] When I turned fourteen, my mother stopped me play in the street. I had to stay home. Every

evening I see the [*Italian*] sunset [*English*] sun go down. Moon go up. I inside.
JOSIE: Ugh, sounds like studying for the HSC. Speaking of which, / Nonna, I should—
NONNA: [*Italian*] Are you even listening, Josie? [*English*] There was girl in my village, friend of my sister your Zia Patricia, she was engage to very nice man—but he die in war. Then her neighbour he was always talk to her, one day he convince her go out at night and then—what can you do—she was finish! [*Italian*] The devil was at her side from that moment. [*English*] She should have stayed in and watched the sun.
JOSIE: What do you mean she was finish? He murdered her???
NONNA: Murder? No. But maybe she die would be better.
JOSIE: Oh my god, what happened?
NONNA: She do things only wife should do and after that night, nobody will marry her.
JOSIE: Nonna, what the hell? You're so dramatic.

But NONNA *can't keep it in any longer. She stands up.*

NONNA: Let me fix your hair.
JOSIE: What?
NONNA: Let me fix.

She reaches for JOSIE*'s hair, just as* JOSIE *ducks.*

JOSIE: It's the fashion, Nonna!
NONNA: Is not fashion. Is wet!
JOSIE: So?
NONNA: So! I see you at beach, Josie! Not I see—but Signora Formosa saw you, she tell Signora Centofante, she tell Signora Fabretti, and she tell Zia Patricia—
JOSIE: Who told you! Of course— [*To us*] the bloody WOG ASIO! Most deadly force known to man. Honestly, they should be recruited— [*To* NONNA] Why was Signora Formosa even in Coogee?? They have a sale on Sopressa or something? I knew I'd seen something.
NONNA: She see you, Josie! She see something! You! With Sergio—Sergio Miloti—he not good boy. I don't want to say, but his family—the Milotis—is not good family.
JOSIE: Nonna, Sergio is Sera's boyfriend.

NONNA: Oh.
JOSIE: Yeah.
NONNA: Boyfriend.
JOSIE: Yes. Sera's boyfriend. My friend Sera, remember? Sergio, *her* boyfriend, just met us at the beach after school.
NONNA: Sera … Sera Russo … the Russos.
JOSIE: Here we go.
NONNA: They think they so much better than us. You know when your Nonno died, they no even come to the Lutto … [*Whispering*] Sera Russo.
JOSIE: Yeah, that could have been to do with Nonno, couldn't it? He wasn't exactly a great guy, was he?
NONNA: [*Italian*] Bite your tongue. Wash your mouth. [*English*] We not speak of the dead like this. We not.
JOSIE: You're the one who brought him up!
NONNA: This attitude. This is your mother talking.
JOSIE: No, Ma never says a thing about Nonno.
NONNA: She been putting poison in your mind.
JOSIE: She doesn't have to! He kicked out his teenage daughter when she was pregnant, how could I not think he was horrible?
NONNA: He not horrible! He try to protect—
JOSIE: And aren't you always going on about how he was so strict and never let you dance in the house. And how you used to be such a great dancer and—
NONNA: [*Italian*] Stop it, Josie! [*English*] He only try to keep me safe. I was—you know nothing of the world, Josie. You not know how your mother ruin our life—
JOSIE: You know, Nonna, if she ruined your life so much, why do you want us here all the time? Like, why am I even here right now??
NONNA: Yes, why you here! Go! Go! If you acting like this, I not want you here, Josie!
JOSIE: Great!
NONNA: Very good!

> JOSIE *grabs her backpack and jumps up.*
>
> NONNA *tries to speak, but can't master herself. She looks away.*
>
> JOSIE *storms off, and collides straight into*—MICHAEL ANDRETTI.

JOSIE: Ow!
MICHAEL: I'm so sorry. / The door was open.
NONNA: / Josie? What happen?

> JOSIE *pulls away from* MICHAEL, *to reveal him.* NONNA *stops, shocked.*

MICHAEL: I should have knocked, I'm sorry.

> *Beat.*

NONNA: [*Italian*] Michael?
MICHAEL: Signora. [*Italian*] The door was open, I'm sorry.
NONNA: I leave open in summer.
MICHAEL: Yes … I remember.

> NONNA *gasps and gets a hold of herself, jolting into her manners.*

NONNA: [*Italian*] Michael! I cannot believe it is you!

> *They walk rapidly to each other to embrace, talking quickly and affectionately.*

MICHAEL: Signora, you look the same.
NONNA: Michael! Michael Andretti! Don't lie.
MICHAEL: The house as well. I feel I have stepped back in time—

> JOSIE *seems suddenly unsteady on her feet, her backpack drops. She looks ashen. She sits down.*

NONNA: Michael—look at you— [*Italian*] It's been so long! [*Italian*] How many years? [*English*] Fifteen—twenty years! [*English, to* JOSIE] So long, Josie! Oh! [*To* MICHAEL] Michael! This Josie! My [*Italian*] granddaughter. [*English*] Oh still so handsome! How your mother and father? They here also?
MICHAEL: [*trying to get a word in*] Uh no, they're still in Adelaide—

> *He looks at* JOSIE.

—your granddaughter? So—
NONNA: You lawyer now. I hear! [*To* JOSIE] He smartest boy Josie from young age. His parents our neighbour long time ago. The Andrettis. Oh! [*To* MICHAEL] Michael! Michael!
Josie want to be lawyer also. But I think not good idea. Oh!— where my manner, Michael?—You want coffee?—Why you here?

MICHAEL: I've—I've moved for work, Signora. Not sure for how long. Depends on how the case I'm on proceeds—

NONNA: [*Italian*] Good! Sit, sit! [*English*] What was I doing? I getting old Michael—

MICHAEL: No, you look the same, Signora.

NONNA: [*Italian*] Michael, you're making me blush. [*English*] Nescoffee? Or espresso? I make Nescoffee.

> NONNA, *chattering away to herself, goes to get the coffee, leaving* MICHAEL *and* JOSIE *alone.*
>
> *Beat.* JOSIE *looks at him, then looks away quickly.*

MICHAEL: So—you're—you must be … Tina's daughter?

> *The name jolts* JOSIE. *She snorts.*

JOSIE: *Tina?*

MICHAEL: Oh, that's what I—I used to—Christina, I meant.

JOSIE: Yeah. That's my mother.

MICHAEL: [*startled*] So she has … but she didn't … I thought …

> *He trails off. Beat.* JOSIE *stares at him.* MICHAEL *tries to recover.*

Why does Katia think you shouldn't be a lawyer?

JOSIE: [*snapping*] I don't know? Maybe because she's a hundred years old and she's crazy! Or maybe 'cause she thinks I don't have much control over my emotions, which is saying something coming from her. Or maybe she just hates anyone who does anything without her approval.

> *She stops, realising she's gone too far.*

I've gotta get home.

> *She starts to pack her backpack, readying to leave.* MICHAEL *scrambles—*

MICHAEL: Oh, okay! Well, nice to meet you, Josie.

> *Small beat.*

And, you know, a lot of lawyers don't have much control over their emotions … so I wouldn't worry about that.

> JOSIE *pauses.*

MICHAEL: Not that I'm saying you were worried.

JOSIE: Do you?
MICHAEL: Do I … ?
JOSIE: Have a lot of control over your … emotions?
MICHAEL: Oh. Generally. Yes.
JOSIE: And you were always like that? Since you were younger?
MICHAEL: I'd say so.
JOSIE: Never got carried away?
MICHAEL: Not more than usual.

>JOSIE *scoffs.*

JOSIE: [*to herself*] So you're a liar too.
MICHAEL: Sorry?
JOSIE: You know, my mother … *Tina* … she had me *very* young.
MICHAEL: Right.
JOSIE: I dunno if you can tell, but I'm seventeen.
MICHAEL: Right …
JOSIE: I'll be eighteen *soon.*
MICHAEL: Oh.
JOSIE: Yup.

>*Beat. She waits for him to process. He is clearly struggling.*

Okay then. Bye.
MICHAEL: Wait—um, Josie—wait—
JOSIE: [*losing it*] No, I can't! I don't have all day, you know! Some of us need to go back to our tiny apartments and study for Year Twelve at our tiny desks so we can go to uni so we can earn money so we can help our poor mothers have a better life someday—
MICHAEL: That's not—that's not fair …
JOSIE: Yeah, 'cause *you* really know what fair is.

>NONNA *comes in with the coffee, as* JOSIE *hoists her backpack and runs out without another word.*

NONNA: Josie? [*To* MICHAEL, *Italian*] I'm so sorry for her rudeness— [*Calling after* JOSIE] —Josie!

>NONNA *looks at* MICHAEL, *embarrassed. They leave, as* JOSIE *loops back into the space and the scene morphs into …*

7. BACK HOME

CHRISTINA *and* JOSIE*'s living room.*

A sobbing JOSIE *flies into* CHRISTINA*'s arms.* CHRISTINA *soothes her.*

JOSIE: I don't know why I'm so bothered! It was just so weird, Ma!
CHRISTINA: [*Italian*] It's okay. [*English*] Of course you are. You've never so much as seen him before.
JOSIE: I had to stand there as Nonna brought him Nescoffee and went on about how he was the second coming of Christ. I didn't give anything away though. She doesn't know.

> CHRISTINA *pulls away from* JOSIE. *A twinge of guilt.*

CHRISTINA: Josie, I don't want you to feel like … you know, I've only kept it from Nonna all these years because it seemed like the best thing to do … but you shouldn't—
JOSIE: Alibrandi! You don't have to explain it to me! After how Nonno and Nonna treated you! She was talking about him too today, defending him. She doesn't deserve to know anything. She'd just use it to find more problems with you.
CHRISTINA: Maybe …
JOSIE: Not maybe. Definitely.
CHRISTINA: You must be starving, Josie. Sit.

> CHRISTINA *busies herself with dinner prep.* JOSIE *looks at her mother—weird response—but she sits.*

JOSIE: I'm sorry I even told him. It just came out.
CHRISTINA: Please, Josie. Don't be. It's natural.
JOSIE: I wish I hadn't. He was just so arrogant. And so, ugh! I think I just got upset he was acting like he was so innocent.
CHRISTINA: [*lightly*] You know, I'm surprised your Nonna hasn't called yet. Running out without saying goodbye, in front of a guest? She's probably plotting to kill us actually.

> JOSIE *stares at* CHRISTINA, *who places some dinner down and joins her at the table.*

JOSIE: What's wrong?

CHRISTINA: What do you mean?
JOSIE: You just seem so ...
CHRISTINA: I'm fine. Come on, eat.

> JOSIE *stares at the bowl of food.*
>
> *Beat.*

CHRISTINA: Is it the croutons? Just go around them.
JOSIE: Ma!
CHRISTINA: What?
JOSIE: Is it 'cause I saw him? Are you upset I saw him?
CHRISTINA: Of course not, Josie. You couldn't help seeing him. And I'm not upset.
JOSIE: Yes, you are. You're always like this when something is up! [*To us*] My mother and I are perfectly attuned to each other. We can always tell what the other is feeling. Even before it's spoken. [*To* CHRISTINA] Something else is wrong, Ma. What is it? Are we being evicted again?
CHRISTINA: Josie, no! Also that was one time, so long ago. The way you still bring it up.
JOSIE: Something with your job then? Did your boss say something creepy? I've always thought Dr Pirelli had another game going with you, asking you to take on all these extra nights.
CHRISTINA: Josie! Dr Pirelli has been very kind to even give me this extra shift.
JOSIE: Women of your generation don't think they have a choice, but you can file for harassment, you know—
CHRISTINA: Josie, the only one harassing me right now is you!

> *Beat.*

I didn't mean it like that.

> *Small beat.*

JOSIE: You saw him. You saw him too.

> CHRISTINA *looks at her, surprised ... and then, she laughs. She reaches over.*

CHRISTINA: My daughter sees through everything! My fault for deciding to raise you like an equal—

JOSIE: Hardly. You don't even let me stay at home by myself.
CHRISTINA: Too much openness and now I can't even keep a secret from a child for a second! Yes Josie, I saw him.
JOSIE: Did he contact you?
CHRISTINA: No, a coincidence. Before work this morning. It was only for a minute or two. At the bus. He said he was visiting 'the old neighborhood'. I said I was going to work and that was all. I didn't even say I had a daughter. Of any age.

She looks down, seems to swallow.

JOSIE: Ma, don't cry!
CHRISTINA: [*snapping back up*] Of course not, Josie. You know I don't cry over silly things.
JOSIE: I hate him!
CHRISTINA: You don't hate him.
JOSIE: I do, Ma!
CHRISTINA: You don't even know him. Seeing him today, Josie ... I just, I think I'd forgotten he was real, somehow ...

She trails off, seeming to quiver again.

JOSIE: Well, I don't wanna know him! And he clearly doesn't want to know me. I could tell.
CHRISTINA: That's ... that's his loss then, kiddo.

Small beat.

He was probably just in shock.
JOSIE: Who cares, Ma? He made up his mind a long time ago— [*Stopping her*] I know, I know—but like you've always said, what kind of Catholic gets his girlfriend pregnant and believes her when she says she'll take care of it? He never even checked up on us. He didn't wanna know us then. And he doesn't wanna know us now.

The phone rings.

CHRISTINA: There she is.
JOSIE: If she asks why I ran out on fucking Michael Andretti, tell her it's 'cause he's fucking boring and fucking ugly.
CHRISTINA: Josie! Language!

The phone rings.

JOSIE: Seriously, when's Nonna gonna realise that if she wasn't so bloody worried about what people would think all the time, our lives wouldn't be in this mess in the first place?

CHRISTINA pauses. The phone rings. Then stops.

CHRISTINA: Do you think our lives are a mess, Josie?

JOSIE: What? No! That's not what I— [*To us*] Aaaaah! My mother is a perfect angel and honestly, I'm such a brat sometimes, like I just forget what she's been through and just say anything. [*To* CHRISTINA] That's not what I meant, Ma. Sorry. [*To us*] My new year's resolution was to become a better person before I was eighteen but so far I think I'm failing. [*To* CHRISTINA] I'm gonna think more before I bloody speak. I promise, Alibrandi.

CHRISTINA takes in her daughter, softens.

CHRISTINA: Oh, you're fine, Alibrandi. And … I'm fine too, Alibrandi. Okay?

JOSIE nods. The phone rings again.

JOSIE: I can pick up.

CHRISTINA: No, just leave it. I think we deserve some dessert.

She picks up her keys.

JOSIE: You … have the devil in you, Alibrandi!

They hug, laugh and walk off.

The phone rings on and on and morphs into the sound of a klaxon, beeping. A flurry of movement on stage, students move across the space—

8. HAVE A SAY DAY!

An event space, Sydney CBD.

It's Have a Say Day—an inter-school event for students across Sydney.
SISTER BERNADETTE *crosses the space, blaring into a megaphone, barking directions at the flurry of bodies.*

SISTER BERNADETTE: Attention all students, please assemble in an orderly fashion to your designated rooms. Sera Russo! What are your hands doing to your chest?? John Barton, shouldn't you be in the green room?

JOHN BARTON, *deep in his palm cards, looks up, surprised at being addressed.*

JOHN: Just waiting for someone, Sister.

He spots JOSIE *and waves, lighting up, just as she does.* JOSIE *runs over.* SISTER BERNADETTE *rolls her eyes—she has no time for young love ... or whatever this is. She glides away in haste.*

SISTER BERNADETTE: Everyone, in your designated rooms, now please!

JOSIE *and* JOHN *ignore her and hug. Then, she punches him.*

JOHN: Ow. What was that for?

JOSIE: For not getting in touch all summer! I thought you were in some palazzo in bloody Europe but then I find out you've just been here. Not hanging out with me.

JOHN: Here in body, maybe. But in spirit? Thanks to the election being called early, all I did was fundraise up and down the coast with the old man. I've eaten enough lobster to last a lifetime. Did you have a good summer?

JOSIE: Mmm, mine was much the same. Too many finger sandwiches. Too much champagne. Too many luncheons with members of the Senate.

JOHN: The Senate? Josie, your Australian civics is still terrible.

JOSIE: [*laughing*] I know! It's just *fucken* boring. [*To us*] God, he's so smart. Normally, that would piss me off. But with John, it's never been a competition. We just connect and want each other to get through all the bullshit together. [*To* JOHN] How are you feeling about your big speech? Ready for your close-up?

JOHN: I guess.

He gestures to his palm card.

'Australia should not be a Republic' [*Sarcastically*] Real barn-raiser. What's yours?

JOSIE: I'm doing the one on AIDS and the church I did at assembly that time, remember?

JOHN: Oh yeah, that was great! An incisive critique of Catholic values, sexuality, and the Vatican while somehow still praising the role of abstinence. They'll love it.

JOSIE: Yeah, I thought of writing something new but—

JOHN: Nah, best not to take any risks on Have a Say Day. The MOST important day of the year ... when the nation stops to LISTEN to the VOICE of the YOUTH.
JOSIE: Yeah, I'm sure they're taking down everything we're saying in Parliament right now.
JOHN: As an MP's son I can tell you that they are absolutely one hundred percent ... not doing that. Unless—

He gasps and grabs her shoulders.

—you're not a party donor's kid, are you?
JOSIE: I'm so sorry, but no!
JOHN: Too bad.

Small beat, then he sighs.

Honestly, I don't even wanna do mine. Don't believe a word of it. But the media are gonna be here, so ...

He trails off. Small beat.

JOSIE: [*sympathetic*] Your dad?
JOHN: Yeah. Yes. I think he thinks this is my first campaign event. First this, then law school—
JOSIE: With me!
JOHN: That'll be fun, at least, for a few years. But then ... junior minister, then Prime Minister. That's House of Reps.
JOSIE: Yeah, or you could just skip all the boring politics, and we can open our own firm after we graduate.
JOHN: Don't make any promises you can't keep, Josie.
JOSIE: What? Why wouldn't I?

Small beat. JOHN *backtracks.*

JOHN: I just meant ... life is long. Things change.
JOSIE: Not for me! I've always known what I've wanted and that's not gonna change.
JOHN: [*laughing*] You are definitely the most passionate person I know. I wish I had a quarter of your decisiveness.
JOSIE: You don't need it, I've got plenty for both of us. Just stick with me.
JOHN: Sounds perfect. But for now, I should probably—

He gestures offstage, to exit.

—honestly you should be the one up there, not me.

JACOB: Why don't you give it up then, mate?

> JOSIE *and* JOHN *swivel to look at* ... JACOB COOTE, *who entered while they were speaking.*

JACOB: Heya Josie—

JOSIE: Ugh. [*To us*] Jacob Coote. Total shit head. Used to throw eggs at Sera and I when we first started at St Martha's.

JOHN: Jacob.

JACOB: Barton. So? You think it's fair, do you? Some of you doing your speeches to camera in that fancy camera room, and us plebs having to 'have a say' to the other plebs out here.

JOSIE: Only captains do the speeches on TV, Jacob—that's how it's always been done.

JACOB: Not all captains. I'm captain at Cook High.

JOSIE: Yeah, well it *is* Cook High. [*To us*] Public school on the North Shore. Full of delinquents— [*Gesturing at* JACOB] Exhibit A.

> *As she speaks,* SERA *runs in.*

SERA: Oh my god, John! John! They're calling your name over there. Sister Bernadette's losing her shit.

JOHN: Oh thanks, Sera. Guess I'll—

JACOB: Seriously mate, if you don't think you deserve it why don't you give Alibrandi here a chance, or even Russo?—You'd be great on TV, Sera.

JOSIE: No, she wouldn't.

SERA: Oh my god I could never, my father would kill me. [*To* JOSIE] Oi *bellezz*! Have you seen my boobs?

> SERA *points at her chest.* JOSIE *reluctantly looks, and starts.*

JOSIE: Wait—has your dress shrunk?

SERA: Told you it works!

JOSIE: Fucking ridiculous.

> JOHN *clears his throat, readying to leave.*

JOHN: [*to* JACOB] I agree by the way, Coote. It is unfair. Completely. You wanna swap?

He extends his hand. Beat. Then, JACOB *grins and shakes* JOHN*'s hand.*

JACOB: Nah, you're alright, mate. Give the member for Manly my regards!

JOHN: Warringah, actually.

JACOB: What's the bloody difference?

JOHN breaks into a laugh, and starts to leave.

JOHN: Not much, Coote. Not much. Good luck everyone! And Josie, see you soon, yeah? At the dance, maybe?

JOSIE, *crush-struck, yells after him.*

JOSIE: Yes! Dance! The dance! See you there! Good luck, John! And tell Ivy I hope she trips! And dies!

JOHN: [*jokingly*] Shut up.

JOHN *exits and* JOSIE *stares after him, a bit dreamy.* SERA *and* JACOB *clock it, and snigger.* JACOB *pinches* JOSIE*'s palm cards without her noticing and starts to rifle through them.*

JACOB: You don't stand a chance, Alibrandi.

JOSIE: [*starting*] What?

JACOB: Ivy and John—they grew up together, their dads play golf together, their mothers day-drink prosecco together and they're really blonde.

SERA: I'm blonde.

JOSIE: You're Calabrese.

SERA: So what?

JOSIE: It's from the bottle.

SERA: Oh … yeah.

JACOB *interjects, reading off* JOSIE*'s palm cards.*

JACOB: Hah! 'An indictment—AIDS and the Catholic church—abstinence as a path!' This is what you're going with, Alibrandi?

An annoyed JOSIE *snatches her cards back.*

JOSIE: It's a very important topic.

JACOB: You'd do more good teaching people to put on a condom.

SERA: Nah, Josie doesn't know about that! But it's a good idea, Jacob. You got a lot of good ideas, Jacob … Cute.

JOSIE: Are you on heat or something?

SERA: Always, *bellezz.*
JOSIE: [*to* JACOB] What are you even talking about anyway? How women should lean against cars half-naked?
JACOB: Mm yeah, I mean that is something I'm very passionate about—very passionate—

> *He grins at a giggling* SERA.

—but nah, I'm gonna talk about how young people should participate in democracy.

> *Beat.* JOSIE *snorts.*

JOSIE: Okay, good luck. It's all bullshit. No-one's listening unless you're a party donor's kid anyway.
JACOB: So cynical, Alibrandi. I don't think it's bullshit.
SERA: I don't either, Jacob!

> JOSIE *tries to pull* SERA *away from* JACOB.

JOSIE: Ugh, Sera—can you not—why does every girl at school turn to jelly in front of this idiot?
SERA: They got eyes.
SISTER BERNADETTE: [*over the loudspeaker*] And now, from Cook High, Jacob Coote.
JACOB: Shit, that's me.
SERA: Go Jacob Cute!

> SERA *claps.* JOSIE *rolls her eyes.* JACOB *clears his throat and faces us, the scene transforming into the moment of his 'Have a Say Day' speech. He plays the audience, a real charmer and clown.*

JACOB: G'day dickheads! Whew, got that out of the way. Could see the teachers shaking in their little boots—wondering what I was gonna say, but now we don't have to worry, ey. Called you dickhead, what's next? Well, I'm not gonna be as erudite as my esteemed neighbour up there before me, talking bout how the Pope says you gotta keep it in your pants. Look, I'm a car mechanic's son from Redfern. I don't have time to think about his holiness. But I was thinking bout this letter I got the other day—telling me I could register to vote …

> *He pulls it out of his pocket—it's crumpled.*

... yeah alright, first I made it a little ball and I was gonna shoot it in the bin but then I was like if everyone thought like that, and nobody voted, any asshole could run this country, couldn't they? I just hope it's not Damo.

He points to someone in the audience.

Nah, you're alright, mate. And I know there's a lot of assholes already running this country, but at least we get a say in which one it is. Like if you think about what happens overseas—in some countries like China they have one-party systems, and when the people come out and have a say like we're doing today—when they scream and shout and voice their opinion—their own army shoots them. Young people like us.

So yeah, we can be apathetic. We can just chill out and not vote. Say it's bullshit. We can be ignorant and all be proud of that ignorance. Or—

He scrunches the paper up and plays with it.

—we can choose to feel freedom. The freedom to choose our future—the same feeling of freedom I feel when riding a motorbike, or when I'm watching the Rabbitohs play and it gives me a tingle in my balls. Sounds good, right? So what do you say? Let's hear it for the freedom in my balls! And the freedom in your balls! Or non-balls! Yeahhh!!

He's got the audience clapping by this point.

I'm Jacob Coote and I endorse every fucking one of you.

> SERA *whoops as* JACOB *kicks the scrunched up paper like a football. It probably hits* JOSIE.
>
> JACOB *grins at* JOSIE, *as if to say, 'What did ya think?'* JOSIE *tries not to look impressed, but despite herself ... she is.*
>
> *As* SERA *and* JACOB *exit,* JOSIE *stares out at us, breathing to steady herself. For some reason ... she's flushed. The space darkens and the scene morphs into ...*

9. GETTING READY

NONNA's *living room.*

A flurry of giddy movement. We see JOSIE *being pinned and prodded by* NONNA *and* CHRISTINA *as they try to alter her dress for the dance.*

JOSIE: [*Italian*] Nonna! It looks terrible. [*English*] I look like I'm going to mass. Ma!

NONNA: [*Italian*] If you don't stand still, how can I adjust it?

JOSIE: I don't need you to adjust it—I need you to chop off half of it.

NONNA: Why? You want the entire world to see inside you.

CHRISTINA: [*Italian*] Okay, okay—look we can take it up here—easy.

She pins it a little.

[*English*] That looks nice.

She starts to brush JOSIE's *hair as* JOSIE *looks at herself.*

JOSIE: I look hideous. Like a hairy buffalo that's pretending to be a nun.

CHRISTINA: I think this is very sophisticated, Josie. Very grown-up.

JOSIE: Why couldn't I have got my looks from your side of the family? If anything, it's clear I look like him!

She stops short. CHRISTINA *freezes.* NONNA *notices, but isn't quite sure ...* JOSIE *tries to cover ...*

JOSIE: I mean, it has to be him, doesn't it? Whatever he looks like, that's what I've got. Nonna, can you just take this bit up here?

NONNA *moves to do so, grumbling.* JOSIE *breathes out—crisis averted?*

NONNA: [*English*] Is too much, Christina. People will look at her like she's for sale.

CHRISTINA: [*Italian*] It's fine, Mama—it's the fashion.

NONNA: [*Italian*] Que fashion! [*English*] Is many Australian boys tonight, Josie?

JOSIE: Yeah, it's inter-school, Nonna. Skip boys for miles.

NONNA: I not like this.

JOSIE: Nah, it's the best night to catch one.

NONNA *gets up, she's finished altering.* JOSIE *twirls—not bad.*

NONNA: Catch one? [*Italian*] Don't be disgusting, Josie. [*English*] They only want one thing. [*Italian*] Christina, you going to let her go out with them? Who's she going with? How she get home?

CHRISTINA: Sera's father will bring her home, Ma.

NONNA: Ah yes, to rely on the charity of other fathers. This is what we are reduced to. You are inviting the curse into the house. Christina, she so wild. Did I tell you how she ran out here that day?

CHRISTINA: Many times.

CHRISTINA *helps* JOSIE *with a necklace.*

NONNA: I apologise to Michael but I don't think he forgive.

CHRISTINA: [*annoyed, sharp*] Michael's a grown man—if he's upset by a teenager's moods, that's really—that's really his problem, isn't it?

JOSIE *tries to ignore them and keeps getting ready. She starts to do her make-up.*

NONNA: I talk to Signora Andretti and she say you not even go say hello to Michael. He here three weeks already. They were good neighbours for many years, Christina.

CHRISTINA: Yes, I know.

NONNA: Why you both behave like [*Italian*] gypsies. No manners. No tradition. I am the only one keep this family's reputation.

CHRISTINA: What a heavy burden. I think that's enough rouge, Josie.

JOSIE *stops and presents herself to* NONNA *and* CHRISTINA.

JOSIE: What do you think?

CHRISTINA: Perfect.

JOSIE: Nonna?

NONNA: [*Italian*] It is … [*English*] You look nice, [*Italian*] my granddaughter. [*English*] You have Alibrandi beauty, not worry.

JOSIE *hugs* NONNA. *Then,* CHRISTINA:

JOSIE: It's time!

She twirls away, they watch her go.

CHRISTINA *breathes in. She picks up her bag, but then—*NONNA *places a firm hand on* CHRISTINA's *arm, stopping her.*

NONNA: [*Italian, stern*] You wait.

CHRISTINA *and* NONNA *look at each other. A tense moment of stillness as an understanding passes between them.* CHRISTINA*'s breath grows shallow, then—*

The tableau of mother and daughter is overwhelmed by the dance floor beat. They are swept away as the next scene smashes into the space—

10. DANCE!

St Martha's Auditorium.

Joyful, dancing bodies transform the space, as JOSIE *enters, hopeful and self-conscious. She waits on the threshold of the dance, scanning the room for* JOHN *... there he is!* JOSIE *waves eagerly to get his attention, but* JOHN*, by himself in a corner, seems to be staring past her, blankly into the distance, lost in something invisible ...*

Over the music, JOSIE *tries to call out to him.*

JOSIE: John! John! Over here!

She finally catches his attention. JOHN *snaps to for a moment, still a little dazed, then nods at* JOSIE*. She waits for him to come over but ... he simply gives her a half-smile, then looks away. Then, he disappears into the crowd, exiting without a look back at* JOSIE*.*

She stands in place, hurt and visibly confused ... but not for long because SERA *arrives like a hurricane, ready to bring the party—*

SERA: *Bellezz!*

JOSIE *spins to face her friend. They scream, and hug excitedly.*

JOSIE: Sera! Oh, you look great! I'm wearing fabric from my fucking dowry.

SERA: It's all about attitude, Josie. I'd look just as good in a sack.

JOSIE: I mean, it's basically a sack. Did your dad really let you out like that?

SERA: Am I stupid? I changed in the car. Oh! Speaking of how good I look, Josie, when I was trying this on at the shop, I was talking to this sales girl. She was really nice.

JOSIE: Oh, yeah?

> JOSIE *starts to look around again, distracted by the prospect of* JOHN *returning.*

SERA: Yeah, about my cream? Anyway, she was all—oh my god, I could really use something like that—and now I'm thinking, maybe I should develop the formula? Like, I should sell it or something?

JOSIE: [*visibly looking around*] Um ...

SERA: Oi, Josie! You even listening?

JOSIE: What? I—um ... sorry. It's just ... he just disappeared and I was wondering if maybe he didn't really see me even though it seemed like and maybe I should go look ...

SERA: Ahh, okay, this is about John Barton. [*Italian*] Why didn't you say, babe? [*English*] Go, go, be bold!

JOSIE: I dunno ... I feel like he just / didn't want to—

> SERA *spots* SERGIO *and screams.*

SERA: Serge, baby! Here!

> *But she doesn't wait for him to come over, instead running right to him and climbing him like a mountain. He dips her. They swirl away.*

JOSIE: ... Okay.

> *She sighs, just as* IVY *enters behind her, watching her, smug and deliberate.*

> JOSIE *scans the dance floor again. Beat. Then,* IVY *pounces.*

IVY: Looking for someone, Alibrandi?

> JOSIE *groans.*

JOSIE: Oh, great. What do you want?

> IVY *says nothing. She moves to stand next to* JOSIE.

Hello? Can I help you?

IVY: Just taking in the view.

> *She nods in the direction of* SERA *and* SERGIO, *now swirling back onto the dance floor—their moves are extremely ... enthusiastic.*

I see your friend Sera brought a fisherman from the docks with her tonight. Classy.

JOSIE: He's a very nice, young entrepreneur in the construction industry, actually.
IVY: Huh. Pity she couldn't dredge one of those up for you. But I guess the women in your family are used to doing it all alone.
JOSIE: Yeah, and I guess the women in your family are used to doing nothing with their life except organising parties and watching their husbands cheat on them.
IVY: At least my father cares I exist.
JOSIE: It's good someone does.
IVY: And at least I know who he is.
JOSIE: Congratulations.

Beat. JOSIE *looks out again, and* IVY *watches her.*

IVY: He's gone, you know.
JOSIE: What?
IVY: I just wanted you to know that if you were looking for him, for John—
JOSIE: I'm not.
IVY: He already went home.

JOSIE *looks at her, surprised despite herself, which is all the confirmation* IVY *needs.*

Yeah, that's what I thought. Guess he didn't bother telling you, did he?
JOSIE: I'm not his mother. He doesn't have to tell me everything.

Beat. JOSIE *tries to hide her feelings, but ...*

IVY: Aw, are you sad, Alibrandi?
JOSIE: Don't be ridiculous.
IVY: It's okay. I'm sure you'll find someone to straggle home with tonight. Maybe there's another lonely wog out there with a unibrow just dying to whisk you away, make a little unibrow baby, aww … it might even have a tail.
JOSIE: Jesus, what is your problem?
IVY: I'm just saying, like mother, like daughter.
JOSIE: Ivy, if you don't get out of my face, right now—
IVY: Oooh, temper, temper, Alibrandi. Please, a little decorum, we're representing the school tonight. What would Sister Bernadette say? I should go check in with her, actually. Cute dress, by the way.

Before JOSIE *can retort,* IVY *glides away gleefully.*

Pissed off, JOSIE *stomps her way to a table with a punch bowl. She fills herself a cup and starts to drink, just as—*

JACOB: Having a shit one, Alibrandi?

JOSIE *groans—not again. She turns to face* JACOB.

JOSIE: Just got worse.

JACOB: It's this crowd, hey. Boring. Not like you and me.

JACOB *takes a small flask out from his jacket and jiggles it at her, then gestures to the punch bowl.*

Wanna get things going and toss a bit in?

JOSIE: What? No. Maybe? No!

JACOB: Just kidding, Josephine.

Beat.

I already put some in.

A panicked JOSIE *tries to spit out her drink.*

JOSIE: Why would you do that?

JACOB: Don't worry—it's high-quality stuff. Whisky—my favourite by the way.

JOSIE: I don't care! We have to get rid of this. What if someone drives home after drinking this? What if they run someone over? What if someone we know becomes a TAC ad?

JOSIE *starts to empty the bowl, as* SERA *and* SERGIO *roll by.* SERA *is now on piggy-back. They yell at* JOSIE *over the noise and indicate they're leaving the dance.*

SERA: Josie, his cousin's got a new jacuzzi!

JOSIE: So?

SERA: Come!

JOSIE: No!

SERA: We're your lift home! You gotta!

JACOB: I can walk you home.

A surprised JOSIE *looks at* JACOB, *as* SERA *gets pulled away with* SERGIO. JOSIE *turns back to reply to* SERA, *only to find she's gone. Shit.*

Looks like you're stuck with me, Alibrandi.

JOSIE *grabs the punch bowl again.*

JOSIE: I need to finish getting rid of this.

JACOB: Why? It's just juice.

She realises he's been pulling her leg. Despite herself, she laughs.

JOSIE: You're an idiot, Coote.

JACOB *grins.*

JACOB: Sera's right though. This party's a dud. We should get out of here. Race ya!

JOSIE: Huh?

But before she can process, he grabs her hand and starts to run. A shocked but delighted JOSIE *gives in. They speed off into the night.*

11. NONNA AT HOME

A moment in the space.

As the dance floor morphs, we see a glimpse of NONNA *, alone, poring over her albums. Her hair is in painstaking rollers. She smokes.*

She stops on a page of her album. She takes out a photograph. She lingers on it. Perhaps, she holds it to herself.

Her hair rolls out; the cigarette extinguishes. She's about to go, when JACOB *runs back into the space, laughing. For a moment, it's almost like* NONNA *sees him, a ghost from the past ...*

JOSIE *tumbles in after* JACOB, *laughing too. The moment is broken, and the scene snaps to—*

12. WALK HOME

Streets of Glebe / The Alibrandi home.

A giddy JOSIE *and* JACOB—*still in their dance clothes—catch their breath, puffed out from all the running and laughing.*

JOSIE: You started on three! You're supposed to start after three. One, two, three—then go!
JACOB: Nah. Don't be a sore loser.
JOSIE: I'm not! You … won. Okay, you won.

> *They smile at each other. The quiet expanse of the night settles around them.* JACOB *picks up an unlit cigarette dropped by* NONNA, *and they smoke it.*

I'm never really out this late.
JACOB: Aw, you're scared?
JOSIE: No, dickhead. I'm an Italian girl. My mum and my fucking Nonna would kill me if I went out whenever.
JACOB: Shit. Sounds bad. I couldn't put up with that.
JOSIE: It's not bad. It's a little bad. My mum's only so strict 'cause she cares.
JACOB: Yeah, that's nice.
JOSIE: What's your mum like?
JACOB: She's dead.

> JOSIE, *shocked and stricken, struggles to find her words. Then—*

JOSIE: What?
JACOB: Yeah, two years ago now.
JOSIE: Why didn't you say?
JACOB: Well shit, it's not something you slip in like 'good morning'. Morning Josie, by the way my mum's dead.
JOSIE: I—how can you even joke about it? If my mum was … I'd just die.
JACOB: Nah, you wouldn't. At first, you'd feel like it, sure. And then. You go on.

JOSIE *shakes her head, and just hugs him, tight, before she can even think about it.*

Beat.

They pull apart, but they're close. JOSIE *looks offstage.*

JOSIE: Uh—this is—this is my house.

He follows her gaze.

JACOB: It's pretty shitty, hey. You're definitely not like the girls at St Martha's.

JOSIE: Not a stuck-up North Shore ice princess.

JACOB: Yeah. Well maybe a little bit stuck-up.

Beat. They're still close. JACOB *... leans in for a kiss, and* JOSIE *instantly recoils.*

JOSIE: What are you doing??

JACOB: What do you think I'm doing?

JOSIE: I dunno!

JACOB: It's pretty obvious.

JOSIE: Didn't you listen to my Have a Say Day speech?

JACOB: Jesus, you're fucking weird, Alibrandi. You saving yourself for Barton or something?

JOSIE: Fuck off.

JACOB: Whatever. I didn't want to anyway.

JOSIE: Sure acted like you / did.

As she speaks, we see CHRISTINA *and* MICHAEL *in a different section of the space. A loud raging argument between them from 'inside the house' intrudes on* JOSIE *and* JACOB, *who immediately stop talking to listen.*

MICHAEL: What was I supposed to do, Tina? Fly into a rage and demand to see her?

CHRISTINA: It's one thing when you didn't know, but to know—and not even approach me for a month?

MICHAEL: I was in shock! I'm in shock. It's not fair to expect—I do not want to see her. I can't be expected to—suddenly love her.

CHRISTINA: Oh! I have no expectations of you. At all! [*Italian*] I always knew not to!

MICHAEL: A seventeen-year-old girl doesn't need a father anyway!

CHRISTINA: I'm thirty-four—god, turning thirty-five in October!—and I still need a father! I can't even begin to think what my daughter needs sometimes.

> JACOB *looks at* JOSIE.

JACOB: That ... doesn't sound good. Is that your parents?
JOSIE: [*snapping*] How's that any of your bloody business? What are you still doing here anyway?

> JOSIE *turns away from him, as* JACOB, *offended, has had enough and leaves.*
>
> *Beat.*
>
> JOSIE *creeps closer to her parents, listening in the half-light.*

13. CONFRONTATION

CHRISTINA *and* JOSIE*'s living room.*

CHRISTINA *and* MICHAEL *pace around the kitchen table.*

MICHAEL: I thought we had agreed. We had agreed. I do not want a complication in my life, Christina.
CHRISTINA: Don't call my daughter a complication.
MICHAEL: Isn't she? She complicated your life.
CHRISTINA: No, it's *us* who don't want *you* complicating ours.
MICHAEL: You act like I'm the villain here but ... anyone you ask would say that you should have told me.
CHRISTINA: And they'd be idiots. What would you have done? Look at your reaction now.
MICHAEL: It's still not right.
CHRISTINA: You saw what that house was like for me! [*Italian*] Did you really think I had a choice? [*English*] You were gone! You heard what you wanted to hear. I let you hear what you wanted to hear. I let you have your life. Your freedom.

> *The words hit him. He stills. Beat.*

MICHAEL: [*softly*] Tina ...
CHRISTINA: No.

> *He moves closer to her. Beat.*

MICHAEL: I … want to do the right thing. I want to help.
CHRISTINA: Help?
MICHAEL: I'm … very comfortable.
CHRISTINA: [*Italian*] Oh my god!
MICHAEL: What?
CHRISTINA: [*Italian*] Stupid boy! [*English*] We don't need your money. We're fine! I *work*.
MICHAEL: You could still use the help.
CHRISTINA: Always missing the point. So sure of yourself. [*Italian*] You haven't changed at all.
MICHAEL: You haven't either.

> *Small beat.*

You look the same.
CHRISTINA: No.
MICHAEL: Yes.

> *He moves closer still, staring at her, taking her in. Beat.* CHRISTINA *blushes under his gaze. Then, she quickly pulls away, changing the topic, breaking the moment.*

CHRISTINA: My mum knows now.

> *A disappointed* MICHAEL *snaps back to himself.*

MICHAEL: Right. Right.

> *Small beat.*

So she's probably cursing me right now?
CHRISTINA: That's what you're worried about?
MICHAEL: [*jokingly*] The day Katia doesn't frighten me is the day I'm dead.
CHRISTINA: [*snapping, frustrated*] Really? Michael, you have no idea, not one idea what the last seventeen years have been like, do you? You just make light of everything.
MICHAEL: You used to like that about me.

> *Beat.* CHRISTINA *takes him in. Memories flood her.*

CHRISTINA: [*mumbling, unconvincingly*] It was so long ago. I don't [remember] …
MICHAEL: [*Italian*] You look just as you were, Tina.

CHRISTINA: [*Italian*] Stop it.
MICHAEL: [*teasing*] You're supposed to say I look the same too.
CHRISTINA: Mm, I don't want to lie.
MICHAEL: [*Italian*] Brutal. There's the Alibrandi tongue.
CHRISTINA: Your hair is starting to thin.
MICHAEL: You picked up on that? Of course, you did.
CHRISTINA: [*laughing*] The famous Andretti hair. How could I not?

> *She almost reaches for it, but holds back.* MICHAEL *tries to smooth the moment, and they slip into an easy, teasing banter.*

MICHAEL: Uh, well, this is what happens when you work for the skips.
CHRISTINA: Don't blame them! You chose that life.
MICHAEL: They're grinding me to the bone, Tina. [*Italian*] Do you not care?
CHRISTINA: It's your own fault. [*Italian*] Blame them. It's not because you're a stress-head.
MICHAEL: Wait till I'm bald, maybe then you'll feel bad.
CHRISTINA: [*Italian*] I doubt it! I would pay good money to see that.

> *They start giggling, a little hysteric, a little teenage-like themselves.*
>
> JOSIE, *unable to stand it anymore, bursts in.*

JOSIE: I can hear you two on the street!

> *They stop short, and stare at her.*

CHRISTINA: Josie, let me / explain.
JOSIE: [*to* MICHAEL] / Why are you here?
CHRISTINA: I asked Michael to talk tonight.
JOSIE: Why? Have you gone mad?
CHRISTINA: Josie—
MICHAEL: Don't talk to your—

> *They both stare at him—is he really going to finish that sentence? He stops immediately. Small beat.*

Tina just ... called me here to discuss the situation.
JOSIE: Ugh, do you mean to discuss me? I'm not a bloody 'situation'! God, who speaks like that anyway? You're making me puke.
CHRISTINA: Josie—

JOSIE: He says one charming thing and you go straight back into his arms?
CHRISTINA: [*Italian*] Be quiet! [*English*] That's not what's happening.

> *Beat. They glare at each other. Then,* CHRISTINA *sighs and turns to* MICHAEL.

Michael, you need to go.
MICHAEL: I think maybe if we—
CHRISTINA: [*Italian*] Go now.

> MICHAEL *hesitates. Then, he relents and leaves.*

Josie, let's speak.

> JOSIE *quivers with anger.*

14. ENOUGH

CHRISTINA *and* JOSIE*'s living room /* NONNA*'s living room [flashback].*

A rumble, as if the earth is droning. As JOSIE *and* CHRISTINA *look at each other, we see behind them,* NONNA *on the ground, in the darkness, trying to rise—almost like a woman learning to walk again, an almost spectral creature in pain. She murmurs to herself—*CHRISTINA *and* JOSIE *do not see or interact with her.*

NONNA: Every day it's coming nearer. [*Italian*] Do you feel it? Bastard. Bastard. When I left the ship. I was too defiant. [*English*] He didn't let me dance. [*Italian*] Too wild. I roamed. I have nothing. [*English*] I'm a stain on the earth. A stain on the earth.
CHRISTINA: Speak.
JOSIE: I don't want to.
CHRISTINA: Josie.
JOSIE: No!

> CHRISTINA *tries to push back again, but then just deflates. She turns around.* NONNA *rises to face her. She reaches out and holds* CHRISTINA*'s arm.*

CHRISTINA: I called him here to warn him, Josie. Nonna knows now. She—she figured it out.

> CHRISTINA *and* NONNA *look at each other, unwavering, and we are returned to their positions from the end of Scene 9; to their*

tense moment of stand-off after JOSIE *left for the dance. We see the conversation that occurred between them unspooling now ...*

This time, JOSIE *stays to the side, watching them speak.*

Ma ...
NONNA: How did I not see?
CHRISTINA: I didn't let you see.

NONNA *tosses* CHRISTINA's *arm away.* CHRISTINA *flinches.*

NONNA: So deceitful. Michael Andretti. [*Italian*] It was him. I should have seen. But now, I see everything. Everything.
CHRISTINA: Yes.
NONNA: People will talk.
CHRISTINA: They've already talked ... so much.
NONNA: You let me invite him in my house. You tell your daughter! You make her deceitful, just like you.
CHRISTINA: No! It's not like that.
NONNA: You are always making things more difficult for all of us. What did I do to deserve you? [*Italian*] A disgrace. You are a disgrace.

CHRISTINA *tries to fight back tears. Then, she loses it—*

CHRISTINA: [*Italian*] You're a disgrace! [*English*] Look at your life. Look at the way you talk to me! Like an animal. [*Italian*] I've always been an animal in this house. [*English*] Look at us—we're nothing to each other. You just judge and judge. If we kept it from you, it's so we could have a second's peace in our lives!
NONNA: [*Italian*] Excuses, excuses for your shame! Why Michael Andretti, of all the people? [*English*] I was good woman—we tried, we give you everything, but [*Italian*] the curse keeps coming back and back and back.
CHRISTINA: I'm sick of the bloody curse!
NONNA: [*starting to talk to herself, rapidly, Italian*] Every day it's coming nearer. Do you feel it? Bastard. Bastard. When I left the ship. Too defiant. Dancing. Too wild. I roamed. [*English*] A stain on the earth.
CHRISTINA: You know what? You don't have to deal with it, anymore, Ma! Me, your curse on this earth—I'm out! I'm done!

CHRISTINA collapses into sobs, and JOSIE lunges towards her, enveloping her mother in her arms.

JOSIE: Ma, no! I'm sorry, I'm sorry.

NONNA watches them, then starts to fade back into the darkness, muttering as she goes.

NONNA: [*Italian*] I have nothing. [*English*] Do you feel it? Every day it's coming nearer. I have nothing. Nothing. Too wild, I …

She disappears and CHRISTINA and JOSIE are alone in their home, still in an embrace. CHRISTINA collects herself.

JOSIE: Ma …

CHRISTINA: I'm fine. I'm fine, Josie. I just need a second. I'm perfectly fine.

She pauses.

I just … don't think I'll be going to Nonna's for a while. [*Before JOSIE can interject*] Just me, Josie. You still need to … it's important, don't argue with me …

She trails off, then gets up, still a little dazed as she exits. JOSIE watches her mother go, then turns to us, furious and exhausted.

JOSIE: [*to us*] These fucking Italians! I'm sick of it. It's like living in an endless Francis Ford Coppola movie. But I refuse to be another Alibrandi fuck-up. If it's the last thing I do. I won't. I just need to focus on getting out of here. God, I'm getting as far as my feet will take me.

The school bell rings, pealing out, and the scene snaps into—

15. CAREERS DAY

St Martha's Auditorium.

An inter-school Careers Day Fair. Students cross the space, pamphlets in hand, passing them between each other.

An eager JOSIE collects a heap of pamphlets, then sits down, and tries to sort and stuff them into her backpack.

As she does so, a paper plane flies onto stage and lands on the ground near her. She notices, but ignores it. After a small beat, another plane lands at her feet. JOSIE rolls her eyes, and scrunches up the paper plane.

JOHN: Josie!

JOSIE turns to see JOHN standing behind her—the plane-thrower.

JOSIE: John.

JOHN: Those are important pamphlets. You shouldn't be scrunching them up.

JOSIE: Yeah, well you shouldn't be making them into planes either.

JOHN: True, but I don't need that one. Or any of them. In fact—

He gestures at some of her many pamphlets.

—why do you even have so many? You know what you're going to do after school.

JOSIE: It's always good to have your options open.

JOHN: I see. You're not reneging on our plan, I hope.

He sits down next to her.

JOSIE: [*shortly*] If anyone's 'reneging' on our plan, that would be you.

JOHN: No way! Law at Sydney Uni. It's a done deal.

JOSIE: For you, maybe. Some of us have to work a bit harder to get what we want.

JOHN: Okay. I mean—we're doing it together. We better. I won't survive without you.

JOSIE: I'm sure you'll be fine. Ivy will be lurking around campus, I bet.

JOHN: Nah, she wants to do journalism, remember? UTS is better for that.

JOSIE: Sure, whatever. I'm not really keeping track of what Poison Ivy wants or doesn't want.

JOHN: You two are so alike.

JOSIE: Only a fool would ever think that.

She snaps shut her backpack. Beat.

JOHN: Josie—

JOSIE: Why did you ditch me at the dance?

JOHN: I didn't …

JOSIE: Yes, you did.

Beat.

It was really rude.

JOHN: You're right. Unforgivable behaviour for an MP's son.

JOSIE: No—it's not *unforgivable*. It's just plain rude for anyone.
JOHN: [*slightly absent*] Yeah ...
JOSIE: What do you mean 'yeah'? [*Softly*] You really hurt me.
JOHN: Josie ... I wasn't feeling well.
JOSIE: You made me look like an idiot. You could have at least told me you were leaving.
JOHN: I told Ivy to tell you.
JOSIE: And you thought that would be a good idea?

> *Before* JOHN *can speak,* SERA *runs up and places a whole pile of pamphlets down, excited.*

SERA: Oh my god, Josie—I'm so glad you made me come! There's so many TAFE reps here! Hey, John!
JOHN: Hey—yeah, the government's just invested in subsidised places for vocational courses.
SERA: They got everything! Look, hairdressing, make-up, beauty therapy—maybe that's what I should do? The therapy? Really really help people, you know? That's my goal in life now ... like I told you, Josie.
JOSIE: You did?
SERA: Yeah at the dance, *bellezz*. With my cream and stuff. Oh my god, at the afterparty, Sergio's cousin Antonetta Scolio—you know her, the one with the nose? She thinks it could be a legit business. She thanked me with tears in her eyes after trying it! I am scientifically improving people's lives one set of tits at a time.
JOSIE: Jesus.
JOHN: You know, maybe you should do medicine, Sera. If you like science and helping people.

> JOSIE *snorts.*

JOSIE: Okay, John. Don't be mean.
JOHN: I'm not. You should go talk to some of the unis, Sera—before they pack up.

> SERA *seems shocked at* JOHN*'s vote of confidence, but then takes it on, and jumps up.*

SERA: Okay, I'm gonna! Thank you, *bellezzo!*

> *She gives* JOHN *a big kiss on the cheek, and bounds off.*

[*Calling offstage*] Excuse me, do youse guys know where the doctors' stuff is?

JOSIE looks at JOHN.

JOSIE: You just wanted to get rid of her so we can talk.

JOHN: That's not true. But also I love talking to you Josie, so—

Beat. He sighs.

—I'm sorry about the dance. Really. I shouldn't have taken off like that … I had a lot on my mind. You know how my dad is.

JOSIE: I guess.

JOHN seems surprised at her standoffishness, but continues …

JOHN: Well. He wasn't happy with my Have a Say Day speech. According to him, I didn't make an impression. It didn't occur to him that maybe I didn't want to say all those boring, backwards things he'd approved. When I told him that, he just stared at me like I was a piece of shit. Like he / [regretted]—

JOSIE: / Oh, who cares what he thinks, John! You've been talking about him the same way for years.

Small beat.

JOHN: [*stiffly*] I didn't know I was boring you. Sorry, Josie.

He looks crushed. JOSIE instantly regrets her words.

JOSIE: [*to us*] Oh god. There I go again, with my giant mouth. Not that anything I said was wrong. John can get a bit … moody about his dad. It's not moody in the way I get. He's like millionth generation WASP and they do emotion differently. But … I dunno, sometimes I'm like, at least you got a dad. I'd love to have an influential father paving the way for me with money and connections. Actually giving a damn about my future, and not jetting off into the night at the sight of me—

She turns back to JOHN.

—John, no, that's not what I meant.

JOHN: No?

JOSIE: I just meant—we've all got shitty fathers, don't we? Even when you don't think they're shit, they turn up out of nowhere and prove it! Maybe it's just an eternal condition of everyone's bloody life?

JOHN *smiles.*

JOHN: Maybe. You're right. Let's not dwell on boring things when something much more exciting is happening for you.

JOSIE: It is?

JOHN raises a suggestive eyebrow.

JOSIE: What?

JOHN: I heard about, um … you and Jacob Coote.

JOSIE: WHAT. Okay, I don't know what you heard—

JOHN starts laughing at her indignation.

JOHN: Just that you left together.

JOSIE: Right. Well, yes. But that's all. Anyone saying anything else is woefully misinformed. Woefully! Maybe if you want the facts, stick around next time.

Before JOHN can respond, SERA bursts back in, a ball of excitement, and plonks down between them with a huge bundle of pamphlets.

SERA: *Bellezz!!!* Did you know there's universities on the Gold Coast? There's universities on the Gold Coast. Like, I could go to class and then to Wet'n'Wild?! I bet the parties go off. And oh my god, this one—

She taps one of the pamphlets.

—has even got a medicine course you can do in five years instead of six! I'll still be young when I graduate. Maybe we should go to Schoolies there and I just don't come back.

JOSIE: Sera, first semester's already over. If you're serious about the UMAT you can't even be thinking of Schoolies.

SERA: The what?

JOSIE: The UMAT.

SERA: The who-MAT?

JOHN: It's the special exam you need for medicine. You have to sit it before pracs.

SERA: Holy shit! I … I'll be right back!

She peels off again at pace. JOHN looks at her go.

JOHN: God, wish I got that excited about anything. I don't know if I've ever been that excited. Imagine living life like it isn't shit.

He catches her look, and corrects himself.

Sorry, sorry. I know. Just having one of those days.

JOSIE: Okay. [*Then, trying to lighten the mood*] Though, if you want to see shit, you should come over to my house at the moment. My mum and Nonna are at war, and my fa—my father, um …

She trails off. JOHN *is surprised.*

JOHN: Your father? He's … you found out? Josie, that's [massive].

JOSIE: It's nothing. I don't want to …

She looks offstage.

I think Poison Ivy wants to talk to you.

JOHN *follows her gaze and spots* IVY *too. He nods.*

You should go. I have to sort these—

She gestures at her pamphlets.

—anyway.

Slightly puzzled and deflated, JOHN *gets up.*

JOHN: Oh. Well if you ever need to talk. I'm here.

Beat.

Hey, maybe we could go to the USYD campus soon and look around—I could show you the law library, been there a bunch. I have a feeling you'd like it.

JOSIE: Oh. Yeah. That would be nice.

She softens, embarrassed.

JOHN: Done.

JOSIE: [*to us*] Look how kind he is. God, I'm the real moody one. USYD. Me. John Barton. That's the plan. That's the dream. But I've really got to learn some bloody self-control. Can't turn into Nonna fighting with everyone all the time for no bloody reason. Yes, I can feel it; I'm going to be completely calm and serene from now on, no matter what happens.

As she speaks, an angry IVY *walks in, slams her own bag down and interrupts* JOSIE.

IVY: God, Alibrandi, can you go anywhere without making a mess?

JOSIE: [*to self / us*] Why does God hate me?

> *Beat. She gathers herself.*

Ivy.

IVY: I mean, I understand that you can't help your own miserable life, but now you need to make John miserable too?

JOSIE: What are you talking about?

IVY: I don't know how they do things in the old country or whatever fucking mud hut you're from, but you're in Australia now, okay?

JOSIE: I know where I am, Ivy.

IVY: Uh-huh, well you just don't seem to understand we have a way of doing things here, Alibrandi. You and your mum can live off all the handouts in the world, but don't you dare think you can leech off someone with actual worth.

JOSIE: I have no idea what the hell you're on about.

> *Small beat.* IVY *simmers—does Alibrandi really not know what she's saying?*

IVY: Look, all I know is that every time I see John after he's been talking to you, he seems different.

JOSIE: From what? From you? I'd hope so.

IVY: I just wish you'd stop dragging him down to your sad, grubby level.

JOSIE: Are you actually jealous, Ivy? Wow.

IVY: Don't be fucking ridiculous. You know, Alibrandi, I really don't know where you get off acting so full of yourself when—

> JOSIE *gets slightly up in her face.*

JOSIE: When what?

> IVY *takes a breath, a step back.*

IVY: No … no … my mother has always said we need to take a charitable stance with those less fortunate.

JOSIE: I don't need charity from you, Ivy.

IVY: Is that right?

> *Beat.*

My father's donations to the school's outreach fund would beg to differ.

JOSIE: Fuck off. You know maybe John seems different or miserable when he's talking to you because he's, um, talking to you? Did you ever consider that? Like—took him long enough—but maybe he just finally realised you're fucken boring and is sick to fucken death of hearing you talk about Country Road and how you wanna match your handbag with your xenophobia.
IVY: What was that?
JOSIE: Oh, do you not know that word?
IVY: No I just … sometimes I can't … understand with your voice?
JOSIE: My voice is fine, Ivy, and you bloody know it.
IVY: You're right, it is fine. Inarticulate, but fine. It's more the whole package. You can learn as many new words as you like, Josie, but once a dirty wog, always a dirty bastard wog.

At this, JOSIE *can take it no longer. She snaps and punches* IVY.

IVY *goes down, like, face-first into a nearby barrel (of passata). Her body goes limp.*

JOSIE *gapes.*

Beat. Then—

JOSIE: [*to us*] Oh my god. Oh my god. I killed her.

As she says this, IVY *jolts upright, screaming her lungs out.*

Blood (passata) runs down her face, onto her shirt. It looks like her nose is broken.

JOSIE *screams too.*

The bell rings us into chaos, as students start to move about and SISTER BERNADETTE *swoops in. She stares at the two girls, horrified and confused—*

IVY: [*yelling*] What. The. Fuck. Alibrandi.
JOSIE: [*yelling back*] I'm sorry! I didn't mean to hit you. That hard.

—before swooping into action, hoisting them both by their arms.

SISTER BERNADETTE: My office! Now. And not a word till I've called your / parents.
IVY: It's assault! My father's going to sue you and your whole family— you're fucked, Alibrandi!
JOSIE: Call my father, Sister! Not my mother. Please.

IVY: What? She doesn't even have a father! You are so expelled.

> SISTER BERNADETTE *sends* IVY *offstage to be looked after, and motions firmly at* JOSIE *to stay put.* JOSIE *sinks to the ground and looks at us—she's so screwed. As* SISTER BERNADETTE *swoops away ...* MICHAEL ANDRETTI *emerges from behind her.*
>
> *He steps into the space and looks at* JOSIE. JOSIE *looks up at him. Her face freezes in shock.*
>
> *The lights snap off.*

INTERVAL

ACT TWO

16. ENTER ANDRETTI

Sister Bernadette's office.

JOSIE *and* MICHAEL *are where we left them. They stare at each other. Beat.*

JOSIE *crosses her arms.*

JOSIE: I'm surprised you came.
MICHAEL: It's not every day a nun calls the Clayton Utz reception.
> MICHAEL *sits down next to her. Beat.*

I'm surprised you called.
JOSIE: It's only 'cause—I thought Ivy was threatening—I just thought … I needed a lawyer.
MICHAEL: I see.
JOSIE: Also, I thought I should spare my mother. She's been through enough lately. Doesn't need to witness her daughter being expelled on top of everything.
> *Beat.*

MICHAEL: No, I imagine she wouldn't like that. Luckily … you're only being suspended.
JOSIE: You talked to Sister Bernadette?
MICHAEL: Yeah. Terrifying woman.
JOSIE: / Nuns.
MICHAEL: / Nuns.
> *They look at each other.*

Though I think we might be friends now. We had a good chat on the way in.
JOSIE: Ew. What about? How you both think I'm awful?
MICHAEL: She doesn't think you're awful. She … is just disappointed. She said you're very bright. You're deputy captain.
JOSIE: Right.

Beat.

MICHAEL: And I don't—I don't think you're awful.
JOSIE: Guess you have to know someone to think they're awful.
MICHAEL: Yeah, that's right.

Beat.

You'll have to apologise to uh, the Lloyd girl.
JOSIE: I already did! Before you got here.
MICHAEL: Well, again. In front of Sister. Or something.
JOSIE: Ugh, she's gonna love that.

Beat.

MICHAEL: Do you often do this?
JOSIE: Yeah, I'm an Alibrandi. I'm out of control. She called me a wog, you know?
MICHAEL: Sister Bernadette?
JOSIE: Ivy! I told Sister Bernadette and she said nothing! She doesn't get it. A wog! Actually—'a dirty wog'.
MICHAEL: So?
JOSIE: So!
MICHAEL: Aren't you? A wog?
JOSIE: Yeah, but—she can't call us that! And it's how she says it, it's like … you wouldn't understand.
MICHAEL: [*laughing*] Really? Josie, when your mum and I were growing up, we weren't just called wogs—it was spat at us everyday.
JOSIE: And you just took it? You never felt like punching a skip?
MICHAEL: I didn't say that. But you can't let it get to you. It's what they want. You get back at them by—
JOSIE: Being silent.
MICHAEL: By doing well in life.

Beat. JOSIE *looks at this suited man, and sees herself for a moment …*

JOSIE: [*quietly*] I am doing that. I am trying to do that.
MICHAEL: Are you?
JOSIE: But Nonna and Ma, they can't see it! No-one understands that it's not so simple …

MICHAEL *sighs.*

MICHAEL: Yeah. Maybe they don't. But you're not going to get anywhere acting like this. When you're in court you can't just punch opposing counsel, no matter how much you might want to.

Beat.

JOSIE: Ivy said her dad's going to sue us.

MICHAEL: [*suppressing a laugh*] Oh, okay.

JOSIE: No seriously, she said she's going to bring charges. Her dad is a big deal—

MICHAEL: Dr Lloyd, yeah?

JOSIE: Yeah …

MICHAEL: One of our long-term clients. Don't worry Josie, he's not going to bring anything.

Beat.

He was too busy to even make it down here today.

JOSIE's surprised to hear this.

JOSIE: Oh.

Beat. MICHAEL *stands up and jangles car keys.* JOSIE *looks away. He watches her, wrestling with himself. He clears his throat.*

MICHAEL: Well I guess we should get you home home to Ti / na.

JOSIE: / Eugh. Don't call her that.

Small beat.

MICHAEL: To your mother, then.

JOSIE: I can get home on my own.

MICHAEL: And you'll tell her about this, will you?

JOSIE: Yeah. [*At his look*] What? God, the whole point of calling you was so she wouldn't need to know!

MICHAEL: Ah, to spare her the suffering?

JOSIE: Exactly. It would break her heart. She's very delicate, you know.

MICHAEL: That's not a word I'd use for her. Quiet, kind, strong, but delicate— [*Italian*] what an insult.

He gets slightly lost in the thought. In a corner of the space, CHRISTINA *appears, tidying, at home. For a moment, it's like he can see her, or longs to …*

JOSIE: Okay, try not to drool.

MICHAEL: [*snapping to*] You know, if you're serious about this—about your future—the law—
JOSIE: Of course I'm serious.
MICHAEL: You need to see how it all works a bit more. Maybe ... maybe you can come help out at the firm.
JOSIE: What?
MICHAEL: Might stop you smashing in people's faces.
JOSIE: I don't understand.
MICHAEL: There's a lot of copying that needs to be done. It'll mainly be that. And coffees. But you may learn a thing or two about how it works.
JOSIE: Are you bloody serious???

> JOSIE *jumps up, confused but excited despite herself, and* MICHAEL *shrugs, embarrassed but surprised by his own delight at her reaction.* CHRISTINA *turns to them—an expression of pure anger on her face. We snap into—*

17. FAMILY ROUND TWO

CHRISTINA *and* JOSIE*'s living room.*

Back at home, CHRISTINA, JOSIE *and* MICHAEL *face each other, in a triangle again.*

CHRISTINA: Really, Josie? Really? [*To* MICHAEL] And you— You should have called me immediately, Michael. What's wrong with you, Josie? You're nearly eighteen! 'This will be the year I do better, Ma.' Clearly not.
JOSIE: I didn't mean—
CHRISTINA: You're lucky you're only suspended. [*Italian*] I would have expelled you. [*English, to* MICHAEL] Why did you even go— who said you could go?
JOSIE: Alibrandi—
CHRISTINA: Don't 'Alibrandi' me! It's like you don't even bother trying sometimes, Josie. I'm tired of it.

> *Small beat.* JOSIE *wrestles with herself, then—*

JOSIE: Well ... maybe I'm tired of being from a broken home!
CHRISTINA: [*Italian*] What did you just say to me?
JOSIE: I ...

JOSIE *trails off as* CHRISTINA *stares at her daughter, clearly hurt. An uncomfortable* MICHAEL *breaks the silence.*

MICHAEL: [*to* CHRISTINA] I'm sure she didn't mean to say / that.
CHRISTINA: [*laughing, to* JOSIE] / A broken home. A broken home. You don't know the meaning of—And Michael—you—you've done one responsible thing today, and you suddenly think you can—'I'm sure she didn't mean to, Tina'—we're not your clients— [*Laughing more, Italian*] The two of you really …

She looks at them. Beat.

[*Quietly*] The same. A couple of actors. What a show. I thought you took after Nonna but you take after your father. It's your father!
JOSIE: How can you say that? I only called him today 'cause I didn't want to trouble you! You don't know all the things I do to never trouble you. But I never get any thanks for that, do I?
CHRISTINA: What do you do Josie, honestly? What do you lack? [*Italian*] Don't forget where you come from.
JOSIE: Where I come from *is* the problem! I'm—I'm going to work with Michael at Clayton Utz!
MICHAEL: [*surprised*] Oh?
JOSIE: Yeah.
CHRISTINA: Michael? [*Italian*] What is she saying?
MICHAEL: We have interns sometimes, I [offered] …
CHRISTINA: You're rewarding her for this behaviour?
MICHAEL: No it's—no, I—it's not a reward, it's [useful]—
CHRISTINA: You really want to do this, Josie?
JOSIE: It's a great experience, Ma. You'd know if you—
CHRISTINA: No, no, I see.
MICHAEL: Tina, you maybe don't know how useful these—
CHRISTINA: Of course, I don't know! I don't know anything, do I? Stupid, simple Christina. Doesn't know a thing. I really don't. I don't know when my mother will stop sulking and grow up, and I don't know when you started to grow so ungrateful and punch girls at school, or when you—when you decided to slip into our lives, even though you were very clear about the opposite.

Beat.

MICHAEL: I'm just trying to contribute, Tina.

CHRISTINA: Ah, so this is a debt you're paying off. [*Italian*] Careful, Michael.

> JOSIE *looks a bit distraught—she thought he'd offered from instinct, not obligation.*

MICHAEL: No, it's not a debt.
CHRISTINA: Then, what is it?
MICHAEL: I don't know … *she* called me! I'm just … Tina—

> CHRISTINA *raises a hand to signal the conversation is over.*

MICHAEL: [*Italian*] Oh, you want me to leave again, I suppose.
CHRISTINA: [*Italian*] At least you can still pick up on that.
MICHAEL: Well, what if I don't want to? [*Italian*] I have some rights here, Tina.
CHRISTINA: Oh, now here comes the Italian man. [*Italian*] Time to be big and strong and throw your weight around, is it?
MICHAEL: [*Italian*] This is your mother talking.
CHRISTINA: [*Italian*] You say that to me?

> *As they start to squabble with each other,* JOSIE*'s just about had it.*

JOSIE: Oh my god, emancipate me now! I'm going for a fucking walk!

> *She stomps off, exiting. It catches them by surprise.*

CHRISTINA: [*calling out*] Josie! [*Italian*] Get back here this instant!
MICHAEL: [*calling out*] Josie, listen to your mother!

> CHRISTINA *turns and looks at him—it's almost comical, him slipping into this role.* MICHAEL *looks embarrassed.*
>
> *Beat.*

Should I [go after her]?

> *But* CHRISTINA *is winded. She shakes her head. He lingers … should he stay?*

CHRISTINA: You should go home, Michael.

> *He sighs and leaves.*
>
> CHRISTINA *takes a moment to breathe. She looks down, and spots* JOSIE*'s backpack.*
>
> *Careers Day Pamphlets are spilling out of it. She picks up one of them. It's a TAFE pamphlet.*

A flicker of interest and longing on CHRISTINA*'s face as she reads it. The life she didn't have. The life she supposedly doesn't know about.*

She folds the pamphlet and pockets it, then exits.

An Aussie rock song starts as she goes, tilting us into ...

18. JACOB COOTE PLEASE

The Cootes' garage; night-time.

JACOB *saunters on with a tool-belt, in time with the Aussie rock song, and rolls under a 'car' [a table / other part of the set] like he's doing repairs. A couple of beats. Then,* JOSIE, *slightly out of breath, enters the space. She's tied her bloody school-shirt over her waist. Suddenly self-conscious, she stares at* JACOB*'s feet, gathering the courage ...*

JOSIE: Nice shop.

The music stops. JACOB *rolls out from under the car, surprised.*

JACOB: Alibrandi? At this time of the night?

She shrugs. He emerges fully.

Not a shop. A garage.

JOSIE: Okay. Whatever.

Beat.

JACOB: Thought you said Italian girls didn't go out so late.

JOSIE: Screw being Italian.

JACOB: Shit.

JOSIE: It's culture, you wouldn't get it.

JACOB *scoffs.*

JACOB: I think I get culture, Josie.

JOSIE: I didn't mean—it's just different. Migrants are ... fucked in the head.

JACOB: Sure.

JOSIE: I mean, it's not totally our fault. This country. But still.

JACOB: I get ya.

She looks at him. Beat.

JOSIE: I don't know why I'm here.

JACOB: I do. I'm impossible to resist.
JOSIE: Ugh, okay I'm already regretting it.
JACOB: Well, why else?
JOSIE: I dunno. Maybe … I came to tell you, you behaved like a dickhead. Running away from me after the dance.
JACOB: Weeks ago. [*Cheekily*] You still holding on to that, huh?
JOSIE: I'm not *holding* on to it—I just—I think you should know. So you can improve your behaviour. Of being a dickhead.
JACOB: Nah, I kinda like being a dickhead sometimes. It's fun. You should know.
JOSIE: **Me?**
JACOB: Yeah, the news is all over, mate. Your—uh—

He mimes an extended exaggeration of punching himself in the face and blood pouring out and a girl screaming. JOSIE *groans.*

JOSIE: Stop! Stop! You know, I had to apologise in front of my—um—in front of Sister Bernadette—and then I had to go home and take it from my mother. Also Ivy was one hundred percent asking for it!
JACOB: I fucking bet.
JOSIE: Why are you smiling like that?
JACOB: 'Cause I think it's awesome.

Small beat.

JOSIE: You do?
JACOB: Yeah. Wish I'd seen it. Bet you were really sexy.

JOSIE *blushes, and looks away, embarrassed. She makes a slightly high-pitched, wheezing sound.*

JOSIE: Sorry. I've never made that noise before.

JACOB *reaches out to touch her cheek.*

JACOB: Oh, you're going a bit warm, Alibrandi.

JOSIE *looks down at his arm.*

JOSIE: You have goosebumps.

He leans in, starting to whisper …

JACOB: Nah, that's from—it's very cold under a car. Mechanic stuff, you wouldn't get it. The coolant.
JOSIE: [*softly*] Right.

They pause. Then, JOSIE *lunges at* JACOB *and kisses him. He responds extremely enthusiastically. It escalates and ... she pulls away.*

I ...

She runs off.

JACOB: Oi! Wasn't that bad, was I? [*To self*] Nah. No way. [*Calling out to her*] You're fucking mental, Alibrandi!

JOSIE: [*calling out from offstage*] I know!

JACOB *grins. Then he walks off, just as ...*

19. BACK HOME

The Alibrandi living space / kitchen.

JOSIE *bursts in.*

JOSIE: Ma. Ma!

CHRISTINA *enters, hurrying back into the space.*

CHRISTINA: Josie! Is everything okay?

JOSIE *flings her arms around her mother.* CHRISTINA *kisses and squeezes.*

JOSIE: I'm sorry. / I'm sorry. I'm sorry.

CHRISTINA: / Don't ever run out like that again. What's our one rule, huh?

JOSIE: You have more than one rule.

CHRISTINA: Josie!

JOSIE: I know, I know, you need to know where I am at all times.

CHRISTINA: It's more than that [*Italian*] my darling. Yes, I need to know you're safe. Yes, I need to know you're not—in trouble. I couldn't bear it if—

She stops herself.

JOSIE: Ma, it's okay. I'm perfectly fine. I—I ... didn't go far. Just went for a Glebe walk, like we used to. I was safe.

CHRISTINA: If you want to go for a walk, fine—just tell me. Because when we start to hide things from each other ... that's when you really lose someone. And I can't have that. Do you understand?

Beat.

JOSIE: Yeah.

CHRISTINA: I want you to have everything you want in life, Josie.

JOSIE: I know.

CHRISTINA: No. I've—I've been behaving badly. I'm not proud of it.

JOSIE: Ma, you haven't done anything wrong!

CHRISTINA: No ... it's okay to want to see your father, Josie.

JOSIE: But I don't want to.

CHRISTINA: And it's okay for him to want to see you— [*Before* JOSIE *can say anything*] and he does. He does. I know him like the back of my hand. And you do too. Even if you can't see it yet.

Small beat.

You're very alike, you know.

JOSIE: Ma!

CHRISTINA: It's not a bad thing. He's ... I'm angry with him, Josie. Of course. And he's very ... flawed. But ... Michael is still one of the best people I've ever known.

JOSIE: You haven't known that many people, Ma. [*Off her look*] Sorry.

CHRISTINA: And— [*Italian*] I hate to say this, but Josie, he's right. [*English*] He *can* help you. And you should let him. You should grab the opportunity—to learn from him, to know him. To get the life you want.

JOSIE: I can get it without him. I don't want to ... bring him into our lives to cause chaos.

CHRISTINA: It might be chaos. But it could be, maybe, a little wonderful?

Beat. JOSIE *doesn't know what to say. She puts her head in her mother's lap.* CHRISTINA *strokes it.*

CHRISTINA: You know, I had to grow up so fast when I was your age, I'm not used to having a real teenager in the house.

JOSIE: I don't understand how you did it, Ma. You're the strongest person I know.

CHRISTINA: I don't know about that. I never felt strong.

Small beat.

My father, Josie, he ... was not a kind man. He never wanted me, you know. He even missed my birth.

JOSIE: He missed your birth?

> *Beat.*

You've never told me that.

CHRISTINA: I suppose I try not to think of it.

JOSIE: You've told me he used to yell at you all the time. Before he threw you out.

CHRISTINA: That's true. He would ... hit me sometimes too. Not often.

JOSIE: Ma ...

CHRISTINA: It's not as bad as it sounds. It was common for parents back then. I could have handled it easily, Josie, all of his anger ... if he had just looked at me with love once in a while. But he never did. He would pretend sometimes, when we had company, but you know the real look when you see it ...

> *She trails off, lost in a memory.*

JOSIE: I can't believe Nonna never stopped him.

> *But* CHRISTINA *doesn't quite hear her. Beat. She snaps out of it. She kisses* JOSIE *on the head.*

CHRISTINA: I don't want you to miss a thing, Josie. We'll call Mich[ael]—your father—

JOSIE: You sure, Ma?

> CHRISTINA *nods, starts to get up, when—*

You know, he couldn't stop drooling over you.

CHRISTINA: *Josie.*

JOSIE: Seriously, he was practically slobbering when he talked about you.

CHRISTINA: Don't be disgusting.

JOSIE: Personally, with your shared history, I wouldn't advise pursuing his advances. But I thought you should know that it's not just Dr Pirelli—

> *She makes a gesture as if to say 'yuck'.*

—who's obsessed.

CHRISTINA: No-one is obsessed, okay?

JOSIE: If you say so.

> CHRISTINA *gets up.*

CHRISTINA: I do say so. [*Italian*] Now get up and clean yourself. You stink, baby.

JOSIE: Ma!

CHRISTINA: [*grinning*] We'll call him in the morning, Josie.

> CHRISTINA *exits.* JOSIE *stares at us, then gets up, and can't resist ... a smile, as the tempo shifts into something upbeat and the scene shifts into—*

20. MICHAEL TIME [*FANTASY & REALITY*]

A TV interview / MICHAEL*'s office.*

A TV interview on A Current Affair*:* JOSIE *and* MICHAEL *sit in chairs opposite* IVY—*now in the mould of your classic middle-aged Aussie blonde* JOURNALIST [IVY *grown up*]. *Her nose is bandaged.*

JOURNALIST: [*to us*] Hello. Hello. Good evening, everyone. And if you're just joining us, we are here with the infamous father-and-daughter legal duo—Josephine Alibrandi and her father, Michael Andretti.

JOSIE: Thanks for having us.

JOURNALIST: Josephine, you're the youngest—I believe—person to become a barrister in New South Wales.

MICHAEL: All of Australia, actually.

JOURNALIST: My apologies. Someone's proud, I see.

MICHAEL: Of course, but I can't take credit for Josie's success.

JOSIE: He's being modest. My father's legal guidance has opened doors that would have otherwise been closed to a girl like me.

JOURNALIST: Italian?

JOSIE: Sure, or we could just go ahead and say it—'a wog'.

JOURNALIST: [*gasping*] No! I'd never say that. I'd never. [*Whispering to self*] I've learnt my lesson.

JOSIE: Well, it does sound vile coming out of your mouth. But for me, it's kind of a mark of pride. My father taught me that. Right after I smacked you in the face.

JOURNALIST: Incredible. You really have such an amazing dad, Josephine, unlike me. I feel so privileged to have played a small part in this story. Also, are the rumours true? You're representing Kylie Minogue?

JOSIE: Oh. I couldn't possibly say. Confidentiality.

JOURNALIST: Oh, go on. You know you want to.

MICHAEL: Josie's a shark, sorry, you won't get it out of her.

JOURNALIST: Please! I need the scoop Josephine; I haven't had good ratings in months.

JOSIE: I'm not sure what I'm supposed to do about that, Ivy. Maybe you're just not very ... relatable to the Australian public?

JOURNALIST: You're right. It's probably me. If only I knew when it all started to go downhill.

JOSIE: I'm no expert but I'd say it was back at St Martha's when you acted like a racist bitch with no moral compass?

JOURNALIST: [*gasping*] Yes. That's exactly it. God, you're good. Thank you, Josie.

JOSIE: Don't mention it.

JOURNALIST: Well, I guess I'll go now and be alone like the terrible person I am. Thank you both so much for your time. This is Ivy Lloyd for *A Current Affair*, signing off. Forever.

> The JOURNALIST *runs off in campy sobs as* JOSIE *waves goodbye to her, and smiles into the distance.* MICHAEL *gets up and moves his chair.*
>
> *He clears his throat.*

MICHAEL: Josie!

JOSIE: Mmmm.

MICHAEL: Do you have the print-outs? Of the orders?

JOSIE: [*still dreamily*] What?—

> *She starts.*

—Oh!—sorry, I was, yes, here, just a sec ...

> *She grabs a bunch of paper and hands it to* MICHAEL, *who flips through them quickly.*

MICHAEL: Good work.

> JOSIE *beams.*

JOSIE: Really? No mistakes?

MICHAEL: Yeah.

JOSIE: Oh thank god! First time this month.

MICHAEL: That's still impressive. This is pretty difficult stuff.
JOSIE: I really like it though. I thought it would be boring 'cause you don't do murder and shit but … it's not.
MICHAEL: If you're interested in … murder … 'and shit', you should keep your options open. Get an internship during uni. I could talk to a friend or two.
JOSIE: Nah, I wanna work with you. We could open our own firm some day.

Small beat. MICHAEL *tries not to smile.*

MICHAEL: Well, I don't know if we'll crossover quite in time.
JOSIE: I'll be done in five years!
MICHAEL: Well, my plan is to go hard for the next ten years then buy a vineyard outside Adelaide.

JOSIE*'s face falls.*

JOSIE: Adelaide?
MICHAEL: Yes, have you been?
JOSIE: No, why would I? It's Adelaide. This is *Sydney*. The best city in the world?
MICHAEL: You think so? What about London or Paris?
JOSIE: Ugh, whatever. You're crazy if you wanna go back to Adelaide. What do they even have there?
MICHAEL: That's where my life is, Josie.

He pauses, realises what he's said—sees her face.

I mean—that's where a lot of my life is. It's not in my hands anyway. I go where the firm tells me to.
JOSIE: Right. Sure. The firm.

She busies herself with some papers. Small beat. MICHAEL *tries to lighten the mood …*

MICHAEL: You know the partner you met earlier?
JOSIE: Mmm.
MICHAEL: Don't tell anyone but he likes to put on a white wig late at night in the office when he thinks no-one's looking.
JOSIE: [*snapping to it, delighted*] What? That's mental!
MICHAEL: Takes all sorts.
JOSIE: Did you catch him?

MICHAEL: Nah, Camila in Mediation told me.

JOSIE: Oh, is that the Spanish one?

MICHAEL: Yeah. The only competent one on her team, between you and me. Sometimes she pretends her English is bad to not deal with her senior. I should have done that.

JOSIE: She's very pretty. Bosomy. Spanish.

MICHAEL: I suppose.

JOSIE: Is she your girlfriend?

MICHAEL: What? No!

JOSIE: Just saying. It's not very responsible. To acquire a girlfriend and then abandon her and go to Adelaide.

MICHAEL: Well, thankfully I haven't.

JOSIE: Also I saw her eating spaghetti with a spoon once. So. What a dickhead.

MICHAEL: *Josie.*

JOSIE: What? It's a dickhead thing to do.

Small beat. MICHAEL *offers her a chair and sits down too.*

MICHAEL: Josie, you know, even if I leave. I'll be coming back all the time. Not for work. To see you.

JOSIE: You will?

MICHAEL: This has been, probably, one of the best months of my life.

He looks away, blinking—not used to this. JOSIE*'s lip trembles.*

JOSIE: God, you're soft.

MICHAEL *laughs.*

MICHAEL: You're so much like Tina sometimes. She used to tease me mercilessly.

JOSIE: I can see that.

He smiles ... the memories returning ...

MICHAEL: She used to rag on my essays, you know? English Lit. She loved poetry and all that highfalutin stuff. I would have just read *Archie* comics for the rest of my life if she hadn't looked at me like I was an idiot from time to time. She was so smart, much better at school than I was ...

JOSIE *watches him, sees the joy in his eyes.*

You know all the boys wanted to be with the beautiful Christina Alibrandi, but she never talked to them. She was so quiet and aloof … until you got to know her. Until she *let* you know her, and then—

He takes a breath and tries to shake himself out of it.

JOSIE: Michael, did you really not know?

Beat. He knows what she's asking.

MICHAEL: I'm—Josie … I can be—in law, we'd call it … wilfully negligent? I *should* have known. Maybe I—maybe I did. Like she said, what else would a good Catholic girl have done? But, I wanted … the world, I suppose.

He breaks, puts his head in hands. JOSIE *reaches out and touches his shoulder.* MICHAEL *starts, then half-smiles and exits. The school bell rings, and the scene shifts into …*

21. NEW SERA

St Martha's Library; study period.

JOSIE *and* SERA *in the library.* SERA *is buried deep in books, furiously taking notes, while* JOSIE *chatters on, oblivious.*

JOSIE: So yeah, I guess I feel weird 'cause I was so sure that John was it and then I'm out there kissing Jacob at all hours of the day. Not that I get to see him as much as I'd like with work, and he gets grumpy about that, but I find it kinda cute? I dunno. *And* I'm keeping it from my mother, which is so weird of me too. The whole thing is just weird, right? Like yes, she'd freak out but I think it's more than that. Like if it was John, I wouldn't hesitate. But Jacob's so … you know. And she's gone through enough this year with my father and Nonna, so … Sera, hello? Are you even listening?

SERA: [*starting*] What? Yes, sorry—I know—John Coote, Jacob Barton—it's very difficult. You gotta kiss them all.

Beat.

JOSIE: [*annoyed*] What's wrong with you? I only ever see you in study period anymore and half the time you use it to go to the library.

SERA: We can't all be like you, Josie! I have to study. The UMAT is really hard. Some of us actually have to try.

JOSIE: You're really going through with this?
SERA: Of course, I am! Look at my roots. They're fucked. You think I'd have this regrowth otherwise?
JOSIE: [*sighs*] Well, are you following my schedule? I made you a timetable.
SERA: Your schedule makes no sense! It's crazy! I just think Calabrians and Sicilians operate in different time zones.

SERA frantically opens more books. JOSIE watches. Then—

JOSIE: I wonder if the problem with Jacob is 'cause his mother's not around so he's just a bit unfocussed and like, has no goals. Maybe he just needs someone to help him. I should make him a schedule.
SERA: Oh my god, Josie! Do not do that. There's nothing wrong with Jacob. You're just a snob, *bellezz*.
JOSIE: What? Oi!

She snatches SERA's book off her.

SERA: Hey!
JOSIE: I am not a snob.
SERA: Give it back.
JOSIE: My Nonno worked in a factory!
SERA: Everybody's Nonno worked in a factory!

SERA grabs her book back.

JOSIE: My family are outcasts? Your dad won't even talk to me directly when I'm in your house—'Hi, Mr Russo.' 'Your mum's a whore.'
SERA: He's old-fashioned. Your dad's a lawyer. Just like everyone else at St Martha's!
JOSIE: Well, that's a new thing.
SERA: Still true.
JOSIE: You know, I've had to work harder than anyone to get here. I'm going to be the first Alibrandi woman to go to university.
SERA: [*snapping*] Yeah, well I'm gonna be the first Russo to not join the concreting business—it's not easy for me either!
JOSIE: Okay, you seriously need to chill out and go see Serge or something.
SERA: I can't, Josie! He's a distraction! I just have to stay on task! I have to focus. Holy fuck—

She grabs her chest and wheezes in a big breath.

—I think I took too much No-Doz!

JOSIE: Have we swapped brains??

Beat. The girls glare at each other. Then they burst into laughter. SERA *exhales.*

SERA: I think we didn't just swap brains, we swapped bodies. Literally.

JOSIE: Literally?

SERA: Yeah, 'cause I've banned Serge from seeing me in private. It's too dangerous. And he's been really sweet 'bout it and really respected my space. But as a result I can tell you I have one hundred percent become a virge again. Like it's actually regrown.

JOSIE: Yeah, you should know that's not medically possible.

SERA: Nah, it's a miracle. I'm the reverse Virgin Mary. I got closed up by God.

JOSIE: [*laughing*] I'll call the Vatican then?—Oh, shit.

She's just realised the time.

SERA: What?

JOSIE *gives her a look, and starts to pack up.*

JOSIE: Remember, I'm at the library with you.

Ah, right—of course. SERA *winks and salutes.*

SERA: You got it, *Porca Madonna*.

JOSIE *grins and rushes away.*

22. MORE JACOB

Streets of Glebe / CHRISTINA *and* JOSIE*'s living room.*

JOSIE *and* JACOB *run around the space—the streets of Leichhardt and Glebe—ducking and weaving as Wog ASIO trail them.* JOSIE *leads* JACOB. *The chase is tense, but ... they finally find a satisfactory place, out of breath, and collapse.*

JACOB: You're mental.

JOSIE: It's life or death, alright? I don't even know I brought you here—it's very dangerous.

JACOB: You like the excitement.

JOSIE: Okay, one, two, three—go!

They run and burst into JOSIE*'s kitchen, laughing. Beat. They settle.*

JACOB: I've definitely never walked through Glebe that way before.

JOSIE: Four p.m. is peak Wog ASIO time. They're always watching, but at four? They're waiting for all of the grandchildren to come home from school to see if there's anything to report. Boyfriends, girlfriends, cigarettes, cleavage, who's eating McDonald's before dinner …

JACOB: Right.

He looks around.

You sure your mum won't be back?

JOSIE: Nah, she picked up another reception night shift. More money.

JACOB: Fair enough.

Beat.

Can't believe I'm standing in the kitchen THE Josephine Alibrandi grew up in.

JOSIE: Yeah, you're very lucky. Oh—this—is where I threw up for the first time.

JACOB: Beautiful.

JOSIE: And once I ran into this door and smacked my forehead. It started bleeding

JACOB: Have you got a scar?

JOSIE: Yeah, just here …

He leans in to look and kisses her forehead. They kiss. It gets a bit heated. JOSIE *pulls back and clears his throat.*

JOSIE: Where are my manners?

She grabs a couple of mugs and starts to fill them. She places one in front of JACOB. *He stares—what the hell … he takes a sip and scrunches his face.*

JACOB: What is this?

JOSIE: San Pellegrino.

JACOB: Don't like it. Tastes like it's trying to be beer but gave up. D'yu have a real beer?

JOSIE: You've barely had any. It's an acquired taste.
JACOB: I'm good.

> *Beat.*

JOSIE: How's school going?
JACOB: What?
JOSIE: Isn't it insane we have like a few weeks left? Have you put in your preferences?
JACOB: Nah.
JOSIE: I guess there's a little bit of time.
JACOB: Yeah, I dunno? That's only for uni, isn't it?
JOSIE: Yeah.
JACOB: I think I'm just gonna help my dad out. Maybe do my apprenticeship.

> JOSIE *stares at him. Then, she gets up and retrieves a pile of pamphlets.*

JOSIE: I mean, I'm sure he wants you to help out, but you don't have to, you know. I—I got a whole bunch of these, even though—huh, thought I threw this TAFE one out? Weird. But you could do that too, actually. TAFE. There's lots of options.

> *She puts the papers down in front of him. He stares at her.*

JACOB: Is this like a roleplay thing? Like we're in an office? I watched a porno once with a secretary—two secretaries actually, and—
JOSIE: No! Stop talking about pornos. I'm trying to help you. You're very smart, Jacob. Your Have a Say Day speech—
JACOB: Yeah that got you going, didn't it?
JOSIE: You could do whatever you wanted to, really. I mean—

> *She finds a pamphlet.*

—look, electronics, that's like cars, and then it converts into engineering—USYD has a great engineering school.

> JACOB *gets up with a frustrated grunt, and turns his back to her. Then turns back.*

JACOB: I thought we were going to have fun today, Josie.
JOSIE: We ... did.
JACOB: When?

JOSIE: This is our future.

JACOB: It's not mine.

JOSIE: Why are you being so stubborn? What—you wanna hang out in Redfern your whole life?

JACOB: What's wrong with that? Redfern's awesome.

JOSIE: Look, I'm supposed to visit the USYD campus with John Barton soon. Why don't you come? You'll see. It's so great.

JACOB: Yeah I'd love that ... I'd love that as much as dunking my balls in a jar of acid.

JOSIE: Oh my god! I'm sick of hearing about your balls all the time.

JACOB: Yeah, bet Barton never talks about stuff like that, does he?

JOSIE: I haven't seen him much lately but yeah, he definitely does not.

JACOB: Makes sense, see you gotta have some balls to talk about them.

JOSIE: He's got plenty of—ugh, no—I don't wanna talk about either of your bloody balls—ew—I can't believe you've made me say that ... look, don't you wanna be together next year?

Beat.

JACOB: Josie, we're not even together now.

JOSIE: Meaning?

JACOB: I don't see how we can be together if ... I mean all we've done is hang out and hide behind a deli and avoid your bloody Nonna. And drink this stupid thing that tastes like piss.

JOSIE: Right.

JACOB: Josie ...

JOSIE: Uh-huh. Sorry if I'm too much trouble for you.

JACOB: I didn't say trouble. I like trouble!

JOSIE: Just too much of a bloody ethnic, I guess.

JACOB: That doesn't work on me, Josie. It's not about 'too ethnic'. But you're definitely ... too much of something.

JOSIE: You know what Jacob, why don't you just go back to your usual conquests? I'm sure they'd love to talk about your balls all day.

JACOB: Yeah, but see, they don't really *talk* about them. That's the point.

Beat.

[*Off the expression on her face*] That's a joke, man.

JOSIE, *disgusted, turns away, looks out at us.* JACOB *shakes his head and leaves.*

JOSIE: [*to us*] What's wrong with me?

> *From the corner,* NONNA *enters the space, album in hand.* JOSIE *squeezes her eyes shut, tries to steady herself.*

It's—it's for the best. He's not on my … level. And I'm way too distracted. I should be focussed on my … ugh, why can't I just shut the fuck up and just touch him???

NONNA: What you say!

> JOSIE*'s eyes fly open and we snap into the next scene.*

23. BACK AT NONNA'S

NONNA*'s living room.*

JOSIE *spins to face* NONNA.

JOSIE: Nothing, Nonna!

> NONNA *plonks her album down in front of* JOSIE. *They sit down.*

NONNA: Long time you no come. Very busy. Too busy for Nonna.

JOSIE: Practice exams are like literally around the corner, Nonna. I shouldn't even be here. Even Sera Russo's studying more than me!

NONNA: [*Italian*] Don't mention that family!

> *Beat.*

[*English*] So you study lot? Don't let Michael Andretti distract you. Is he distract you? You see him lot?

JOSIE: No, he doesn't distract me. Sometimes I think he's more obsessed with my marks than I am.

NONNA: Good, good.

> *Beat.*

And your mother also, she not come long time. At least you have excuse.

JOSIE: I think she has an excuse, Nonna.

> NONNA *goes silent. Looks at the albums. Starts to try to open them.*

NONNA: Yesterday, I bring more from upstairs. I carry all myself but [*Italian*] thank god, I not break my back. [*English*] My neck but, oof.

JOSIE: You could have just asked me to bring them down.
NONNA: [*Italian*] How? You are never here. [*English*] Always busy ...
    JOSIE *sighs.*

JOSIE: [*to us*] Okay truth be told, I have been avoiding her. But after how she treated Mama! And, not that it's a problem currently, but I was afraid she'd sniff out Jacob on me too—I mean, what does she have to do all day but sit around and gossip and cry about how beautiful she once was? She's primed for detection.
NONNA: Josie, yes, see this—I want show you.
    JOSIE *glances over dismissively, expecting to see another of* NONNA*'s younger day photos. Except—*
JOSIE: That's Mama!
NONNA: Yes, is when she [*Italian*] baby.
JOSIE: She looks the same. The eyes. Well, your beautiful Alibrandi eyes.
    JOSIE *looks through the album eagerly.*
Oh. There's only one.
NONNA: Yes. Only one photo of Christina. Nonno—he did not think you should take many photos. He not like.
JOSIE: But I've seen photos of Nonno. In his big suits. There's literally one now—
    She taps the book, then looks closer.
—Oh!—it's not Nonno. He's too handsome. Who's the dish?
NONNA: Dish! [*Italian*] Don't be disgusting, Josie. [*English*] This some man who come help us sometimes to do handyman work when men too busy on farm. He was man from Ingham.
JOSIE: A skip?
NONNA: Sometimes ... they are good ones. This one, he good.
JOSIE: Can't believe you had a skip friend.
NONNA: Noooo, he more Zia's friend. You know how she is big flirt.
JOSIE: Zia Patrizia??? *Our* Zia Patrizia?
NONNA: Yes, big flirt.
JOSIE: I ... cannot imagine.
    She looks back at the photo.
He's got a nice smile.

NONNA: His name was Marcus Sanford.
JOSIE: Marcus Sanford?
JOSIE: He very kind man.
>   *Beat.*

NONNA: Anyway, Nonno not like photos.
JOSIE: Oh, that's you and Zia! You look so happy.
>   *She squints.*

And dirty.
>   *Beat.*

I've never seen these photos before. Where have you been hiding these?
NONNA: [*agitated*] I not hide anything Josie! You take no interest, you never come here. And I not dirty, [*Italian*] if you knew what real work is, you would know. [*English*] I work on farm with Zia in Ingham—
JOSIE: Oh yeah, near Brisbane.
NONNA: [*more agitated*] Not near Brisbane! Ingham is distance from Italy to Belgium!
JOSIE: I don't think that's true.
NONNA: Is very far, Josie. But we must go! We get down from the boat and I meet man I am engaged to for first time—your Nonno. But then we not stop, he immediately take me train and bus to Ingham. Is not city, just farm. Full of Italians working in field—I was shock, but Nonno say you don't know how lucky you are—he was in camp in World War before I come—the Australians lock all Italian in camp, Josie. What they think our men do? Kill them with tomatoes? So then I understand what Nonno say and I quiet.
JOSIE: [*to us, looking slightly at* NONNA] God, sometimes I think of the silence of Nonna's life and feel insane.
NONNA: Oh! My first house, sometimes the snakes come in. It is miracle Zia and I not bitten and die. When she pregnant with your cousin Roberto, I worry every day.
>   JOSIE *peers into the album where* NONNA *is pointing.*

JOSIE: God, she's massive.

NONNA: Well, Roberto very big ugly child. And now he big ugly man. [*Laughing*] It not from our side, it his father's.

JOSIE: Zio's not that bad.

NONNA: No no, he good man. I thankful my sister marry good man. I so sad when she and Zio stay in Queensland and Nonno move us to Sydney—he want to work factory, no more farm.

JOSIE: Well I'm glad we live in Sydney. [*To us*] Me in Queensland, can you imagine?

NONNA: [*smiling sadly*] Yes, I only go back farm one time, to visit for one Christmas. Then stay for January for tomato picking. Then Christina born later that year, then too busy. Then Zia move here, so no more.

She closes the album.

You right, Josie. Christina do have my eye …

JOSIE: [*bursting forth, impatient*] Nonna, oh my god, you're so obvious. I mean, you bring down this sad sack album? With a literal photo of Mama looking like some exorcist baby bride of Christ! Just admit you overreacted and you miss her.

NONNA: I not miss anyone.

JOSIE: *Mannaggia!* [*English*] I'm so sick of being the only adult in this family. [*Deliberately*] Mama's birthday is coming up. October first. If you remember?

NONNA *looks at her—of course she knows* CHRISTINA'*s birthday.*

Come to our house.

Beat.

We'll celebrate.

NONNA *looks away.* JOSIE *sighs—there's no use trying with these two. But then—*

NONNA: I make lasagna.

JOSIE *squeals and hugs* NONNA.

They part. JOSIE *picks up her bag and the scene morphs into* …

24. JOHN BARTON

USYD campus.

JOSIE *and* JOHN *at Sydney University, in the thick of the sandstone campus.* JOHN *gets* JOSIE *a coffee.*

JOHN: Careful, it's hot.

They take a sip.

JOSIE: Mmm … maybe I prefer Nescoffee.
JOHN: This is the finest coffee on campus! Probably isn't saying much.

JOSIE *looks around.* JOHN *looks at her. Small beat.*

JOSIE: There sure are a lot of ugly old dude statues here.
JOHN: It's not all ugly old dudes. That one's a horse.
JOSIE: Oh yeah!

Beat.

Oh no, is one of the old dudes your grandpa or something? I bet it is.
JOHN: Actually …
JOSIE: Oh my god, really? Sorry I didn't mean to insult your lineage!
JOHN: It's okay, I forgive you … it's true, my grandfather … was *that* horse.
JOSIE: You're an idiot.

They laugh. They settle. A content beat as they gaze out into the horizon.

It's so nice here.
JOHN: Yeah. I actually like the campus. Very peaceful. Green.
JOSIE: Full of possibility.
JOHN: Yeah.

Small beat.

God, this year has been a blur.
JOSIE: Oh my god, I was thinking the exact same thing! [*To us*] It's nice you know, we haven't seen each other ages but … we're still in sync. Like always. [*To* JOHN] It's just gone by so quickly, hey. And so much has happened. My life is completely … different. And

not to brag, but I think I've single-handedly fixed my family. Okay, no. But ... things aren't shit right now apart from ... I am kind of behind on my prac exam prep.

JOHN: Me too, don't worry. Been so hard to concentrate.

JOSIE: Tell me about it.

Beat.

Hey, John?

JOHN: Yeah.

JOSIE: Sorry we didn't get to see each other more this year. I've missed you.

JOHN: You too. And that's okay, Josie. We have now.

JOSIE: That's right. And next year. And then like four years after that. And then our whole lives.

JOHN: [*quietly*] Yeah.

Beat.

JOSIE: We should make this our spot—like come here between classes to talk or stuff. Or hide from Ivy.

JOHN: I think she's more likely to hide from you. Post-nosegate.

JOSIE: Hmm, come to think of it, I guess she has been avoiding me at school. I didn't even notice. Turns out violence is the answer.

JOHN: There you go. Sometimes you just have to take drastic measures.

Beat. They drink their coffee.

JOSIE: John?

JOHN: Yes, Josie?

JOSIE: Thanks for bringing me. Sorry I kept putting it off.

JOHN: You have to stop saying sorry. We made it. All that matters. Besides, you've had a lot on.

JOSIE: Yeah, god, my—my dad—Michael—I keep switching between the two, but only 'Michael' to him—it's been a lot but it's also been ... kind of ...

She trails off. Almost too embarrassed or overwhelmed to say 'great'. JOHN *smiles.*

JOHN: I'm so glad to hear that, but ... that wasn't what I meant.

He grins at her. He's talking about ...

JOSIE: Jacob. Right. Yes. You probably heard that we'd been hanging a bit?
JOHN: I'd heard a rumour. And then a rumour it was off. And then a rumour it was on again?
JOSIE: I ... can confirm those rumours. It's been a bit—

She gestures up and down.

—but right now, it's back (on). I can't seem to ... not? I dunno what I was even thinking, jumping into it in the first place. Like, he's ...
JOHN: Jacob Coote? [*Laughing*] Come on, Josie. Nothing to *think* about there. We all have eyes.
JOSIE: John!

Small beat.

I dunno, for some reason, I feel like I should have told you? Or like I should say sorry? Sorry! Didn't mean to say it again ... I ... for some reason feel like I need to explain it to you ...
JOHN: About Jacob?
JOSIE: Yeah. 'Cause you and I, we've always been ...
JOHN: Great friends?
JOSIE: Yeah. Yeah ... I don't know my own head sometimes, so(rry)—

She stops herself. He smiles at her. Small beat.

JOHN: You know Josie, if it helps, I thought I had a crush on you for all of Year Ten. And a bit of Year Eleven.
JOSIE: Oh my god, me too! But more recently than that ... till year ... earlier this year actually ... okay, embarrassing.

Beat.

Friends is good though, isn't it?
JOHN: Friends is perfect.
JOSIE: Forever then. Well, until we both die and get our own statues side by side.
JOHN: That a pigeon shits on.
JOSIE: [*noticing the pigeon shitting*] Oh yeah! Look at it go.

Small beat as they watch.

John.
JOHN: Yep?
JOSIE: You seem, I dunno, happy?

JOHN: Do I?

 JOSIE *nods.*

JOSIE: Are things better, at home?

JOHN: Same old.

 JOSIE*'s face falls.*

 Aw, don't look so guilty, Josie! It's not your fault he's a prick. I'm happy your dad drama turned out so good. But, as for home … It's the same. Same old expectations. Same unhappy mother. Same old political dinners. Which I've realised is just as it is. 'Cause nothing will ever change in that house. But it also has nothing to do with me. I can't let it take me down with it, you know?

 She squeezes his arm.

JOSIE: Exactly. I can see that. I'm so proud of you. And next year, all of that will feel so far away. We just have to get through the next few months, ignore all the bullshit bits of life and everything's going to be great. I'm sure of it.

JOHN: I love how sure you always are of everything, Josie. You should get everything you want.

JOSIE: You should too! Oh—what's this?

 JOHN *hands her an envelope.*

JOHN: I—I wrote you something—seems like the moment—it's a letter about, I guess, everything I hope for. In the future.

JOSIE: Oh. Wow.

 She takes it and starts to open it.

JOHN: No—I—I thought you could open it after the final exams. And also, you could write me one. And then—

JOSIE: We open them after we're finished, to celebrate! That's so lovely John. I'd love to.

 Beat.

 You can't give me a hint but?

 He laughs and gets up, helping her up too.

JOHN: Hmm. I think it's about my—what's that word you like?—*emancipation.*

JOSIE: Ooh. 'The Emancipation of John Barton'. I do like that. And what's the emancipated John Barton gonna do with his life, hey?
JOHN: Anything he damn well wants, Josie. Anything he damn well wants!

> *They whoop, and hug, tight.* JOHN *leaves.* JOSIE *watches him go.*
>
> *Darkness falls, and the scene starts to morph. Festive music begins to play. Behind* JOSIE, NONNA *walks out, a lit-up birthday cake in her hands ...*

25. SURPRISE PARTY!

CHRISTINA *and* JOSIE*'s living room.*

JOSIE *turns to face* NONNA *who immediately thrusts the cake at her, and begins to order her around, as she takes over* CHRISTINA *and* JOSIE*'s living room in preparation. They squabble at pace, loudly but joyfully. Finally, everything's ready.*

NONNA: Where she?
JOSIE: She's doing the evening shift Nonna. It only finishes at eight.
NONNA: It eight-fifteen. Lasagna get cold.
JOSIE: You literally just heated it.
NONNA: She should not be work this late—
JOSIE: Oh my god, Nonna—wait—shhhh—I hear something!

> *They scramble and get into position, ready to surprise. Offstage, the sound of laughter ... but it's not just* CHRISTINA*'s. It sounds like she's talking to someone. There's two voices. One unmistakably a man's.*

NONNA: You invite Michael?

> JOSIE *shakes her head. Then, she's delighted—thinking it's her dad and mum.*

JOSIE: [*whispering*] I knew it. I knew they were hanging out. You haven't seen his face, Nonna, but whenever I mention Mama ...

> *They listen for a second before* CHRISTINA *enters. She turns around and —*

Surprise!

CHRISTINA: [*truly shocked*] Josie! Ma??
NONNA: [*Italian*] Surprise. Happy birthday to you.
> *They move to embrace her but* CHRISTINA *quickly takes a step back.*

CHRISTINA: Uh—one second.
> *She turns and motions to someone offstage.* JOSIE *sneaks a cheeky glance at* NONNA. *We hear whispers. Then,* CHRISTINA *turns back.*
> *They look at her.*

JOSIE: Ma! Call him in.
CHRISTINA: What?
> JOSIE *starts to walk past her as if to go out and call her dad back.* CHRISTINA *stops her.*

Josie, no, please—I just want to enjoy this ... wonderful surprise with the two of you. Ma, [*Italian*] I don't think you've been here in years.
> JOSIE *is puzzled, but relents. She ushers her mother back to the table where the cake waits.* NONNA *is oddly stony-faced.*

JOSIE: [*to* CHRISTINA] Ooh, you smell nice.
CHRISTINA: Oh. Thanks, Josie.
JOSIE: Look what we made, Ma. Okay, Nonna made. I suggested we do the sparklers instead of thirty-five candles.
CHRISTINA: Well, we don't want to call the fire brigade.
NONNA: What you wearing?
CHRISTINA: A dress.
JOSIE: You look amazing. Doesn't she look amazing, Nonna?
> NONNA *says nothing.* CHRISTINA *avoids her glance.*

CHRISTINA: Right, well, should we cut the cake?
NONNA: You wear this to work?
> CHRISTINA *ignores her.*

CHRISTINA: Josie, let's do the cake. It looks delicious.
NONNA: Or you wear this *after* work?
JOSIE: God, Nonna, why are you so obsessed with the dress? Obviously, Ma dressed up for—

NONNA: [*cutting her off*] No, no, Josie. She would not wear *this* for Michael Andretti.

JOSIE: What are you talking about, Nonna? [*Looking at her mum*] God, she's gone—

> JOSIE *stops short, seeing* CHRISTINA's *face. Small beat. She knows her mother ...*

That wasn't ... ? Wait—who was that?

CHRISTINA: Does it matter, Josie?

NONNA: [*Italian*] See, I told you! I knew it.

CHRISTINA: [*Italian*] Congratulations, Ma! [*English*] I went out tonight. Yes. I went out with a man tonight. I am thirty-five years old and I went out with a man tonight.

NONNA: [*Italian*] Disgraceful. [*English*] Finally your daughter has a father and you don't have the decency to keep your legs shut.

CHRISTINA: [*Italian*] Don't you start with me. [*English*] It's not enough you insult me in your house, now you come here and insult me in mine.

JOSIE: Dr Pirelli! Oh my god, it's Dr Pirelli, isn't it?

CHRISTINA: What, Josie? What do you have an opinion on now? What is so wrong with Dr Pirelli that doesn't meet your standards?

JOSIE: I can't believe this. All this time I thought you were working evenings.

CHRISTINA: I have been working. Josie, how can you even [say that]—

JOSIE: I got Nonna to come to our house. I have a prac exam tomorrow! And I spent my time doing all this. And you're off with—God, do you even care about my future?

CHRISTINA: You're such an unreasonable child, Josie. One day you'll understand.

JOSIE: No, I won't understand how you can just bring some strange man into our house to do God knows what.

> CHRISTINA *looks like she's been slapped.*

CHRISTINA: [*to* NONNA] Well, there's your influence—you hear that? Are you happy? Josie, I'm your mother—but I'm also a woman. Who deserves to have a life. Or at least a little bit of a good time for once. Around people my own age.

NONNA: [*Italian*] We are eternally cursed.

CHRISTINA: Yes, we're cursed, and I'm the curse, Ma.
JOSIE: Why do you do this now—after everything?
CHRISTINA: I'm not living on your schedule, Josie.
JOSIE: That's what mothers are supposed to do!
CHRISTINA: Well, maybe sometimes I don't want to be your mother!
NONNA: [*Italian*] Bite your tongue, Christina.
CHRISTINA: Or your daughter!
JOSIE: Well maybe you'd be happy if we both died!
CHRISTINA: For god's sake, Josie. When did you become such an entitled brat?

> JOSIE *stares at her mother.* NONNA *tries to put a hand on her shoulder, but* JOSIE *shrugs her off. She grabs her backpack.*

CHRISTINA: Where do you think you're going?
JOSIE: I'm going to my father's.

> *Small beat.*

Or maybe I'll go to Jacob's. You remember him, Ma? Jacob Coote? That boy who used to throw eggs at the St Martha's girls? Yeah, well, he's my boyfriend now! I wanted to be sure before I told you, but what does it matter? Oh and Nonna, he's definitely not a good Italian boy.
CHRISTINA: Josie!
JOSIE: What?
CHRISTINA: Please. Please don't go to this boy's—to Jacob's. You're being silly. Please. Go to your father's if you must. Josie, don't—don't make my mistake.
JOSIE: If you can be free, why can't I?
CHRISTINA: Because you're seventeen years old.

> JOSIE *stares at her, then just leaves.* CHRISTINA *starts to tremble and sob. She speaks through her tears.*

And now she treats me like everyone has my whole … that's all that was left … [*Italian*] Don't say anything, Ma!

> *But* NONNA *is silent, oddly withdrawn.*

NONNA: I have nothing to say. What could I say?
CHRISTINA: [*Italian*] Don't start. [*English*] You must be so happy. This is what you're always warning about. That I'll ruin her.

NONNA: [*quietly*] No, Christina. Everything is already ruin. Long time ago.
CHRISTINA: Of course. How could I forget the mistake I made when I was sixteen years old for one second?

Small beat.

NONNA: I am an old woman. I am tired of fighting.
CHRISTINA: And I am a young woman! And I am tired of being old! Why can't you understand how I feel for once, Ma? Why can't—

She stops herself—it's too much. She leaves. NONNA *stares out into the darkness, remembering something from a long time ago.*

NONNA: I understand Christina, more than you think I do.

She leaves too, just as JOSIE *re-enters the space.*

26. LIQUID COURAGE!

Streets of Glebe.

JOSIE *adjusts herself, trying to look nice. She keeps an eye out, as always, for Wog ASIO.*

She holds out her hand, as if waiting for something, and another hand surreptitiously thrusts a bottle at her. Then, the hand is followed by ... SERA *popping her head out and grinning.*

SERA: Any ASIO spot you?
JOSIE: Past their bedtimes.
SERA: Okay, so you gotta eat something first before you chug that or you'll throw up.
JOSIE: Thanks.
SERA: No problem.

Beat.

It's twenty bucks.

JOSIE *hands over the money.*

JOSIE: You seem … relaxed.
SERA: Oh my god, Josie, I'm so relieved now UMAT's over. Exams gonna be nothing compared to. I think I did well, but. Like, I could tell. It's the first time I've been able to tell. Also, Sergio came over

last night. It was actually our six months, can you believe? Never thought I'd be spending it doing a maths practice prac while Serge slept. For our three months, we went to Wonderland and he got in a fight with a Scooby-Doo and they threw us out. Aw, it was a really nice night.

> *She sighs happily.* JOSIE *smiles, but she's distracted. Beat.*

JOSIE: Does it hurt?
SERA: Oh! Yeah it does. But it's fun after a bit. Don't be scared, *bellezz*.

> *A tender smile between the two friends.* JOSIE *looks at the bottle in her hands, hesitant.*

But you can stay at my place if you change your mind?

> JOSIE *shakes her head. She's going to do this.*

JOSIE: Bottoms up!

> *She opens the bottle and swigs.*

SERA: You go, *bellezz*!

> *Music kicks in, the bass deepens, as the scene morphs into ...*

27. JACOB & JOSIE

JACOB*'s room.*

JACOB *spots* JOSIE *across from him. They walk to each other and begin to strip.* JOSIE *forcefully makes out with him. He reciprocates. It escalates ... and then she pulls back.*

JOSIE: So where did you say your dad went again?
JACOB: You want to talk about my dad?
JOSIE: He's a very nice man.
JACOB: He's alright. He's gone to his sister's.
JOSIE: Oh, why?
JACOB: Uhh, she had a baby.

> *Beat.* JOSIE *keeps looking at him so he continues.*

They all thought she was too old to have one but one day she threw up at work and now there's a baby.
JOSIE: Wow. So, she just got pregnant, like that, by accident.
JACOB: Yeah, guess my family's just very fertile.

JOSIE: So's mine. I mean, I haven't really asked my mother how many times she slept with my father before uh, me ... but it can't have been that many times 'cause they were quite supervised ...

JACOB: Josie ... this conversation is weird. And I don't mean weird in a fun-weird-Josie way. Like, just weird.

JOSIE: You're right. It's just important to be safe. You know.

JACOB: Oh! Shit. Of course. Never fear, Alibrandi.

He takes out a condom wrapper.

JOSIE: Oh, good.

She peers at it.

Large. Like a tampon. Hey, do you ever wonder what it would be like to have a period? I can tell you it's not fun.

JACOB: Josie, we're going weird again.

JOSIE: Right.

She kisses him hard. It escalates. She bites his lip.

JACOB: Ow! What? Why?

JOSIE: Sorry!

JACOB: I think I'm bleeding.

JOSIE: Quick, put some of the alcohol on it to disinfect it.

JACOB: What the fuck—

Before he can speak, she's dabbed some whisky on his lip—it burns.

Ow. Josie, what the fuck—what's going on?

JOSIE: What do you mean? We're having sex!

JACOB: Are we??

Beat. JOSIE *looks away.*

JACOB: Don't get me wrong—I want to—I really really want to—I'm so happy you showed up here tonight. I just, I don't wanna be a dickhead. I want it to be nice.

JOSIE: Who said you were a dickhead?

JACOB: Ah you don't have to say it, a real dickhead knows they're a dickhead.

Small beat.

And it's in how you're acting. Like, do you even want to?

JOSIE: I don't think you're a dickhead. And I also really really want to.
JACOB: Come here.

*They kiss again, they get into position—*JACOB *on top—*

JACOB: Fuck.
JOSIE: [*wobbly voice*] What?
JACOB: Are you crying?
JOSIE: No ...

He gets off her. She sits up, snotty with tears.

Sorry, I know this isn't very sexy.
JACOB: Yeah, no shit.

Small beat.

You don't have to be sorry.
JOSIE: I'm just so defective. It's my fucking family. It's ...

JACOB *puts a cover over gently.*

JACOB: Why are you even here, Josie? It's your rest night. Pracs start tomorrow.
JOSIE: You read my schedule?
JACOB: Yeah, took me a while—couldn't bloody make heads or tails of it—the thing looks like it's written in code.

She stares at him.

JOSIE: I love you, Jacob Coote.

JACOB *pauses.*

JACOB: I love you too, Josie.

They smile, hold hands.

JOSIE: So um, what do you want to do?
JACOB: What do *you* want to do?
JOSIE: I don't wanna go home. I want to be with you.
JACOB: Yeah?
JOSIE: Yeah. I'm ready now.

She starts to kiss him. He pulls away.

What?
JACOB: I ... need to tell you something.
JOSIE: Oh god.

JACOB: It's nothing bad. Well—but I'd feel bad if I didn't. You know Cook High's pracs were last week? Yeah, I didn't do them.

JOSIE: Why not?

JACOB: Didn't feel like it.

JOSIE: That's a really stupid reason.

JACOB: Yeah. Thought you'd say that.

JOSIE: Of course I would. You don't have to go to bloody uni—I'm fine with that now, but you should at least keep your options open.

JACOB: Thanks for being fine with that now.

JOSIE: Jacob—

JACOB: Maybe I don't want to keep my options open, Josie. Maybe I don't want where those options go at all. Maybe I don't want a life of bougie dinner parties and speaking French in cafes or always answering to the man every second of the day or … maybe I just want to rest for a while, Josie.

JOSIE: Rest? From fucking what? You're seventeen!

Beat. JACOB *looks at her.*

JACOB: Some of our seventeens are different from others.

Beat.

Some of us have had other stuff going on.

JOSIE *looks embarrassed. How could she forget about his mother …*

JOSIE: Yeah. Sorry. I can get—a little—

Beat, she turns back to him.

Forget I said anything.

JACOB: I don't know if I can.

JOSIE: What do you mean? I've just said sorry. Look, it's fine. We're gonna have a great time next year, no matter what.

JACOB: I'm sure you'll have a great time, Josie.

JOSIE: Okay …

JACOB: I just think—

Beat.

[*Quietly*] —I just think … I don't know, like … you know, what I said about rest? And I've been watching a lot of 'Married with Children'.

JOSIE: What?

JACOB: It's this terrible American show. It's on every night at six.

JOSIE: Yeah, I know what it is.

JACOB: And I was like ... not always, but sometimes, I feel like we're those guys. Like they fight all the time. And not in the Italian way you're always telling me is normal.

Beat.

[*Quietly*] I don't want that.

JOSIE *stares at him.*

JOSIE: Well, yeah. I don't want that either.

Is that it then?

They look at each other. Then, JACOB *takes* JOSIE's *hand, he gives it a little kiss, and puts it back down. They smile at each other—it's painful, but it's over.*

Beat.

Is it okay if I stay? I just need to be free of ... things. For a bit.

He nods—of course. They fall asleep, holding each other.

28. FIRST EXAM

JACOB's *room / St Martha's.*

The next morning. The school bell keeps ringing. JOSIE *bolts upright.*

JOSIE: Oh shit, shit, shit.

She gathers her things hurriedly and looks at JACOB, *still asleep for a second, but then—she has to go.*

She's swept up into the flurry of bodies in the space, as the scene morphs into the school environment of St Martha's. Students walk with purpose, on their way to exams.

JOSIE *takes a deep breath and looks at us.*

[*To us*] It's here. I can't believe it.

Just then, SERA *walks by, head in a book.*

[*Calling out*] Hey, *bellezz*! Good luck! [*to us, incandescent*] Thousands of teenagers decide their lives today. And I'm one of them.

She takes another breath, looks around.

Everything feels different in the day, doesn't it? The horrors of last night somehow feel so far away now and all that matters is this. First paper. Two weeks till freedom. I feel—

She smiles.

—suddenly nervous. But in a good way.

She spots IVY *huddled in a corner.*

I even feel good will towards Poison Ivy. Wow, I really have grown. [*To* IVY] Hey, Ivy! Ivy!

Good luck today!

IVY *shudders and runs off.*

Uh, okay, rude. You smash a girl one time and … you know, I actually feel sorry for her. Some of us just aren't ready for the new Australia I guess.

She looks around. Where is everyone? It's suddenly gone … deadly quiet.

Huh. Did the exam bell go? Already?

She looks at her watch—no, there's still time.

An eeriness begins to encroach. A guttural drone. Slowly, SISTER BERNADETTE *walks into the space.* JOSIE *looks surprised—is the nun walking towards her?* SISTER BERNADETTE *stops next to* JOSIE, *and puts a deliberate, heavy hand on her shoulder.*

Uh, Sister! Would love to stop and chat but I'm on my way to the exam now, so …

SISTER BERNADETTE *leans down and whispers in* JOSIE*'s ear.*

As she does so, a white sheet billows out above them. Perhaps it slowly starts to colour blood-red.

JOSIE *jerks away, and stares at* SISTER BERNADETTE *in horror.*

SISTER BERNADETTE: I'm so sorry, Josephine.
JOSIE: No, he wouldn't. John wouldn't. He wouldn't. I just saw him … a few weeks ago and—he just wouldn't, Sister. He …

SISTER BERNADETTE *leans down and envelops* JOSIE *in a tight hug, muffling her hysterical repetition.* JOSIE *starts to sob, unable to breathe.*

JOSIE: I don't understand, I don't understand, I don't understand.

JOSIE *sinks to the floor, out of* SISTER BERNADETTE*'s grasp. The nun steps gently away.*

SISTER BERNADETTE: We're gathering the Year Twelves in the library, Josephine.

JOSIE: No, he's just—he's faking it—he's run away. He—it's probably a fight with his father or something. John always gets—

SISTER BERNADETTE: His parents found him this morning ... I'm very sorry.

SISTER BERNADETTE *turns to the sheet. It billows; she grasps it. She slowly pulls it away to reveal ...*

29. THE FUNERAL

A moment in the space.

A row of mourners in black. They move through the space, in a funereal march.

JOSIE, *still collapsed on the floor, watches them pass.*

Their march gains in rhythm, in intensity.

She rises unsteadily to join them. She can't. She stops, still.

The procession surrounds JOSIE. *She merges within them.*

It moves through and vanishes from the space.

We see JOSIE *has gone too.*

The stage is bare of any bodies for the first time.

The absence hangs thick for a moment.

Then, we hear the sound of a kettle whistling and ...

30. AFTERMATH

Alibrandi living room.

CHRISTINA *walks on. She moves some of her papers to the table. The kettle whistles. She turns around to turn it off. A noise behind her. She turns, expecting* JOSIE. *Then, she sees it's* MICHAEL.

CHRISTINA: [*Italian*] Oh, it's just you.

He stands still, looking offstage, despondent.

MICHAEL: She didn't say a word. Just let me in, and stalked off.

CHRISTINA *sits down, pushes a tea cup out towards him deliberately.* MICHAEL *walks over and sits down with a sigh.*

CHRISTINA: How's the new place? All furnished?

MICHAEL: Uh yeah, it's fine. Two-year lease, so that's the main thing.

CHRISTINA: I'm sure Josie will be glad to hear that.

MICHAEL: [*suddenly agitated again*] Has she—it's been weeks—and—[*Italian*] this is mad, Tina!— [*English*] How are you so calm?

CHRISTINA: What do you want me to do, Michael? Drag her from her room and force her to smile and study?

MICHAEL: [*Italian*] I've just never seen her so silent—she loves to talk— [*English*] She normally doesn't shut up, and now … this is an extraordinary circumstance, I know! But it's important to choose life at these moments. It's not like I don't know what this world is like, how things can get to you …

CHRISTINA: [*quietly*] Yes, I think I know that too.

MICHAEL *puts his face in his hands.*

MICHAEL: Ugh, [*Italian*] I know. I know you do. [*English*] Tina, I feel like my heart is on the outside of my chest all the time.

CHRISTINA *looks at him tenderly.*

MICHAEL: What?

CHRISTINA: Welcome, Michael Andretti. You're a parent.

MICHAEL: It's horrible.

Beat.

It's wonderful.

Beat.

I don't know how you've done it. Tina, I'm, I'm …

He trails off; keeps running his hands through his hair.

CHRISTINA: You should stop doing that, you know. We talked about the thinning.

He looks at her.

MICHAEL: I feel like I should—I don't know how to but, I feel like—for all the years—for all the time—for that time eighteen years ago—I—

CHRISTINA *leans forward to check his forehead—like he might have a fever.* MICHAEL *looks confused.*

MICHAEL: What?

CHRISTINA: Michael Andretti. I never thought I'd see the day. You're trying to apologise, aren't you? [*Italian*] Have the heavens opened up?

She laughs, and he joins in. The laughter dies down. He looks at her intensely.

Stop staring.

MICHAEL: Can't help it, there's still that beautiful girl at her window. Even more beautiful now.

CHRISTINA: Michael, please.

MICHAEL: What? You know I don't just say things—well, not to you anyway.

CHRISTINA: I know. But you don't know what you're saying. I couldn't be more different. You—you think I'm calm? I've—I had to be. And I've *not* been—I've been [*Italian*] crazy [*English*] this year, Michael. You've seen it. Everytime you've been over, I've lost my mind. But now, now … you know the night before Josie's friend—that poor boy—after you left— [*Quietly*] it got worse. I said horrible things. I lost my mind.

MICHAEL: It's normal. You're a parent.

CHRISTINA *raises an eyebrow.*

Sorry.

CHRISTINA: I've been losing it for a while actually. I thought it was you, first. Bringing back memories. But it wasn't just that. Making sure that everyone was fine—Ma, Josie—no-one should have to pay for my mistake. But I was paying for it. I've been so busy trying to raise a daughter and not go mad, that I hadn't realised I had no idea what I wanted. I haven't done what I wanted since, well—

She looks at him. He seizes the moment and holds her hand. She gazes down at their hands together.

You know, the night that Josie stormed out and said she was gonna stay at a boy's house—at her boyfriend's—

MICHAEL: What boyfriend? Why didn't you tell me?

CHRISTINA: I'm telling you now.

Small beat.

I thought I'd failed. I'd failed again. But I hadn't. I know I haven't; I know my daughter; I made sure our lives were different. Even if that meant I disappeared for a while. A long while.

Beat.

She just needs time, Michael.

CHRISTINA *withdraws her hand.* MICHAEL *stares at his, now empty. Then withdraws too—she's made a decision.*

JOSIE *enters, looking like she's been in bed for a long time, listless, heavy.* CHRISTINA *and* MICHAEL *stand up immediately.*

JOSIE *grabs a drink. They watch her. Beat.*

JOSIE: You guys can sit, you know.

They look at each other, and hesitantly sit down. Beat.

[*To* CHRISTINA] How's your assignment going?

CHRISTINA: It's—it's going.

JOSIE: [*to* MICHAEL] Are you distracting her?

MICHAEL: I, uh …

JOSIE *slumps into a seat next to them.*

JOSIE: Just kidding, Michael.

MICHAEL *looks agitated.* CHRISTINA *looks at him as if to say— you wanted to talk, now talk.*

CHRISTINA: You know, I think TAFE recommends all trust accounting be done on the balcony. With a Cinzano Rosso. So—

She gets up, gathers her stuff and exits.

JOSIE and MICHAEL sit for a beat. A nervous MICHAEL breaks the silence.

MICHAEL: How's your prep going?

JOSIE: Fine. I've been prepped forever. There's nothing more to do.

MICHAEL: Don't say that, Josie.

JOSIE: What? It's true. I couldn't be more prepared. I didn't think of anything else for years.

Beat.

And now look …

MICHAEL: This is what I mean, Josie. You've got to—you can't just give up.

JOSIE: Why not? John did. Did he not think that sometimes I was depressed and hated life or hated myself? How dare he?

Beat. MICHAEL is not coping.

MICHAEL: This is what I'm saying— [*Italian*] I told Tina— [*English*] she needs to take this more seriously / — [*Italian*] Josie, listen—

JOSIE groans.

JOSIE: Please leave Ma out of this. [*Quietly*] I've put her through enough.

Beat.

MICHAEL: It's just, Josie—your mother doesn't understand, as you've said … the difficulty of what you've been trying to do. I know the cost of it. It's tough, I don't want you giving up on that dream.

JOSIE looks at him. Then, suddenly annoyed, launches into him.

JOSIE: Is it tough? Is it? I think you and I have it easy, Michael. As for dreams, well you know, John's father sure had a lot of dreams for him too. I'm sick to death of fathers.

MICHAEL recoils.

MICHAEL: I know I haven't been the best but—

JOSIE: No, that's not what I meant.

She stops, quietens.

Sorry. You've been a good father. Recently.

MICHAEL *looks like he's going to cry.*

MICHAEL: You make it simple to be a good father, Josie.

JOSIE: Well, that's the first time I've made anything simple.

Beat.

It's not the child who's supposed to make things simple, is it? Look at John. Or Ma! She was the perfect daughter and her father was horrible to her.

MICHAEL: [*Italian*] Yes, Tina did not deserve that monster.

Beat.

[*English*] I never want to think about that man, and even less now. He made me so angry when I was fifteen. How could he treat this quiet, kind girl who just wanted to read books and be loved like that? Never looking at her, never giving her care. Once on her birthday, he even locked her out of the house.

JOSIE *looks at him.*

JOSIE: On her birthday?

Small beat.

MICHAEL: Yes. He always seemed cruellest to her around that time. It's like he was angry she was even born, can you imagine?

JOSIE *shakes her head.*

I can still see Tina's shoulders shaking. She wasn't crying. She never cried over 'silly things'—it's what she used to call anything that hurt her. But it was cold—there was still a winter chill even though it was the start of October—and she was shivering. I—I think of her like that a lot now actually.

Pause, gathering himself.

He made me so angry then, but now that I have—

He gestures to JOSIE.

—I wish I could murder him. I can't believe a father would treat his own child the way he did. I sometimes can't believe I left her there—I can't believe I did nothing to stop him for all those years—I— [*Italian*] God forgive me.

JOSIE *looks to him and then to us—the words settling in, something clicking ... she gets up suddenly.* MICHAEL *looks at her, surprised.*

JOSIE: I need to—I need to think.

Beat.

MICHAEL: Okay, Josie. You think. I'm here.

He leaves. She stands in spot, the thought sinking deeper. Then—

31. THE CONFESSION

NONNA'*s living room.*

JOSIE *spins around to face* NONNA, *now in the space.* NONNA *starts, surprised to see her granddaughter.*

NONNA: Josie! [*Italian*] I didn't know / you were coming—
JOSIE: How could you, Nonna?

 NONNA *stops short.*

How fucking could you? Marcus Sanford?

 NONNA *is still.*

How dare you?

 NONNA'*s face begins to crumple. She tries to reach out to* JOSIE, *but* JOSIE *recoils.*

NONNA: Josefina. Please. Please. I want—I wanted so many times—to tell you—
JOSIE: No, you didn't.

 Beat.

You've had my whole life. You've had all of Mama's life! You let her think it was her—that she was unloved—that she was a curse!
NONNA: No—no! Never. I protect her, Josie.
JOSIE: You let him throw her out of the house! You haven't protected us a day in our lives.
NONNA: Josie—Josie—you not know, you not know—
JOSIE: Know bloody what, Nonna?

 NONNA *shrinks. Silence. Then, she gathers herself. Slowly, she starts to speak ...*

NONNA: You not know … how your Nonno was, Josie. When they tell me there is man for me in Australia, I all smiles. He so nice in his letter. On boat here, I laugh and dance, excited. I dream my new life. But when I come here. On first night, he slap me. In front of everyone. I think maybe is because of camp, maybe not happen again. But he always the same. When in farm, all Italian wife sad their husband have to work so much, and I say I was sad also, but I not sad he away. My body … [*Italian*] For fifty years he treated me like an animal [*English*] like an animal in his house Josie, only there to feed him food and for … even when I don't want.

Then Marcus come to Ingham and it different. He teach me better English, he not laugh. Never anyone … touch my body like that. I know it was wrong, but so many years later I can still feel the touch on me. I don't want to give it away. Even though I know I am stained. When I pregnant with Christina, Nonno beat me all the time. And I not know why, why he not happy, but one day he tell me he know she cannot be his child. Because he always know that he cannot have children. But he never tell me till that second.

But how we tell anyone? Where we go in society? Do we live on street? … Will the Australian help us? They hate us … Marcus write one time say—come I take you away—but I say no. I already cursed.

NONNA *collapses, her body broken.* JOSIE *breaks too, and rushes to hold her.*

JOSIE: You should have told Ma, Nonna.

NONNA *says nothing. She sobs.* JOSIE *holds her.*

You should have gone with him.

NONNA: I wish, I wish I go with her. My heart, when I see her pregnant with you. But I make sure Christina stay with Zia. It better for her. Who knows what Nonno do to her? After all I try, I still pass the curse to her. I have to protect her. Protect you.

Beat.

I see Marcus every time I look at her. Where you think her gentleness come from, Josie?

Beat.

Please, Josie. Don't tell her. I will tell. I tell.

JOSIE *nods.* NONNA *disappears into the darkness.*
JOSIE *looks at us. She breathes in. Then—*

32. THE LETTER

JOSIE*'s room /* JOSIE*'s space.*

JOSIE *jolts, as she remembers she still has ...* JOHN*'s letter!*

She looks down at her jacket—the same jacket she was wearing on the USYD campus that day—and reaches shakily into a pocket ...

It's there. She pulls it out: the letter, still in its envelope.

JOSIE: [*to self*] I can't believe I forgot.

She hesitates to open it.

[*To us*] I'm so scared to read this.

Small beat.

Then, she opens it and silently reads it. A few seconds pass.

JOSIE *looks up at us.*

A spasm of anger seizes her.

She starts to speak, tearing the letter into little pieces as she does, and throwing it into the wind.

Eventually, the pieces start to float over the space and rain back down on her.

[*To us*] I was so angry at John. From the second I heard the news. The only time I didn't feel angry ... was the brief moment between remembering I had his letter and reading it.

Not sure why. Maybe I was hoping it would—bring him back into colour for a moment. So I could erase the constant questions in my mind of—how they found him, how his face would have looked, how he felt when ... erase the feeling of vomit in my throat.

If he could just be there—

She gestures, a spot close to her.

—for a moment—so I could call him a dickhead and see him react like it's the nicest thing anyone's ever said to him. So I could graduate with him. We'd throw our hats in the air. So I could tell him, tough luck, I beat you in the HSC—

She breaks at this thought of the future ... he will never take the HSC ... she will never beat or lose to him again ...

Beat.

She gets a hold of herself, or at least, tries to ...

[*To us*] But it didn't feel like anything like that, reading this ... piece of paper. I read it and it said nothing new. Nothing I didn't already know he hoped for. Nothing he hadn't said to me in some way before.

And it didn't even tell me what I'd missed. 'Cause I must have missed something right? I must have.

They were just his words from a different life, a life I'd wished was mine a thousand times before.

The space darkens.

I lay in the dark for a long time.

The space morphs. Time passes.

And slowly, I started to think about everyone's words—not just John's—but my mother's, and Nonna's words, everyone's but theirs especially, for some reason—so clear and bright. And mine, too. Always mine. Not so clear. My stupid words. The way I spoke. The things I wanted.

And then ... their words, their lives, started to make mine ... make sense.

I've felt the wrong shape for so long, and I've been trying, just trying for so long to make myself what one society or the other wants. And I've not been perfect along the way. But ... then I saw it ... neither has any Alibrandi woman.

And I fucking like that. I fucking love it. 'Cause that's how we survived. Every time we did something someone thought was horrible, everytime we were absolutely mental, I think we were grasping at our freedom, we were surviving.

Pause.

And that's all anybody can do.

Pause.

That's what I wish everyone could do. And I'm lucky to come from people who took all that pain—and it bent them, yes—but they're still here. Screaming. Confused. Loving me.

Beat.

I hoped my friend was at peace. And that he knew he was loved. And I—I'm glad now—I'm glad now to have the world I have, even though I'll still hate sometimes.

But I'm going to try to stand still more and just see it.

Beat.

God, I sound like a bloody saint!

33. *PASSATA FOREVER*

NONNA's *kitchen.*

The lights snap to bright. We see CHRISTINA *and* NONNA *in full swing, making passata.* JOSIE *crosses to them.*

CHRISTINA: [*Italian*] Josie, the washed tomato bucket, please.

    JOSIE *starts taking over.*

JOSIE: I've got it, Ma. Stand back.

NONNA: This year we're going to do nothing, Christina. We watch—is all up to Josie.

CHRISTINA: Haha, very funny.

JOSIE: It's true, Ma, I'm going to do the whole thing. Nonna said.

NONNA: Yah. We not say one word.

    Beat. CHRISTINA *looks at each of them.*

CHRISTINA: Are you—I don't think it's a good idea. I mean I'm glad you want to do more Josie but [*Italian*] we don't want to be poisoned, right? [*English*] Maybe if I just get it started …

    NONNA *and* JOSIE *can't fake it any longer—they laugh. They've been tricking her.*

JOSIE: Ma, you're going soft! As if! I literally burnt water yesterday.

NONNA: [*Italian*] She's a disgrace, Christina. [*English*] Is our fault! Is our fault!

> JOSIE *and* NONNA *giggle together, congratulating themselves on their prank, as they turn away and continue working on the passata.*
>
> CHRISTINA *shakes her head, and then joins them. The three woman bicker and chatter, as music fills the space.*
>
> JOSIE *pulls apart slightly, taking in the scene of her mother and grandmother, and the moment of them all together.*
>
> *She turns around one last time, looking at us, briefly, almost like she might speak, but then—*

CHRISTINA: Ma, did Josie tell you about the Russo girl—she's going to be a doctor—

NONNA: [*Italian*] What? That family! [*English*] Is this a joke now also?

> JOSIE *grins, and turns away from us, joining the conversation with gusto.*

JOSIE: Nah, it's true Nonna, swear on the Virgin Mary. In fact, Sera actually got a half mark more than me.

> NONNA *gapes at* JOSIE *for a second, then, with all the ire in her body—*

NONNA: *Vaffanculo!*

> *The lights snap out.*

THE END

MALACAÑANG* MADE US
by Jordan Shea

* Presidential palace, Philippines

JORDAN SHEA is a writer, performer and teacher. He holds a Bachelor of Arts (Theatre) and a Masters of Secondary Teaching (English and Drama) from the University of Notre Dame, and a Masters of Writing for Performance (Honours II) from the Victorian College of the Arts. As co-writer, he collaborated with Callan Purcell on *Before the Sun Comes Up* (NSW Department of Education) and Kenneth Moraleda on *One Hour No Oil* (KXT/kwento). He was a co-writer on *The House at Boundary Road, Liverpool* (Old 505 Theatre) and *Intersection* (ATYP). Additional credits include: *Malacañang Made Us* (Queensland Theatre), *Diwa* (Performing Lines & Australian Plays Transform) *CAGE* (Old 505 Theatre), *Ate Lovia* (kwento/Old Fitz) and *Kasama Kita* (Belvoir). Awards include: the 2025 Queensland Premier's Drama Award (*Malacañang Made Us*), and the 2024 Notre Dame Alumni Award. His play *They're not listening* won the Writing NSW Fellowship and was runner-up for the Australian Theatre Festival's New Play Award. Jordan's practice has been supported by the Ian Potter Cultural Trust, Create NSW and the City of Sydney. In 2025, he was the keynote speaker for Currency Press Festival of Playwrights, as well as making a triumphant return to performing in musical theatre, starring as Franz Liebkind in Joshua Robson Productions/Hayes Theatre's *The Producers* and Neglected Musicals' *The Witches of Eastwick* as Clyde Gabriel. Jordan lives on Wangal Country (Ashfield) and is a proud Filipino-Australian.

Writer's Note

In 2022, Claro De Los Reyes from the Atlantic Pacific Theatre in New York City emailed me to be part of a series of online readings with Filipino playwrights. It was through this 'Currency Exchange', that the early scenes of this play were born. From a combination of the book *Bayan Ko,* lovingly passed onto me by Alfredo Nicdao, my love for intergenerational storytelling, and my own family's immigrational history connected to the Martial Law period, this play was written.

Over three years, the work has gone through rigorous development. Beginning at Melbourne Theatre Company and continuing on at FilAm Arts Los Angeles, Atlantic Pacific Theatre and Queensland Theatre. I acknowledge the huge number of creatives and cast that have put themselves and their practice into this work. So many of them have left a clear imprint on dialogue, structure and authenticity. Thank you for your patience and dramaturgical eyes over the past three years. It's been an effort, but it has been nothing short of a triumph each time, and each time I've walked away ready to write bigger, and more truthfully.

On a personal note, and a professional one, my working relationship with Kenneth Moraleda has ensured the last three years have seen growth in this work at a very steady pace. We go back to my first professional script development in 2017, where he has continuously provided feedback on my work for the betterment of my practice. I also want to thank the entire team at Queensland Theatre for taking such special care of me and my story. With their generous support, and the Queensland Government/Griffith University's landmark sponsorship, winning the Queensland Premier's Literary Award has allowedme to be ambitious in my craft. It has enabled me to lean into something that a playwright can steer clear from because they're scared their work will never get put on.

And finally, this work is a story that I hope gets people to look to their own histories, whoever they may be. History can bind us, for better or for worse. It's something I think about a lot, even more since writing this. My love for history, particularly the personal colliding with the political, comes from my upbringing. My parents have equipped me with stories as diverse as my mother witnessing the declaration of Martial Law, to my Father riding a horse down the streets of Wollongong in the seventies. I think this did something to me—no matter how extreme or spectacular the stories were, they have led me to believe we all know someone, or are someone, that holds lore that we are closer to than we may think.

Ingat,
Jordan Shea

Thank You

Griffith University, Claro De Los Reyes, Merlynn Tong, Atlantic Pacific Theatre, Alfredo Nicdao, Tamara Lee Bailey, Zoey Dawson, Aubrey Flood, Rhys Velasquez, Matt Edgerton, Jenni Medway, Ray Martin, Melinda Giveen, Kimberley Hodgson, Phoebe Parker, Melba Marginson, St Vincent's College Ashfield English Department, Doron Chester, Giovanni Ortega, Grace Talusan, Ian Potter Cultural Trust, Aysa Garcia Wong, Josh Wong, How Ngean Lim, Michael Shea, Agnes Shea, Liz Hobart, Madolyn McCarthy, Benjamin Warmuth, Sharne McGee, Dr Deborah Ruiz Wall, Currency Press, Raimondo Cortese, David Williamson, Kenneth Moraleda, Abe Mitchell, Ari Palani, Dan Evans, Saffron Benner, Jane Youngs, Courtney Stewart, Lee Lewis, Stevie Rodgers, Triona Calimbayan-Giles, Malou Aguilar, Cristina Atiga, Peter Charlesworth, Delia Zarate.

Malacañang Made Us was first produced by Queensland Theatre at the Bille Brown Theatre, Jagera and Turrbal Country, Brisbane, on 18 October 2025 with the following cast and creatives:

YOUNG ERNIE / @BUNSOYBBY	Marty Alix
LEO	Mark Paguio
ERNIE / @GWAPOBOI	Marcus Rivera
YOUNG MARTIN / @SISIGKWEEN	Miguel Usares
MARTIN / @NOTANURSE03	Mike Zarate

Director, Kenneth Moraleda
Set and Costume Designer, Jeremy Allen
Associate Set and Costume Designer, Madeleine Barlow
Lighting Designer, Christine Felmingham
Assistant Lighting Designer, Briana Clark
Composer and Sound Designer, Sam Cheng
Video Designer, Nevin Howell
Cultural Safety Advisor, Katrina Irawati-Graham
Design Placement, David Wotherspoon
Stage Manager, Jacinta Way
Assistant Stage Manager, Tia-Hanee Cleary

CHARACTERS

MARTIN CABAERO—a railway worker, fifty-five, male-identifying, Leo's father.

NOTANURSE03— an anxious online activist, late teens.

ERNESTO 'ERNIE' CABAERO—a flight attendant, fifty-four, male-identifying, Martin's brother/Leo's uncle.

GWAPOBOI—a masc online activist, late teens.

LEOPOLD 'LEO' CABAERO—a student, eighteen, male-identifying. Martin's son.

YOUNG ERNEST 'ERNIE' CABAERO—an activist, nineteen, male-identifying.

BUNSOYBBY—a fierce online activist, late teens.

YOUNG MARTIN CABAERO—an activist, eighteen, male-identifying.

SISIGKWEEN—an online activist, late teens.

CAST NOTES

The text has been written with the following doubling in mind:

Martin/NotaNurse03
Ernie/Gwapoboi
Bunsoybby/Young Ernie
SisigKween/Young Martin

Cast size: five.

All attempts in casting Filipino/x performers should be made, otherwise consulted with the author and other creatives.

SCRIPT NOTES

Context and information are denoted by footnotes.

A forward slash / indicates the point at which the next speaker interrupts.

INTERNET & DIGITAL LANGUAGE NOTES

If the text dictates that there is more than one question mark and exclamation mark, these are spoken as 'question mark, exclamation mark' only in the internet/digital world and scenes.

Ellipses, question marks and exclamation marks are all spoken in the internet/digital world.

@ is spoken as 'at' and # is spoken as 'hashtag'.

References to emojis are read out.

Any text in capital letters is prefaced with the words 'all caps' only in the digital world.

TAGALOG NOTES

Some Tagalog lines are immediately translated by the character in English, as seen in the text.

Tagalog lines that are not immediately translated in the text are translated in footnotes. Some of these translations from Tagalog are not precise translations to English. These non-precise English translations should inform the tone and delivery of the line.

Leo refers to Martin as 'Tay', which is an abbreviated version of the word 'Tatay', meaning Father.

Ernie refers to Martin as 'Kuya', meaning older brother.

Ernie refers to Leo as 'De', which is a nickname he's given him since childhood.

Mike Zarate as Martin, Mark Paguio as Leo and Marty Alix as Young Ernie in Queensland Theatre's production of Malacañang Made Us, *2025 (Photo: Morgan Roberts).*

SCENE 1: A BRIEF YET SPICY HISTORY OF THE PHILIPPINES

2022. Sunnybank, Brisbane.

LEO *films a three-part video in his room.*

PART ONE:

LEO: 'A Brief Yet Spicy History of the Philippines'. Part One.
There is an actual reckoning.
Seconds ago, OG nepo baby: Bongbong Marcos—AKA 'BBM'—has been 'elected' President of the Philippines, which is leaving Filipinos across the world literally gagged.

An image of Bongbong Marcos appears in LEO's *video.*

But this didn't just happen tonight.
BBM and his family have been around since forever.
Okay so, in 1965, this guy: Ferdinand Marcos Senior, BBM's daddy, is sworn in as the President of the Philippines.

Images of the swearing in of Ferdinand Marcos Senior in 1965 plays in LEO's *video.*

Initially popular, and let's be real, kind of hot, he oversaw huge developments and created close ties with the United States and even went to Harold Holt's funeral.

Picture of Marcos with Lyndon Baines Johnson appears, followed by a picture of Harold Holt emerging from the water, all on LEO's *video.*

Follow for Part Two!

PART TWO:

Footage of Ferdinand Marcos being inaugurated in 1969 appears in LEO's *video.*

YOUNG MARTIN *and* YOUNG ERNIE *watch the second Marcos inauguration and exit at its conclusion.*

LEO: That was 1969, when he was elected for a second term by a landslide. But all of this starts to change when he and his wife, Imelda...

A picture of Imelda appears in LEO*'s video.*

... Use close to fifty million dollars of public money to boost his election campaign, leaving the country broke, and the Marcoses extremely rich.

They've purchased over sixty properties across the United States, Europe, Australia and Asia.

Picture of the Marcoses' opulence appears throughout LEO*'s video.*

The Marcoses also had a massive amount of jewellery, and yes, an iconic yet lowkey-problematic collection of shoes.

Then, Malacañang Palace, the Presidential house, gets completely redesigned to suit the family's needs. Including future President Bongbong.

Picture of a young Bongbong Marcos appears in LEO*'s video.*

Also, there was this like, rock stone-face thing that the Marcoses built in Baguio:

Picture of the bust of Ferdinand Marcos along the Aspiras-Palispis Highway in Tuba, Benguet, Philippines, appears in LEO*'s video.*

Creepy.

Anyway, with all this, like, insane amount of money being spent, people begin to fight back, and fight back they did.

Swipe for Part Three.

PART THREE:

LEO: In 1972, Marcos declares a state of Martial Law, which leads to fourteen years of censorship, starvation, torture and disappearances.

Images of Marcos declaring Martial Law appears in LEO*'s video.*

As of today, close to ten billion dollars of the money spent by the Marcoses has never been recovered.

But, Marcos *did* have opponents. Mainly his former friend, this guy: Ninoy Aquino.

A picture of Ninoy Aquino appears in LEO*'s video.*

Known as 'the greatest President we never had', Aquino travelled the world calling out the Marcos government. He tried to return to challenge Marcos, but—

A picture of Ninoy Aquino's death/murder appears in LEO*'s video.*

YOUNG MARTIN *and* YOUNG ERNIE *run through* LEO*'s world.*

The Marcos announces a snap election and declares himself the winner. This triggered the 1986 People Power Revolution, which was …

Ah! You got some reading to do. Maybe I'll do it for you.

See you soon for Part Four.

Byeeeeeeeee!!!

BUNSOYBBY *appears via the internet.*

LEO *and* BUNSOYBBY *chat. It's high excitement.*

BUNSOYBBY: @Bunsoybby! GURL! *skull and crossbones emoji* #omg #youwentthere.
LEO: @LeoCabaero. I know right!!
BUNSOYBBY: You got in so quick. The hook, Bongbong, everything. People are gonna go crazy for this!
LEO: Are they??
BUNSOYBBY: You're literally like, a million miles away right now, but you are being seen everywhere!
LEO: What's it like tonight? Back home? *Filipino flag emoji, Filipino flag emoji, Filipino flag Emoji*
BUNSOYBBY: Okey lang gurl, wala pang nangyayari.[1]
LEO: Mhm. Mhm. English.
BUNSOYBBY: GURL ARE YOU SERIOUS?!
LEO: Oh my god, I'm trying.
BUNSOYBBY: Bakla, I-Google Translate mo na lang.[2]
LEO: Okay, okay.
BUNSOYBBY: You really went there with the whole, like, property vibe.
LEO: It's literally on the internet.

---
1. It's okay girl. Nothing is happening yet.
2. Queen, just use Google Translate.

BUNSOYBBY: Oh no totally, I'm just like, it's all laid out in front of you.
LEO: Oh my god it might make a good reel. Like if I got photos of the mansions, and like, rated them for like style and like location and then, like—boom—put the price tag on them.
BUNSOYBBY: BITCH!!!
LEO: Okay I'm going to do that one next. No, wait. People Power first. Maybe like Aquino needs his own reel, right? Like he wasn't as hot as Marcos but like kinda. Like, if I was into nerds …
BUNSOYBBY: Mhm. Mhm. Yes. Yes, I like it. You want the BBM tea?
LEO: Bitch you know I want the tea about BBM. *nail polish emoji*

They shriek with excitement.

BUNSOYBBY: Okay.
LEO: Go.
BUNSOYBBY: Alright.
LEO: Yes?
BUNSOYBBY: So, BBM is apparently coming to you. Like next week. *heaps and heaps of kangaroo emojis*
LEO: Here, like, Australia here?!
BUNSOYBBY: Yeah Vincent is going to college in Melbourne. They're coming to Brisbane for a quick little vacay.
LEO: Vincent is?
BUNSOYBBY: The least cute one!
LEO: His son Vincent?!
BUNSOYBBY: Yeah they're leaving here in like a few days.
LEO: You're lying.
BUNSOYBBY: Nope.
LEO: OH MY GOD.

MARTIN *enters* LEO*'s room. The chat ends.*

SCENE 2: U.P.

2022. May 9. 1 a.m. LEO*'s room,* MARTIN*'s apartment in Sunnybank.*

MARTIN: Leo, it's one a.m.!
LEO: Why are you in my room? Oh my god. Boundaries.
MARTIN: It's my house.
LEO: I'm trying to get exchange sorted.

MARTIN: Excellent! Where? King's College, London. McGill, Canada, Georgetown, the United States of / America.
LEO: U.P.
MARTIN: The University of the Philippines? You get a full scholarship, every opportunity at your fingertips, and you go with U.P? Why are you trying to kill me?! WHY?
LEO: My scholarship will be fine.
MARTIN: We don't play with gold.
LEO: I'm on the brochure. If they take it away, that is literal racism.
MARTIN: Yeah but U.P., Leo? Really?
LEO: I have friends there.
MARTIN: Who?
LEO: Friends. Online. The internet. A computer. It's a big night for them.
MARTIN: Sure.
LEO: Sure?! We should denounce his election! We have now elected and remain complicit in an oligarchy!
MARTIN: We?
LEO: The people.
MARTIN: Of Sunnybank?!
LEO: You don't need to set foot on one of the seven thousand islands to be moored to them /
MARTIN: Hai naku /
LEO: To know them, to breathe them, to sense them, to fight for them.
MARTIN: Napaka arte.[3]
LEO: It's 2022. Shouldn't we live as a safe people?
MARTIN: We? When did you wake up and become Jose Rizal?![4]
LEO: Shouldn't we be free from the shackles of our past? We as people are not confined to our history, and nor should we be. The fight is in our blood, Tay.
MARTIN: WHO ARE YOU TALKING TO?! If he won, he won.
LEO: Ah-ha! You said *if.*
MARTIN: Don't pick at my words.
LEO: Don't use a conjunction without thinking. Period.
MARTIN: It is a privilege to sit and watch all of this from the bottom of the world. NYU, Sheffield, Birmingham. These are great schools.

---

3. Oh dear. Such a performer.
4. Filipino literary giant

LEO: Yeah cute, just offer me up to the colonisers!

MARTIN: I would have killed for these opportunities, anak. If you want to get your education from a country that the world doesn't look twice at—go ahead. You go to U.P. and you'll end up driving Ubers or working in a hotel. You go to one of *these* universities, you will be set for life.

LEO: They're a literal exchange partner.

> YOUNG MARTIN *enters.*
>
> LEO *leaves.*
>
> *He shouts toward* LEO's *room.*

MARTIN: I didn't work for eighteen years so you could go back to the Philippines!

> YOUNG MARTIN *stands, looking around at what the world is about to become.*

The students there are no good.

> YOUNG MARTIN *beckons for* YOUNG ERNIE *to join him.*
>
> YOUNG ERNIE *joins* YOUNG MARTIN.
>
> MARTIN *looks on, watching* YOUNG ERNIE *and* YOUNG MARTIN, *before he leaves.*

SCENE 3: REVOLT

1986. February 22. Early evening. Epifanio de los Santos Avenue (EDSA), Manila, Philippines. A huge crowd has gathered.

YOUNG MARTIN *and* YOUNG ERNIE *on a light pole, watching EDSA from above.*

YOUNG MARTIN: Look! A vision!
YOUNG ERNIE: A beautiful one.
YOUNG MARTIN: The crowd heaves.
YOUNG ERNIE: Like a huge school of fish.
YOUNG MARTIN: Every shape, every job.
YOUNG ERNIE: Teacher.
YOUNG MARTIN: Doctor.
YOUNG ERNIE: Garbageman.

YOUNG MARTIN/YOUNG ERNIE: Opera singer.
> YOUNG MARTIN *tries to sing in a high pitch.*

YOUNG ERNIE: Babies, lolas.
YOUNG MARTIN: All of life!
YOUNG ERNIE: Bodies squeezed!
YOUNG MARTIN: Together in unity.
YOUNG ERNIE: The sweat.
> YOUNG MARTIN *wipes his brow.*

YOUNG MARTIN: The joy!
YOUNG ERNIE: Whirled together.
YOUNG MARTIN: In a cocktail of impending liberation.
YOUNG ERNIE: The nuns! They are praying!
Both pray.
YOUNG MARTIN: Mothers with babies in one hand.
YOUNG ERNIE: The other raised in the air!
YOUNG MARTIN: Like a dream being sketched in front of you.
YOUNG ERNIE: Freedom in reach.
YOUNG MARTIN: I think I see them! Our kapatids!
YOUNG ERNIE: Over there!
YOUNG MARTIN: Guys! Guys! Up here! Prino! Ver! Renee! Edwin!
YOUNG ERNIE: Passion and anger merge on EDSA!
YOUNG MARTIN: They merge like cars.
YOUNG ERNIE: Like the cars that clog this avenue every day!
YOUNG MARTIN: All of us shed our snakeskins of happy-go-lucky schoolboy.
YOUNG ERNIE: And today we are men!
YOUNG MARTIN: Activists.
YOUNG ERNIE: Warriors.
YOUNG MARTIN: ONOFRE! WALLY! GUYS! UP HERE! WOOOOOOOOO! GUYS! LOOK UP! UP! HEY!
YOUNG ERNIE: What is that? A ripple comes through the crowd. Heads turn, confusion erupts over the two million-strong. Kuya Martin! Kuya Martin, what is happening?! I see troops marching through us.
YOUNG MARTIN: It's war. It always was but now it is real. I must be ready. I am ready.

YOUNG ERNIE: A line of camouflage peels through the people. EDSA freezes with fear.
YOUNG MARTIN: Don't be scared, get behind me! It's alright. Stand together. We've got this.
YOUNG ERNIE: No! Look!
YOUNG MARTIN: Behind the masses of the army.
YOUNG ERNIE: Two men, who we always thought lived in our television sets.
YOUNG MARTIN: Yes! YES! They are here to protect us. Like Cardinal said. They will follow the word of someone who speaks to God!
YOUNG ERNIE: Fear becomes victory.
YOUNG MARTIN: Two million people begin to clap.
YOUNG ERNIE: Begin to cheer.
YOUNG MARTIN: It's Enrile!
YOUNG ERNIE: Marcos' trusted Defense Minister!
YOUNG MARTIN: And Ramos!
YOUNG ERNIE: His faithful general!
YOUNG MARTIN: Here they are. Turning against Marcos.
YOUNG ERNIE: Standing with us as the crowd roars with triumph!

> YOUNG MARTIN *and* YOUNG ERNIE *watch in a trancelike state.*
>
> *The crowd begins to move.*

YOUNG MARTIN: A murmur of plans build quicker than the Marcoses' billions.
YOUNG ERNIE: They are whispering.
YOUNG MARTIN: What are they saying?
YOUNG ERNIE: I can hear it, but I'm not sure. What are they saying, Kuya?
YOUNG MARTIN: I can hear it.
YOUNG MARTIN: One word rises to the top.
YOUNG ERNIE: Malacañang.
> The next stage grows.

YOUNG MARTIN: A dream for so many of us, now in reach. To scale the gates, to take it back!
YOUNG ERNIE: We should go home.
YOUNG MARTIN: What?!
YOUNG ERNIE: We're here, we did it.
YOUNG MARTIN: Don't be stupid, we are going to Malacañang. I'll be with you.

YOUNG ERNIE: What about Ma?
YOUNG MARTIN: She would want us to go there.
YOUNG ERNIE: She will be so worried.
YOUNG MARTIN: Ma will be fine. I am here.
YOUNG ERNIE: Kuya, I want to go home.
YOUNG MARTIN: I will keep you safe.
YOUNG ERNIE: I'm scared.
YOUNG MARTIN: Don't you want to see where they live?
YOUNG ERNIE: We could do that?
YOUNG MARTIN: You and me. Tonight. We will sit on their thrones and laugh like they did while everyone else starved!
YOUNG ERNIE: What if they are still there?
YOUNG MARTIN: There are more of us.
YOUNG ERNIE: Let's go home.
YOUNG MARTIN: Don't be a baby.
YOUNG ERNIE: Kuya.
YOUNG MARTIN: I will be with you.
YOUNG ERNIE: Kuya, please.
YOUNG MARTIN: Don't be a coward!
YOUNG ERNIE: I am not!
YOUNG MARTIN: Prove it.
YOUNG ERNIE: Kuya, we don't have to go.
YOUNG MARTIN: I'll go without you. Look, everyone else is already leaving.
YOUNG ERNIE: No! Wait!

    YOUNG MARTIN *extends his hand.*

YOUNG MARTIN: You can't miss this.
YOUNG ERNIE: You won't leave me?
YOUNG MARTIN: Never.
YOUNG ERNIE: It is history.
YOUNG MARTIN: Yes, kap!
YOUNG ERNIE: Today.
YOUNG MARTIN: Tomorrow, and the next!
YOUNG ERNIE: It is history!
YOUNG MARTIN: Say it kap, yes!
YOUNG ERNIE: History! It is history!

    YOUNG MARTIN *grabs* YOUNG ERNIE, *hugging him.*

YOUNG MARTIN: This is a bloodless day. Listen to them.

The roar of the crowd bellows over them.

They both run off to join the revolution.

MARTIN *enters his memory, and trails behind* YOUNG MARTIN *and* YOUNG ERNIE.

The memory fades.

SCENE 4: SAFE

2022. May 10. 10 a.m. Living room. Sunnybank. LEO *on his phone.* MARTIN *enters.*

MARTIN: I had a great idea!
LEO: Oh … and …
MARTIN: You want to experience the Philippines?
LEO: Are you serious?
MARTIN: Why not!
LEO: When?
MARTIN: Tomorrow!
LEO: Tomorrow.
MARTIN: Yeah! Let's go!
LEO: You'll come with me?!
MARTIN: That's the plan.
LEO: Don't joke with me, Tay.
MARTIN: No, we are going!
LEO: You won't even spend money to go to the Gold Coast.
MARTIN: I got time off work.
LEO: For real? I have to pack.
MARTIN: Great. We're going to Kusina![5]
LEO: Kusina. The restaurant? In Browns Plains?!
MARTIN: You loved that place when you were a kid.
LEO: Tay.
MARTIN: Your Tito Onofre will take care of us. You'll be Filipino by the afternoon.
LEO: Yeah, funny. Kusina closed anyway.

---

5. Kitchen

MARTIN: What?
LEO: Like two years ago.
MARTIN: I gotta call Onofre.
LEO: He's in a nursing home.
MARTIN: Since when?! He's my age! No-one told me!
LEO: You don't talk to anyone.
MARTIN: I have his number somewhere.
LEO: Tay, I'm pretty sure he's got dementia.
MARTIN: Do you still talk to his daughter? Tell her to call me.
LEO: I literally do not have the time.
MARTIN: Come on, it's important.
LEO: Well, why don't you do it?
MARTIN: It's easier for you. You're so much better at all this.
LEO: I'll see if I still have her number.
MARTIN: How do you know he's in a nursing home?
LEO: I saw something she posted, I don't know.
MARTIN: On the Facebook?
LEO: I'll put you on it, and you can see for yourself.
MARTIN: No, no, it's okay.
LEO: I can do it. You might find old friends.
MARTIN: I wouldn't know what to say to them.
LEO: You should try.
MARTIN: I might get addicted.
LEO: Or connected.
MARTIN: No, it's all good. I got all the connection I need right here.

    LEO *shoots an awkward smile.*

You thought about those other schools?
LEO: I'm busy.
MARTIN: These chances don't come around all the time. You should use your head. U.P. students go to rallies over classes.
LEO: It's a highly ranked school with a great history.
MARTIN: All they did was use their voices. The staff encourage it!
LEO: And that's bad … ?
MARTIN: It's not what a university is for. U.P. students are reckless. They do crazy things. I didn't raise you like that.
LEO: This is my choice.

MARTIN: If someone came up to me when I was your age with a golden ticket to the world, I would be jumping out of my / skin.
LEO: Can you just ...

They stand awkwardly.

MARTIN: I want you to be safe.

SCENE 5: JOY

1986. February 23. Midnight.

YOUNG ERNIE *and* YOUNG MARTIN *walk through the streets of Manila, toward Malacañang.*

A rat scurries across, they jump.

YOUNG MARTIN: I thought the rats were all gone.
YOUNG ERNIE: A flurry of pamphlets, declaring our countries split, drift aimlessly.
YOUNG MARTIN: Words are ours now.
YOUNG ERNIE: We bear witness to the revolution at hand, we are gifted the ability to talk freely, to communicate.
YOUNG MARTIN: To rebel.
YOUNG ERNIE: At last. The fork becomes one road that we paved.
YOUNG MARTIN: This country will shed its skin in a weekend. It will be a snake no more. Countries around the world finally see us as one of them.

    YOUNG ERNIE *and* YOUNG MARTIN *smile at each other.*

    YOUNG ERNIE *and* YOUNG MARTIN *hear a growing crowd.*

YOUNG ERNIE: Boys, just like us.
YOUNG MARTIN: They grow closer. Ernie.
YOUNG ERNIE: Quicker.
YOUNG MARTIN: A herd. Ernesto.
YOUNG ERNIE: An army.
YOUNG MARTIN: Kapatids.
YOUNG ERNIE: Kuya.
YOUNG MARTIN: We must be them.
YOUNG ERNIE: We need to get out of their way.
YOUNG MARTIN: We will be respected.

YOUNG ERNIE: No, no, Kuya, we need to be safe.
YOUNG MARTIN: Praise will come to us.
YOUNG ERNIE: Kuya we have to stay together.
YOUNG MARTIN: We will become textbook, a benchmark. We are that crowd.
YOUNG ERNIE: Gunshot-like footsteps.
YOUNG MARTIN: Lion-like roars.
YOUNG ERNIE: WAIT, KUYA!

The crowd pierces the brothers, separating them.

The dust settles.

KUYA?!
KUYA?!
KUYA, COME BACK!
Take me with you!
Mum will be so mad!

ERNIE *arrives at the Pasig River.*

Our smell, running from the slums to the waterways, traded with … freedom?
The Pasig River is so still.

YOUNG ERNIE *inhales.*

Fish float on the surface.
Across it, Malacañang stands proud in its sweeping glory as the city ripples with our revolution.
I wish I could swim there.
To be with him.
I can taste the mud, the soil …
But the thought of reclamation dances across it.
Not worth drowning for.
No-one has died tonight.
Tonight, the palace and an inch of its loot will be returned to us.
It will line the pockets of the people.
The farmer with his jewels.
The worker with his cash.
The schoolgirl with her shoes.
My brother on his throne—

KUYA?!
KUYA!

2022. ERNIE *enters* MARTIN*'s apartment, carrying his bag. He whispers for* MARTIN.

ERNIE: Kuya, are you home?

> ERNIE *looks around the apartment.*

YOUNG ERNIE: Kuya?

> YOUNG ERNIE *continues to wander the streets.*

ERNIE: Martin?

YOUNG ERNIE: I'll meet you there, Kuya.

> *Fireworks shoot up to the night sky, exploding.*
>
> YOUNG ERNIE *swings between happiness and worry.*
>
> *Eventually,* YOUNG ERNIE *lies down in the street, fireworks exploding into the air.*
>
> ERNIE *continues to look to see if* MARTIN*'s home. Eventually, he lies down in the apartment.*

SCENE 6: REUNION

2022. May 11. 3 a.m. MARTIN*'s apartment in Sunnybank. Darkness.* ERNIE *sleeps on* MARTIN*'s couch.* MARTIN *returns home from work.*

MARTIN: AH!
ERNIE: AH!
MARTIN: AHH!
ERNIE: AHHHHHHHH KUYA!

> ERNIE *throws his arms around* MARTIN. *They reunite.*

ERNIE: How are you? You're so big now!

MARTIN: Shhhhh! Pano ka naka pasok. How did you get in?!

ERNIE: You haven't changed the locks in years! Where's Leo? Wake him now!

MARTIN: You need rest. I need rest.

ERNIE: Bitch, please. I'm on slip time. I want to go out! Gusto ko nang rumampa!

MARTIN: When do you fly out?
ERNIE: I got laid off. Two thousand of us. Last week. Gone. Heaps of the girls went to Disneyland, a few went to Paris. Nah baby, this flying kangaroo had to come and see my gorgeous big brother! Syempre[6], business class.
MARTIN: Shhh!
ERNIE: Wake up Leo! Come on, we got lots to catch up on.
MARTIN: You haven't been here in ten years.
ERNIE: And we're off!
MARTIN: You missed Leo's graduation.
ERNIE: I watched the Zoom.
MARTIN: Ma's last days.
ERNIE: I made my peace, Kuya. I got to see her when she still remembered me.
MARTIN: Buti ka pa. Lucky you.

> ERNIE *flamboyantly gestures for him to stop talking. He places his duffle bag on the table, unzips it, and takes out twenty thousand USD.*

Is this money clean?
ERNIE: Oh for god's sake.
MARTIN: Did they pay you out?
ERNIE: I flew with them for thirty years.
MARTIN: No more twenty-four-hour trips to Disneyland.
ERNIE: I did one last weekend. We got in at eight-thirty, left the bags at the Sheraton, on Splash Mountain by ten.
MARTIN: I always liked Space Mountain better.
ERNIE: Splash Mountain any day of the week.
MARTIN: I know why you hate Space Mountain. Remember?
ERNIE: Don't!
MARTIN: Remember!
ERNIE: Don't be cruel!
MARTIN: HA! You do!
ERNIE: Don't!
MARTIN: When we turned that sharp corner on Space Mountain, music playing, lights flashing.

---

6. Of course.

They laugh.

And you let out that little scream.

ERNIE *laughs.*

And shit your pants.

MARTIN *laughs.*

ERNIE: BITCH! That's why I LOVE Splash Mountain! That and 'It's a Small World'. CAAAAAAAMP! Remember that doll in 'It's a Small World' that I'm obsessed with? I thought about stealing her this time. And she looks like Imelda Marcos, all she needs is those tiny handcuffs!

> ERNIE *places his hands in a handcuff formation.*
>
> MARTIN *laughs and shushes* ERNIE.
>
> MARTIN *takes the money and puts it in a drawer. Changes his mind and places it under the couch cushions.*

MARTIN: It's going to straight to the bank.
ERNIE: You REBEL, Kuya!
MARTIN: Not anymore.
ERNIE: I flew all this way. Come on. Let's go.

> ERNIE *takes the money out of the drawer.*

All we need is a couple of hundred for a good time, let's go.
MARTIN: Put it back.
ERNIE: It's mine!
MARTIN: You gave it to me.
ERNIE: Alright, it's ours.
MARTIN: What are you gonna do for a job?
ERNIE: Who's gonna hire a fifty-four-year-old who's been with the same airline for thirty years? I want to retire. Here. With you. Besides, there are fifty younger queens ahead of me ready to get all the Mabuhay Miles.[7] But hey, bitch! May asim pa ang lola n'yo. I'm still here.
MARTIN: Where are you going to live?

> ERNIE *gestures around to the apartment.*

No.

---

7. Loyalty program for PAL

ERNIE: Come on, Martin. You're all I have here.
MARTIN: What about one of your many friends?
ERNIE: I should be around him.
MARTIN: Leo's just started uni, he needs the space.
ERNIE: Space I'm paying for. Uni I'm paying for. He'll move out one day. All that money he could make from living his life online. Nagpapalaki ka ng isang munting aktibista. A little activist.
MARTIN: What?
ERNIE: Four hundred and fifty thousand followers, hey girl!
MARTIN: Four hundred and fifty thousand?!
ERNIE: He's got good reach.
MARTIN: Is he famous?
ERNIE: I'd say more influential.
MARTIN: I should sign up to the social medias. It's free, isn't it?
ERNIE: That's the beauty of it. You can be rich or poor and say whatever you want to say.
MARTIN: Payag kaba dito. Do you approve this?
ERNIE: He's safe here. It's fine.
MARTIN: Not if he goes to U.P.
ERNIE: Your alma mater— [*Sings*] U.P. naming mahal, pamantasang hirang!⁸
MARTIN: Shhhhh! Don't say anything stupid while you're here.
ERNIE: Don't you trust me?
MARTIN: I trust that you never shut up.
ERNIE: RUDE!
MARTIN: The last place I want him to go to is U.P. He'll go there and make the same mistakes I did.
ERNIE: You're acting like you didn't have any fun.
MARTIN: It was a long time ago.
ERNIE: Don't worry, Leo's shouting into his phone.
    Bongbong won by a landslide.
MARTIN: Are you surprised?
ERNIE: I would love a decent human in Malacañang in my lifetime.
MARTIN: They're all the same.
ERNIE: They are not.

---

8. U.P. beloved, thou Alma Mater dear

MARTIN: They are all born with money. They live with it; they die with it. Their grandchildren will govern long after we are ghosts.
ERNIE: People have short memories.
MARTIN: Not me. Not you. Not Wally.
ERNIE: I saw Wally last week in Makati.
MARTIN: 'Musta na s'ya? How is he?
ERNIE: We had a big reunion.
MARTIN: Who was there?
ERNIE: Edwin, Prino / Pierre, Renee. Ver flew in from Perth.
MARTIN: Prino?! Pierre!
ERNIE: It was great. Still fighting the good fight. All they talk about is politics.
MARTIN: They were good guys. We all were.
ERNIE: Kausapin mo naman sila. Talk to them.
MARTIN: I wouldn't know what to say.
ERNIE: People often start with 'Hello, How are you?'
MARTIN: You know what I mean.
ERNIE: Alright, come on, enough. Where are we eating?
MARTIN: It's three a.m.
ERNIE: Where are we eating tomorrow?
MARTIN: We'll go to the Outback Steakhouse.

    ERNIE *does 'shock horror'.*

ERNIE: I haven't been here in ten years and you want to subject me to that?! Besides, your son's a vegan now. We don't raise vegans. I wouldn't, anyway. COME ON! Let's take Leo out! The Beat, Wickham, Sporties, Fluffy! You can wear some of my stuff. Wait, I hope you're not working. Please, god, tell me you're not working.
MARTIN: Someone has to, now.
ERNIE: The trains will run without you.
MARTIN: I don't work on the trains anymore. I'm in the office now.
ERNIE: Uy? Bakit?[9]
MARTIN: I got a promotion a couple of years back.
ERNIE: Uy! More reason to celebrate.
MARTIN: I gotta get back to work in ten hours.
ERNIE: Take the day off, Martin.

---

9. Oh, why?

MARTIN: I love my job!

ERNIE: You're lucky to have one.

MARTIN: I'm a now a Senior Quality Control Agent. Yeah, it's great fun. I record the number of times a train comes late. Then I table those numbers. Then thoroughly inspect those numbers for anomalies and numerical masses.

ERNIE: Thrilling.

MARTIN: I like the quiet.

Don't worry. I'm okay, I'm good. You're my little brother, why are you so worried about me, ah? Relax, it's all good!

ERNIE: I am relaxed! Wooooooo!

ERNIE throws a bottle of Johnnie Walker Black Label to MARTIN, who just catches it.

ERNIE dances a little then feels a pain in his knee. MARTIN guides him to the couch.

MARTIN exits to get a blanket.

If I were younger, I'd be on the streets right now.

ERNIE gets himself ready for bed and lies down.

MARTIN returns.

MARTIN: It would be good for you to see him.

MARTIN exits as ERNIE lies down to sleep.

SCENE 7: PALACE

1986. February 24. Early hours of the morning. YOUNG ERNIE *walks the streets of Manila toward Malacañang.*

ERNIE *remains on* MARTIN's *couch in 2022.*

YOUNG ERNIE: The line snakes down the street, around the corner.

A slice of the country, ready to step into Malacañang.

The humidity rocks my brain, playing with it.

A nun passes around a sawn-off metal container, a quick sip of the murky water.

To alert me.

ERNIE: Para gising ako.

ERNIE *is now awake, and watches* YOUNG ERNIE.

YOUNG ERNIE: As the night grows older, it grows us.
 The palace gates, with crowns of thorns on each pike.
 The iron bent down, as if a giant has played with it like rubber.
 I imagine my brother as the giant bending the iron as we pour through. We are water through a burst pipe.

YOUNG MARTIN *appears, still searching for* YOUNG ERNIE.

ERNIE/YOUNG ERNIE: KUYA?!

YOUNG MARTIN *exits.*

ERNIE: Kuya, look at this!

YOUNG ERNIE: Our soul sweats it out, we want Malacañang back.
 Our people emerge from a place we dream about.
 It is a choir of cheering, of laughter, of celebration.
 The last of his supporters stand guard.
 They look at us with bloodshot eyes.
 A nervous whisper.

ERNIE: Marcos parin …

YOUNG ERNIE: Marcos still …

ERNIE: Marcos parin!

YOUNG ERNIE: Marcos still?!

ERNIE: MARCOS PARIN!

YOUNG ERNIE: MARCOS STILL!
 A galaxy of American cameras beaming this moment back to the comfort of the West, and we realise:
 The world is watching us.
 The world is looking to us to learn.
 His supporters stand firm, but there are more of us.
 We are armed.
 Planks of wood, nails twisted at every angle, barbed wire.
 They run.
 Not away.
 Towards us.
 And we run.
 Towards them.
 Two are taken down. Quickly. In those few moments, I pray they have changed sides as they lie there, giving their last breaths.

They muster the strength to rise, but one of them collapses with the weight of our country.
We can't leave him!
His eyes fill with blood, his breath heavy.
That close to death, to still life.
This man, this boy, this corpse-in-waiting.
Our countrymen hold him as his body begins to say:

ERNIE: Tama na.
YOUNG ERNIE: That's enough.
The dead man lies at my feet.

YOUNG ERNIE hums in prayer.

YOUNG ERNIE's hum changes as ERNIE sings:

ERNIE: Totoy makinig ka, wag kang magpagabi.
Baka magkamalan ka't humandusay d'yan sa tabi
Totoy, alam mo ba kung ano and puno't dulo
Di matatapos-tapos na kaguluhang ito?

YOUNG ERNIE: I want to dance.

YOUNG ERNIE's hum changes.

ERNIE: Hindi pula't dilaw tunay na magkalaban
Ang kulay at tatak ay 'di s'yang dahilan.

YOUNG ERNIE: I want to fuck everything that moves.
ERNIE: Hangga't marami and lugmok sa kahirapan
Ang hustisya ay para lang sa mayaman.

YOUNG ERNIE: I want to PARTY!

YOUNG ERNIE's hum changes.

ERNIE: Habang may tatsulok at sila ay nasa tuktok
Hindi matatapos itong gulo.

ERNIE leaves the memory.

Each step towards the palace brings us closer to fantasy.

YOUNG MARTIN enters the space looking for YOUNG ERNIE.

We can become like the Kings and Queens we read about.
Our Camelot.

YOUNG MARTIN: ERNIE!
YOUNG ERNIE: We will sit on their thrones. My brother will sit next to me.
YOUNG MARTIN: ERNEST! ERNESTO?!
> ERNIE *exits.*

He is here, somewhere. I pray he is not lost in the alleyways, the highways or the underpasses. Without me.
ERNIE!
ERNIE, WHERE ARE YOU?!
I run past the same street signs, the same passed out people, the same empty bottles of Jack Daniel's. Too many times … where is he?!
It is a ghost town, souls nowhere to be seen.
But no more curfew.
Now we are free.
Free to raid their fridge, steal the strongman's shirts.
Malacañang is still in reach.
But I feel him.
He has to be near.
ERNIE?!
Malacañang is still ours.
ERNIE!
MALACAÑANG!
DON'T GO HOME, KAPATID!
MALACAÑANG!
WE MEET AT MALACAÑANG!

SCENE 8: COMMUNICATION

2022. May 12. Midday. LEO *in his room. He names the chat:*

LEO: BBM Brisbane *Filipino flag emoji , Kangaroo Emoji, Kangaroo Emoji, Kangaroo Emoji*
> @LeoCabaero!
>> BUNSOYBBY *enters.*

BUNSOYBBY: @Bunsoybby!
> LEO *and* BUNSOYBBY *squeal with excitement.*

Gurl, what is this?

LEO: We need a place to dump all the BBM Tea.
BUNSOYBBY: Oh my god, yes!
LEO: Yeah like reels, content, live.
BUNSOYBBY: Oh my god, yes!

    SISIGKWEEN *is added to the chat.*

SISIGKWEEN: @SisigKween!
BUNSOYBBY: This is my cousin.
SISIGKWEEN: Hiii haha, just tell me when and where lmao.

    GWAPOBOI *is added to the chat.*

GWAPOBOI: @Gwapoboi.
SISIGKWEEN: This is my friend from church. #prayers.
GWAPOBOI: YO YO YO!

    NOTANURSE03 *is added to the chat.*

NOTANURSE03: @Notanurse03.
BUNSOYBBY: My second cousin. I think.
NOTANURSE03: IhavetobequickbecauseImmeanttobestudying.
SISIGKWEEN: I am SUCH a fan!
NOTANURSE03: Me too! I watch your videos all the time.
GWAPOBOI: Are you actually tall? Your videos make you look like your tall. #heels.
BUNSOYBBY: They are all keen to protest!

    Fire emojis flood the chat!

LEO: Sorry, protest?
SISIGKWEEN: We have to!
BUNSOYBBY: AGAINST BBM! #NEVERFORGET #PEOPLEPOWER.

    They all raise their fists in order, LEO *a beat behind.*

Hang on, we need to change your name!
LEO: What, why?!
NOTANURSE03: I can't believe this is happening! #howreal #soreal.
BUNSOYBBY: If we start planning we can't use your real name.
SISIGKWEEN: Totally.
LEO: Okay. So … ?
GWAPOBOI: Just think of a name. It's not hard. #seriously.

NOTANURSE03: It always takes time. I went through thirty-four names before I got mine. Haha!

NOTANURSE03 leaves the chat quickly and then comes back.

Pause.

Sorry my mum was checking I'm doing my homework. Phew.
BUNSOYBBY: What about ... Jollyboii?!
LEO: Nothing like, gendered please. Lmao.
SISIGKWEEN: Okai!
LEO: Oh! Jollybby!
BUNSOYBBY: Done.
LEO: Alright, okay cool. @Jollybby!

The whole chat applauds in support.

Okay cute, but this is happening kind of fast.
BUNSOYBBY: BBM is coming this weekend! *plane emoji*
NOTANURSE03: So many people will join in once they see it's you!
SISIGKWEEN: All of us are gagging to hear you speak and do your thing!
LEO: All of you? How many?
SISIGKWEEN: Right now we have like ... four people.
GWAPOBOI: The other side has way more.
BUNSOYBBY: Shhhhhhhh!
LEO: Wait, where are all of you?
SISIGKWEEN: Mount Gravatt.
LEO: Oh my god, near me!
NOTANURSE03: I'm in Chermside!
SISIGKWEEN: Oh my god, what church do you go to?
NOTANURSE03: I'm an altar boy at Saint Joseph and Saint Anthony. *Latin Cross emoji* Okay wait, when are we protesting?
SISIGKWEEN: STOP! Wait.

The chat becomes encrypted.

Okay. We're good. Sunday.
NOTANURSE03: NO! I can't, I'm serving!
ALL *except* NOTANURSE03: SERVING!

The entire chat clicks, except NOTANURSE03.

SISIGKWEEN: King George Square?

LEO: King George Square!?!?
SISIGKWEEN: You want to do this right?
LEO: It's in like, four days!
   No, wait, just, sorry, can you all send like pics of yourselves or something?
SISIGKWEEN: Serious?
GWAPOBOI: I totally knew he would be like this. Like, nervous.
   LEO *breaks off into another chat with* BUNSOYBBY.
BUNSOYBBY: Don't go between chats, it might freak them out a bit that we aren't responding so / quick.
LEO: You need to vouch for them.
BUNSOYBBY: I know them all.
LEO: I know, but just can you get them to send me a photo or something? You taught me to vouch. I don't know who they are?
   Back to the normal group chat.
NOTANURSE03: Guys! Come to my house after the protest and say we met at youth group! I'll make lumpia.
LEO: Wait, were you serious about King George Square?
GWAPOBOI: You know, where we always protest.
LEO: I've never actually done this.
SISIGKWEEN: Seriously?
GWAPOBOI: I knew it!
SISIGKWEEN: You've posted about them before!!!
LEO: Like, I've been to them, I just haven't been *in* them, you know?
BUNSOYBBY: First protest?! CUTE!
NOTANURSE03: I just signed my sixth petition this week. Under a different name. *Shh emoji*
SISIGKWEEN: Protesting intergenerational dictatorship for the first time is SLEYYYYYY. RECLAIM YOUR CULTURE BBY.
   The whole chat goes crazy.
LEO: Okay, okay let's do it.
   The whole chat goes crazy.
   Yep, let's do it. Do we, like … What do we do next?
SISIGKWEEN: You just share the event. We'll turn up.
LEO: Event?

GWAPOBOI: That's usually what happens for a protest. #virgin.
BUNSOYBBY: Put it on your story.
NOTANURSE03: Guys, I gotta go. My mum is at the door!

>NOTANURSE03 *leaves the chat.*

SISIGKWEEN: Byeeeeeee guys!

>SISIGKWEEN *leaves.*

GWAPOBOI: Yeah I've got water polo practice.

>GWAPOBOI *leaves.*

BUNSOYBBY: I know they're intense but they're actually all really cool.
LEO: But is it right for me to do this?
BUNSOYBBY: Oh my god, stop. Of course it's right! Girl, you got the followers, you got the content, you will be fine. This is like your next step.
LEO: Yeah but, speaking? In front of like a crowd, with a sign. Like, can I just do it in my room lmao.
BUNSOYBBY: This is you!
LEO: No, I know.
BUNSOYBBY: This is literally you! They need you!!!
LEO: I've never met any of these people.
BUNSOYBBY: You got this.

>LEO *puts his phone away.*

SCENE 9: GIFT

2022. May 12. MARTIN*'s apartment in Sunnybank.* LEO *sits.*

ERNIE: [*offstage*] De, darling!

>ERNIE *enters.*

>So, before this whole political era, you were totally into vintage clothing, right? Like that was a thing, di ba?[10]

>>ERNIE *dumps a duffle bag full of his old clothes on the floor. He wells up.*

>Go and enjoy! Run free, child. RUN! But remember, it ALL used to fit me.

---

10. Is that right?

LEO: They're that old?
ERNIE: BITCH! But yes, they're all relics. It all deserves to be in a museum. Okay lang, enjoy.

LEO *pulls through the clothes and finds a yellow T-shirt with a cartoon picture of Ferdinand Marcos, and the words 'NEVER AGAIN' under it.*

LEO *excitedly tries it on.*

LEO: I love it.
ERNIE: Take it off before your father gets home.
LEO: This is all I need.
ERNIE: There are better clothes in here!
LEO: I'll wear it to the BBM protest.
ERNIE: Excuse me?
LEO: Protesta.
ERNIE: When?
LEO: Sunday.
ERNIE: Girl. It's the weekend! Footy, Pub, Retro's, Enigma, Sporties, Wickham, The Beat. Fluffy. Come on, my shout!
LEO: Ew. At least two of those venues perpetuate stereotypes that are dangerous to the queer POC community, plus it places the dominant white gay alpha male at the top of the queer paradigm.
ERNIE: Hot.
LEO: BBM is coming here. His son is going to uni in Melbourne. He's stopping here first.
ERNIE: Oh please, Filipino presidents don't travel to Australia.
LEO: Marcoses in 1967, Ramos in 1996, Arroyo in 2007, Aquino in 2012.
ERNIE: Okay, girl!
LEO: We just need to find out where he's staying.
ERNIE: Or you know, enjoy life. Your dear old Tito flies all the way back to see you and all you want to do is chase baby dictators around Brisbane.
LEO: We'll find out where he is.
ERNIE: It's clearly a personal visit, not a state one. It won't last long. Arroyo and Aquino used to fly to Boston all the time on commercial.

You watch. He'll try to blend in as much as possible. No motorcade, take the back streets. He might even walk. He won't be in some fancy hotel.

LEO: Okay, girl.

ERNIE: Give me back that T-shirt.

LEO: I thought this was a gift?

ERNIE: Do you know what this is?

LEO: It's yellow so it's clearly Aquino.

ERNIE: I just liked the colour.

LEO: Not the message? You and Tay would have been, what? Eighteen, nineteen?

ERNIE: I was still in utero in 1986!

LEO: Were you guys there? At EDSA?

ERNIE: Ask your father.

LEO: Even if he was there, he'd never talk.

ERNIE: You have to ask the right questions.

LEO: I don't have time to think about how to ask questions.

ERNIE: You're eighteen. Why protest? Go out, smell the roses, fuck something!

LEO: You were my age when Marcos was thrown out.

ERNIE: Perhaps.

LEO: The people threw them out then, why can't we throw them out now?

ERNIE: The Marcoses have had years to look good. Bongbong uses TikTok to brush over his father's years and call them the golden age, and there are generations of people who choose to forget the thirty-six years in between.

LEO: There will be protests in Sydney, Melbourne and here.

ERNIE: Protesting what?

LEO: Him.

ERNIE: What about him?

LEO: His election.

ERNIE: Celebrated as a landslide.

LEO: His history.

ERNIE: You ask anyone on the street what they remember about the Marcoses and all they say is: 'Oh, the shoes!'

LEO: I know what I'm doing.

ERNIE: Think, De. Is it that they never gave back the billions of dollars stolen? The houses all over the world? What about him are you against? Find that out and you'll have a better idea about you're fighting for. Shirt.

Keep the shirt. But just ... just be smart about it.

LEO *looks proudly at the T-shirt.*

I hate that you get old and still look young. BITCH! Look at you. Look at you, De! Napaka kisig! So handsome.

LEO: Oh my god, you are literal chaos.

ERNIE: Last time you had this little high voice! This little high voice. [*In a high pitch*] Hi Tito, excuse me Tito, can you help me with my English assignment Tito? Now it's all very— [*In a low pitch*] Hey guyzzzzz welcome to my channel. Only seems like yesterday you were born. At nagayon, isa ka nang Aktibsta.[11]

LEO *looks blankly.*

Nagtatagalog ka ba?[12]

LEO *uses his fingers to indicate 'little bit'.*

You spoke it all the time as a kid! [*In a high pitch*] Tito, paki-tali ang sapatos ko. Nadadapa ako palagi, eh?[13]

LEO: Okay, this is a literal attack.

ERNIE: Oh please!

LEO: Aray ko, ang laki![14]

ERNIE: Oh god, what has your father been teaching you?!

LEO: Okay, so you need to understand. Language is always being unlearnt.

ERNIE: You don't have to 'unlearn'. We switch our tongues to survive. We are the chameleons; we are the shapeshifters.

LEO: Like, language doesn't have to exist within a rigid / construct.

ERNIE: [*in a high pitch*] Please, uncle. My shoes. Girl, I knew you were bakla the day you were born.

LEO: Wow.

---

11. And now you're an activist.
12. Do you speak Tagalog?
13. Uncle, please tie my shoes. I trip all the time.
14. Oh my, you're too big!

ERNIE: De, darling. We ran so you could walk. I never wanted to imagine that word when I was a kid. Okay, but now, NOW ... you see it, everywhere. Bakla have their own language, they are in pageants, they are the moment. It's a celebration, girl! *Bakla's back, ALRIGHT!*[15]

LEO: I'm aware of the reclamation of bakla. I did a two-part video on the reclamation of bakla.

ERNIE: Your generation is always reclaiming something. Use it gently, round here De, your father might think 'Sobra na yan'.[16]

LEO: Did I really speak like that?

ERNIE: And with a cute little Amerikano accent. You would fit in in the Philippines. Don't get any ideas though, hey?

LEO: Cool, you've been talking to Tay.

ERNIE: Go somewhere that will make your father proud.

LEO: This is literally not about him.

ERNIE: Don't you want to party with frat boys in Harvard? Or see the castles of Europe?! Or ride down Hollywood Boulevard with no shirt on?! Woooooooo! There are so many exciting places, and you want to go to U.P.?

LEO: It's a great school.

ERNIE: Everyone who goes there is so boring. Look at your father!

LEO: Tay didn't go to U.P.

Oh my god, he went there.

ERNIE: Shhhhhhh!

LEO: This is incredible.

ERNIE: It's just a university.

LEO: I can't believe he went there!

ERNIE: And look what he became. He's never taken a holiday. He doesn't talk to anyone. We both wish we had what you had.

LEO: Me going to U.P. isn't about either of you.

    ERNIE *looks at the T-shirt.*

ERNIE: You really want to protest, don't you? I can find out where BBM is staying. It's not that hard.

LEO: How do you know?

ERNIE: I listen.

---

15. Sung to the tune of 'Everybody' by the Backstreet Boys.
16. Too much.

LEO: To who? You're a flight attendant.
ERNIE: Wally, Prino, Pierre, all those guys. They've never stopped fighting, De.
LEO: Message them.
ERNIE: De, that's a big risk. It's not right. I could get you in a lot of trouble.
LEO: I won't tell anyone.
ERNIE: Don't you want people to turn up to your protesta? Or I could just take you out to dinner and we could just enjoy! Come on! Let's go! Wooo!
LEO: Wait, okay, the address?
ERNIE: If I get you the address, you go somewhere that will make your father proud.

SCENE 10: WORK

2022. May 12. 2 p.m. Brisbane Central Station.

A piece of rubbish appears. MARTIN *makes an announcement on the platform.*

MARTIN: Help out rail staff by avoiding leaving rubbish around the platform. Have a nice day.

> MARTIN *picks up rubbish and drops a pile of documents on the floor.*
>
> MARTIN *pick up one piece of paper, stops, hold it up.*

YOUNG MARTIN: [*offstage*] WALLY! WAIT!

> YOUNG MARTIN *appears.*

MARTIN: Isang kahanga-hangang palasyo.
YOUNG MARTIN: I stand on ornate beauty.

> *It is now 24 February 1986, and* YOUNG MARTIN *is inside Malacañang Palace.*
>
> MARTIN *watches* YOUNG MARTIN *in Malacañang.*

We weigh down the marble floors, our people pour into a foyer once out of our reach.

The works of Picasso, Michelangelo and Monet are spread throughout the palace.

Coloured faces, renaissance figures and water lilies catch our eye, while ten-foot pictures of Queen Imelda watch me.

The real one bound for Reagan's Hawaii, where they welcome the family with open arms.

He gives her the finger.

Line your pockets, kaps! Line them!
Wally! Onofre! Prino! Pierre!
Take it all!
Edwin! Ver! Rene!
Ernie?
Ernie, where are you?

A shower of papers.

My friends pillage the drawers of his study, throwing documents into the air, and they rain down on us.

MARTIN *collects the documents on the floor.*

Wally holds one.

Just one page.

Detailing an inch of the twenty-one years of rule that have led us to this moment.

He pulls a Playboy lighter out of his pocket, the bunny glistening off the marble floors of pure decadence. The flame almost marries the paper …

We will burn it all! Do it outside!

YOUNG MARTIN *runs outside.*

Dance around the flames of lies, cook meat on the fire like our ancestors did on their land.

No, we will keep it all!

MARTIN: Katibayan.
YOUNG MARTIN: For evidence, because tonight, no longer are we paupers.
MARTIN: We are princes.
YOUNG MARTIN: No longer are we beggars.
MARTIN: We are barons!

YOUNG MARTIN *addresses a gathering crowd.*

YOUNG MARTIN: We are here—standing on the shoulders of the known corpses, their ghosts cheering us on from above, a persecuted choir sings our praises.

 A crowd of the free gather beneath me, begging me to jump on the chandelier and swing.

 MARTIN *holds his breath with anticipation.*

It could collapse, smash into seven thousand pieces.

 YOUNG MARTIN *reaches, and grasps.*

 MARTIN *is overjoyed.*

I cling to wealth, swinging like a monkey from branch to branch in Palawan.[17]

MARTIN: Dito matutupad ang ating mga pangarap.
YOUNG MARTIN: We live our dreams in here.
MARTIN: Para sa atin ito.
YOUNG MARTIN: We own it.
MARTIN: Tayo ang bagong kinabukasan.
YOUNG MARTIN: We are the new tomorrow.

 YOUNG MARTIN *and* MARTIN *smile at one another.*

SCENE 11: PLANS

2022. May 12. 4 p.m. LEO *is waiting in the BBM Brisbane chat.*

LEO: @Jollybby! Hello is anyone here?
BUNSOYBBY: @Bunsoybby!!

 They squeal.

GWAPOBOI: @Gwapoboi!
LEO: Vouch pls.
BUNSOYBBY: No, no, he's fine.
LEO: I'm serious, vouch.
BUNSOYBBY: You met him the other day!
LEO: Doesn't matter.

 A selfie of GWAPOBOI *is taken and sent to* LEO.

Okay, hot.

---

17. Island province in the Philippines

BUNSOYBBY: Why did you call us here?
LEO: I'm pretty sure that my uncle was at EDSA.
BUNSOYBBY: OMG stop!
GWAPOBOI: Broooooo. BS!

    LEO *takes snapshot of him wearing the shirt as proof.*

LEO: And don't call me bro.
BUNSOYBBY: Sley sley sley! SLEY THE DAY AWAY.

    SISIGKWEEN *is added to the chat.*

SISIGKWEEN: @SisigKween! Hey, oh my god sorry, I'm here. Oh my god! That shirt is giving 'eighty-six realness!

    NOTANURSE03 *is added to the chat.*

NOTANURSE03: @NotaNurse03 Guys, I gotta be quick, I told my mum—wow! You really are soooo cool!
LEO: And I found out where #BBM is staying!
BUNSOYBBY: Leo, wait!
NOTANURSE03: Hang on!
LEO: Rydges South Bank.
GWAPOBOI: Broooooooo!
BUNSOYBBY: Oh my god.
NOTANURSE03: I am so sweaty right now.
SISIGKWEEN: Wait, wait!

    The chat becomes encrypted.

LEO: What?
GWAPOBOI: Bro, who is this guy?
SISIGKWEEN: Delete that message! Now. Quick.
LEO: Okay, okay! I have!
GWAPOBOI: Who told you the address?
BUNSOYBBY: People are always watching. You know that!
LEO: Sorry.
SISIGKWEEN: The UK sold spyware to the Phils from 2016 to 2018. *British flag emoji*
BUNSOYBBY: #warondrugs #bigkuya.
LEO: I won't do it again. I promise.
GWAPOBOI: Who did you get the address off?
LEO: My people.

GWAPOBOI: Do you trust them?
LEO: Obvi.
NOTANURSE03: You are so cool.
LEO: Oh, thanks. Haha.
SISIGKWEEN: So what are we gonna do with his address?
LEO: We meet at King George Square.
BUNSOYBBY: Nice.
LEO: Then walk to #RSB.

The chat goes wild.

How many people do we have now?
SISIGKWEEN: We'll have more soon.
NOTANURSE03: Once you put it on your story.
LEO: Guys, how many people do we have?
SISIGKWEEN: Twelve.
LEO: That's nothing.
SISIGKWEEN: We have time.
NOTANURSE03: We only have a few days!
BUNSOYBBY: Just follow what Leo says. King George Square and then to #RSB.
GWAPOBOI: Can you imagine if we actually met BBM? Like actually shook his hand.

BUNSOYBBY, SISIGKWEEN *and* LEO *all 'question mark' react* GWAPOBOI's *message.*

LEO: For real?
BUNSOYBBY: Oh my god, why?
GWAPOBOI: I dunno, just like talk to him about what he's going to do?!
LEO: HE IS GOING TO DO EXACTLY WHAT HIS FATHER DID!
SISIGKWEEN: Do you watch any of Jollybby's content?!
NOTANURSE03: I liked when you did recipes.
GWAPOBOI: There are a lot of other people out there supporting him lmao.
BUNSOYBBY: Oh my god.
GWAPOBOI: I'm not pro-Marcos but I'm hopeful. We all should be! It doesn't make any sense if we all believe the same thing.
BUNSOYBBY: No.
LEO: Nope.

GWAPOBOI: None of us actually live there!
BUNSOYBBY: Ahem. *hand-raising emoji*
GWAPOBOI: Okay you do, but like, obvs you think the country has never gotten any better, right?
BUNSOYBBY: How would you know? You've never lived here!
GWAPOBOI: Literally every president has been arrested for corruption.
LEO: BBM is the worst!
GWAPOBOI: He's been talking about infrastructure, uniting the country, finishing projects!
We need to see if he might actually do good stuff!
LEO: I literally can't with this!

 LEO *posts a poll: 'Kick Out* GWAPOBOI*?*

GWAPOBOI: Don't do it!
LEO: **Votes yes**
GWAPOBOI: **Votes no**
SISIGKWEEN: **Votes yes**
BUNSOYBBY: **Votes yes**

 Majority rules. No need for @NOTANURSE03 *to vote.*

NOTANURSE03: We should talk this out!
LEO: No, I'm good.
GWAPOBOI: Leo! Wait!
LEO: Byeeeeeee!

 GWAPOBOI *is removed from the chat.*

NOTANURSE03: Wait here, I'll talk to him.

 NOTANURSE03 *leaves the chat.*

LEO: WILD.
BUNSOYBBY: I know.
SISIGKWEEN: Guys, OMG I'm sorry I brought him but he's not really that bad!
BUNSOYBBY: I'll add him back in soon.
LEO: What?? No!
BUNSOYBBY: We need all the people we can get.
LEO: At least, like, put him in a timeout.
BUNSOYBBY: Okay, vibe! Timeout for supporting intergenerational dictatorship lmao.

SISIGKWEEN: I can't believe you did it!
BUNSOYBBY: You did that, Jollybby!
LEO: Stop! No, wait. Keep going.
BUNSOYBBY: YOU ATE.
SISIGKWEEN: Like a true leader!
LEO: You guys.
BUNSOYBBY: That was incredible.
LEO: I should speak tomorrow, shouldn't I?
BUNSOYBBY: Bby yes!
SISIGKWEEN: You are POWER.
LEO: I am.

SCENE 12: PLANS

2022. May 12. LEO *arrives at* MARTIN*'s work, Brisbane Central Station.* LEO *puts his phone in his pocket when he sees* MARTIN.

MARTIN: Leo. What's wrong, have you eaten?
LEO: Everything's fine.
MARTIN: Oh, good.

>   *Pause.*

The train / came.
LEO: I think the train / is here.
MARTIN: No, you / go.
LEO: No, no. I want to hear about the trains.
MARTIN: Well, they came late today. Heads are gonna roll. That's the twelfth time this week!
LEO: Wow.
MARTIN: I know! I'm going to have to stay late tonight. You take care of your Tito Ernie.
LEO: It was nice to see him again.

>   MARTIN *laughs in remembering..*

MARTIN: Now there's a guy that's always late. When he was starting out, he used to just make his flights. He would go running out of the house putting on his uniform, stuffing rice in his mouth. Your lola and I would joke, saying he would be running alongside the plane. 'Wait! Wait for me!'

MARTIN *does a vocal and physical impression of* ERNIE *doing just that.*

They laugh together.

There are some great stories from when we were young, running around the streets, rolling dice around the sidewalk, playing patintero in Rizal Park.

MARTIN *chuckles.*

LEO: I can see it. He told me what you both went through.

Pause.

Growing up on a pig farm.

MARTIN: OH! Ha! Your Tito told you, did he? Pigs everywhere! You wake up and there would be a pig sitting there. All the pigs eating our scraps. Your lola would want the pigs fed before us. The bigger the swine, the more money we could have.

LEO: Pigs equalled money.

MARTIN: A pig could set you up for life. It did for me. I thought. And we all had to pitch in—me, your Tito Ernie, cleaning out the pigsty every day. Hands covered in dirt.

LEO: Ew.

MARTIN: We'd fling it on each other like crazy.

LEO: So gross.

MARTIN: Your Tito Ernie hated it!

LEO: You were literally rolling around in dirt and poo.

MARTIN: It was fucking filth!

LEO: And now you're here.

MARTIN: You sit there wanting to get out, wanting freedom! Then your lola comes running out of the house, holding a college letter offer to …

LEO: U.P.

MARTIN *makes to leave.*

If you went there, why can't I?

MARTIN: It's because I went that I know it's not right for you, Leo.

LEO: You were there a long time ago, Tay.

MARTIN: Nothing changes in that country. There were students living in poverty, not wanting to study, to do things that could get them out of that country. All they wanted to do was fight.

LEO: Did you fight?!
MARTIN: Me? Come on Leo, I don't even send my order back if they get it wrong.
LEO: You went to one of the biggest protest schools in the world. Didn't you care about anything?
MARTIN: Yeah, of course. Your lola. Tito Ernie. My friends. Wally was one of the earliest computer students at U.P. Onofre was studying astrophysics, Renee and Pierre were incredible basketball players—the best on our team.
LEO: While the country literally was falling apart all you cared about was playing basketball with your friends?
MARTIN: If we played past curfew, troops would come from the shadows.
   We risked our lives playing basketball.
   Pause.
LEO: You've never talked to me about this.
MARTIN: I don't have to.
LEO: I want to.
MARTIN: You think you will get off the plane and feel like you're at home? Feel like you're connected? Feel like you belong? The best thing about us is we can belong anywhere. You will belong anywhere.
LEO: I have a choice.
MARTIN: What if you had no scholarship? What if we had to put every cent into getting you anywhere? You are so lucky, Leo. So lucky you don't have to worry. I came here with nothing but a dream for you. A dream of seeing you thrive.

   LEO *opens his jacket, revealing the T-shirt.*

LEO: Yes, I know ...

   MARTIN *sees the shirt.*

MARTIN: Where did you get that?
LEO: Tito Ernie.
MARTIN: Get rid of it.
LEO: No.
MARTIN: Go get one from the Lost and Found.

LEO: Ew.

MARTIN: You shouldn't be wearing this around Brisbane.

    MARTIN *looks around, as the public passes by them.*

LEO: Yeah, a random on the street knows what this is.

MARTIN: It might upset people.

LEO: You know what this is.

MARTIN: Go change.

LEO: No.

MARTIN: Now, please.

LEO: No.

MARTIN: Do as I say.

LEO: Tay.

MARTIN: Take it off now!

    LEO *removes the shirt and* MARTIN *grabs it.*

LEO: You can't live through me.

    LEO *leaves.*

SCENE 13: REMEMBER

2022. May 12. 5 p.m. MARTIN*'s apartment, Sunnybank.*

MARTIN *enters.*

MARTIN: What the fuck have you done?

ERNIE: I had to talk to him. You don't say anything!

MARTIN: I tell Leo what he needs to know.

ERNIE: Clearly it's worked out very well.

MARTIN: Ernesto!

ERNIE: I don't get why you're so angry about this.

MARTIN: Do I need to take time off and follow you around?

ERNIE: You're so patronising sometimes.

MARTIN: Do I need to make sure you don't say something that could completely change his life?! This. U.P. What's next?

ERNIE: I'm not stupid. Neither is he. When we were his age all we did was ask questions. It made us who we are. Ma, why do we have to queue for hours for rice? Ma, why do we have to be home by nine? Ma, why did that family move away overnight? He will never stop

asking questions.
MARTIN: And look at what happened to us.
ERNIE: He has every right to know who he is.
MARTIN: He has known who he is for eighteen years. Without you.
ERNIE: Alright, fine. I'll just take him out and we can find the dirtiest toilet and do a couple of great big lines.
MARTIN: ERNIE! You do that and you're out of this house.
ERNIE: Where'd you put that cash?
MARTIN: ERNESTO!
ERNIE: Chur lang. It's a JOKE! I made it to my fifties, Kuya. Do you think I'm going to throw it all way now? I'm six years clean and I'm never going back.
MARTIN: That's great, kap.
ERNIE: Not easy when most of your friends from the party days are Duterte's target practice. I dodged bullets. Guilty by proxy.
MARTIN: I wish you said something.
ERNIE: You were raising a son.
MARTIN: Still.
ERNIE: When I'd land back in Manila there'd be another funeral. I begged the airline to keep me out of town for a while. Sometimes when the whole plane was asleep, I'd be staring out to the sky. I'd have that same jolt of danger. The same danger I had in the pit of my stomach the night we were inside Malacañang.
MARTIN: Nakalitgas tayo. We survived.
ERNIE: You did. Because of me. Nailigtas kita.
MARTIN: And you went on. Partied, slept with anything that had a pulse.
ERNIE: Please. I have standards.
MARTIN: You lived. You've got friends.
ERNIE: You can pick up the phone and call any of our old kapatids.
MARTIN: Ilang araw na ang nakaraan. It's been so long.
ERNIE: And thank god they are still with us. I'm sick of saying 'he's very busy with work' to cover for you.
MARTIN: It's not just them. It's any person that even looks like them. Any crowd, any Filo event.
ERNIE: Our kapatids would understand.

Pause.

MARTIN: That night …
ERNIE: I know. You were scared. But I was too. I mean, we're the heroes. Shouldn't Leo know his father is a hero?!
You've got a son with guts. Malakas ang loob n'ya.
MARTIN: You have no say here.
ERNIE: You're all rules, Kuya.
MARTIN: I'm his father. I have made the rules all his life. Without you.
ERNIE: Leo should know what happened that night.
MARTIN: When did we all start telling each other the truth?!
ERNIE: It's what made him.
MARTIN: I made him.
ERNIE: We could tell him what happened. Maybe he won't go to U.P. if he knows that's where it all started.
MARTIN: U.P. led to protesting, protesting got us here. The last thing I want is for him to become like me.
ERNIE: You're a good man Martin, you would have been an activist wherever you went. We changed the country because we took a stand. You should be proud of yourself!
MARTIN: It wasn't just me.
ERNIE: Sure, but you were there.
MARTIN: That moment is like a film I hate watching, but it keeps playing over and over and over again.
ERNIE: I try to forget it, but I can't.
MARTIN: We stood for hours on the streets.
ERNIE: I can't even stand for twenty seconds without sitting down.
MARTIN: We were so strong. Strong enough to swim the Pasig River fifty times.
ERNIE: Or jump from car to car on EDSA.
MARTIN: Swing from a chandelier.
ERNIE: Stuff your pockets full of cash!
MARTIN: Knowing a loyalist, or even better—
MARTIN/ERNIE: A crony!
MARTIN: Could be around the corner, lurking, ready to strike.
ERNIE: Sit on the throne that Marcos claimed every day of his life.
MARTIN: Go into the meeting room, sit where he sold the land to America.
ERNIE: See the pen he used to sign off on the sale.
MARTIN: Imagine the Americans sitting opposite Marcos.

ERNIE: Closing your eyes and imagining the sucking of cigars.
MARTIN: The clinking of whiskey glasses.
ERNIE: The laughter of complicity.
MARTIN: And then the crash of the people coming!
ERNIE: Ready to take it all back.
MARTIN: All of us! Prino, Onofre, Wally.
ERNIE: Rene, Pierre!
MARTIN: Edwin, Ver!
ERNIE: We swarm the palace!

> YOUNG ERNIE *and* YOUNG MARTIN *appear.*

MARTIN: And they fly above you one last time, whisked away, waving and crying.
ERNIE: Watching their islands be ours.

> MARTIN *makes to leave and is stopped by* ERNIE.

Remember what that night made us.

> YOUNG MARTIN *and* YOUNG ERNIE *enter 2022, still separated, and they call out to each other.*

SCENE 14: WORLDS

2022. May 13. 5.30 p.m. Sunnybank. MARTIN*'s apartment.*

LEO *attempts to film a video, trying to master angles, and consistently fixing his hair and himself.*

He begins to film Part Four of 'A Brief Yet Spicy History of the Philippines'.

ERNIE *hovers, watching* LEO.

LEO: BBM. Remember him? Okay, so in 1986 OG nepo-baby tells his daddy to order an air strike by two F-Thirty-Fives on Camp *Crame*, where literally thousands of civilians are gathered.
 Plot twist, Marcos refuses.
 In an even BIGGER plot twist, Cardinal Jamie[18] Sin, via radio, asks two million civilians who are swarming Metro Manila, to protect two of Marcos' most trusted / cronies.

---

18. Pronounced Jay-me

ERNIE: I think it's *Jaime*.[19] And Camp *Crame*.

    LEO *stops filming.*

What's this one about today?
LEO: Part Four. 'A Brief / Yet Spicy History of the Philippines'.
ERNIE: 'Spicy History of the Philippines'! I've been waiting for Part Four.

    ERNIE *fixes* LEO's *appearance.*

LEO: I'm fine.
ERNIE: You could look better.

    LEO *continues to fix his hair.*

    ERNIE *gestures for* LEO *to sit.*

It's all about patience, my dear. You don't want to look like dogshit. We used to take three, maybe four hours to get ready.

    ERNIE *fixes* LEO's *hair.*

LEO: Okay, are you sure this is / right?
ERNIE: Bitch, you want more followers or no?!
LEO: Bitch, followers aren't the problem here.

    LEO *smiles.*

ERNIE: You lucky thing. You still have your baby hairs. They were so fine.
LEO: You were there?
ERNIE: Hm?
LEO: You were there the day I was born.
ERNIE: Oh yeah, it was a great day. We were all there. Kuya, me, your lola. Your mother, obviously.
LEO: Dad told me she was sick. I was like twelve years-old when he said— [*Impersonating* MARTIN] The shame killed her! The shame.
ERNIE: It's more like— [*Impersonating* MARTIN] THE SHAME KILLED HER! THE SHAME!

    They laugh.

I can tell you it wasn't shame. She was very free.
LEO: I gave up asking when I was thirteen. He wasn't going to talk.
ERNIE: She brought a spirit out of your father.
LEO: I've never seen that.

---

19. Pronounced Hai-may

ERNIE: They were both in love.
LEO: What, like, really in love?
ERNIE: It was special. It was real.
LEO: I can't picture him in love.
ERNIE: Be nice, De.
LEO: Special?
ERNIE: She was gorgeous, darling. Simply beautiful.

ERNIE *continues with the hair.*

Your father should tell you more about her. The world stopped whenever she walked into a room. And she could argue about anything. And so passionate. Like you.

ERNIE *finishes.*

Do my greys.
LEO: My rates have gone up since ten years ago.
ERNIE: Fine.

LEO *agrees to pluck* ERNIE's *greys.*

I used to do this with your lola back home.
LEO: Sometimes I imagine that when I go home, I will understand everything.
ERNIE: You don't know what 'home' is like.
LEO: But I will.
ERNIE: There are so many other great places in the world. OW!
LEO: You guys are ridiculous.
ERNIE: Excuse me. Wasn't the T-shirt enough? The address? U.P.? I went out on a limb for you, De.
LEO: I know.
ERNIE: Do I get a thank you, at least? OUCH!
LEO: Thank you.
ERNIE: Get your head out of the whole one hundred years of Filipino political mess. Ouch! Jesus, you're rough.
LEO: Five-hundred-and-ninety years of it.
ERNIE: It's not that bad?
LEO: We will always have something to fight against.
ERNIE: De, I've lived there all my life.
LEO: Look at Duterte's War on Drugs.

ERNIE: I was there.
LEO: We all were.
ERNIE: It is not the same through your phone. OW!
LEO: Hold still.
ERNIE: You should care, you should react, you should believe. But it's not the same.
LEO: There were over twelve thousand killings.
ERNIE: More.
LEO: Our country shouldn't be in the hands of two families.
ERNIE: Some people would argue that Duterte cleaned the / country up.
LEO: Oh my god.
ERNIE: Some would argue he improved it.
LEO: Do you think that?
ERNIE: He passed a surveillance act that meant ninety days of watching people that should be watched.
LEO: But could detain anyone for up to a month.
ERNIE: Yeah, that one.
LEO: Using software sold to the Philippines by Britain.
ERNIE: Geez Leo, you're on it.
LEO: I like to know what's going on back home.
ERNIE: People can be flagged the minute they get off a plane. Remember that if you wanna go. It's Bongbong's game now.
LEO: I've got followers that will support me the minute I arrive.
ERNIE: And you expect them to turn up at the airport ready to embrace you? Go somewhere with freedom. Go somewhere where you can live. Ow!

    LEO *finishes.*

LEO: I've already sent in my application to U.P.
ERNIE: What? I gave you BBM's address!
LEO: You can't take it back. That's not how this works.

    ERNIE *pays* LEO.

    LEO *stands waiting, hand outstretched.*

    ERNIE *pays* LEO *again.*

ERNIE: Just like your mother.

SCENE 15: PERMISSION

2022. May 13. 11 a.m. LEO's *room. The group chat:* **BBM Brisbane** **Filipino flag emoji and heaps and heaps of kangaroo emojis**
@NotaNurse enters the chat.

NOTANURSE03: @NotaNurse03! Guys! Is anyone here? We are protesting on Sunday, right?? Have we protested already?!

    SISIGKWEEN *joins the chat.*

SISIGKWEEN: @SisigKween! We're going to sley this protest. PERIOD!

    LEO *enters.*

LEO: @Jollybby. Oh my god. Hi? Wait, where's Bunsoybby???

NOTANURSE03: They haven't been active for two days.

LEO: What! Why?

SISIGKWEEN: They like don't check their phone sometimes, for like, their mental health.

LEO: Okay, weird. But I am SO excited!

    NOTANURSE03 *and* SISIGKWEEN *cheer.*

Okay, we gotta get organised.

    GWAPOBOI *is added to the chat.*

GWAPOBOI: @Gwapoboi! Sorry I'm late. It's leg day.

LEO: Oh. Is the timeout already done?

SISIGKWEEN: Okay, we need water for people.

GWAPOBOI: HYDRATION!

NOTANURSE03: We've got massive bottles in our garage.

GWAPOBOI: First aid kits?!

LEO: It's a Filipino protest. There will be nurses.

GWAPOBOI: I can do signs.

SISIGKWEEN: What about flags?!

NOTANURSE03: Temu has large ones on sale for four dollars ninety-five.

LEO: YES!

NOTANURSE03: Wait, Amazon it's more expensive but it will get here in two hours.

SISIGKWEEN: This is going to be MASSIVE!

They all cheer.

NOTANURSE03: What about trying to get a lola or lolo to speak?!

SISIGKWEEN: What about Tita Cecile?!

GWAPOBOI: She would fall asleep before it started.
Didn't you say your uncle was at EDSA?

LEO: Actually my dad could have been as well.

The chat gasps.

SISIGKWEEN: OMG you have to!

GWAPOBOI: Ask them! Do it!

LEO: It's not that easy.

GWAPOBOI: Did they go to Malacañang?

LEO: I don't know.

SISIGKWEEN: Get them to speak!

NOTANURSE03: The crowd will go crazy!

LEO: How many have we got for Sunday?

SISIGKWEEN: … Twenty-one.

LEO: Twenty-one people?! We can't do this with twenty-one people!

NOTANURSE03: Did you count me?

GWAPOBOI: Twenty-three if you've got the balls to ask your dad and uncle!

LEO: Excuse me?

GWAPOBOI: You haven't even put it on your story yet!

NOTANURSE03: We don't have a lot of time!

LEO: OKAY I WILL!

GWAPOBOI: Right! I'm heading to Officeworks to get stuff to make signs. It's two Ks there and back.

GWAPOBOI *exits.*

NOTANURSE03: I'm gonna go steal my dad's speaker system for the titos!

NOTANURSE03 *exits.*

LEO: I haven't even talked to them yet.

SISIGKWEEN: You have to get your tito and your dad to talk tomorrow.

LEO: But like, I don't really need them.

SISIGKWEEN: It's like a meeting of the past … AND THE PRESENT.
Literally, the three of you, standing there, together. IMAGINE.

LEO: Okay it would be pretty sley.

SISIGKWEEN: Don't you want them there?!

The chat ends.

SCENE 16: CARE

2022. May 14. 3 p.m. MARTIN *and* ERNIE *wait in* MARTIN's *apartment.* LEO *enters.*

MARTIN: A protest?
ERNIE: He's doing it.
MARTIN: Are you serious? Against BBM.
ERNIE: Right on time for his 'personal visit'.
MARTIN: Don't be silly, he would never come here.
    LEO *enters unseen by* MARTIN *and* ERNIE.
ERNIE: Kuya Martin. Darating s'ya. It's all over his TikTok. Even Karen Davila from ABS-CBN picked it up.
LEO: You should both speak. With me. King George Square. There's twenty-one of us. There will be more.
MARTIN: Twenty-one stupid kids running around unsupervised in King George's Square?
LEO: What if thirty thousand proud Filipinos show up? What would you say?
MARTIN: Every emergency room in Brisbane would be understaffed.
ERNIE: Darling. Maybe we aren't ready to turn up anymore. Maybe the election made us realise the Marcoses would always return.
LEO: Don't be like him, Tito.
MARTIN: Excuse me?
ERNIE: Don't talk about your father that way.
MARTIN: You are more stupid than I thought.
ERNIE: Let me handle this. Kuya! Ako nang bahala.
MARTIN: BBM won by a landslide. There is nothing you can do.
LEO: There will be rallies against BBM in every major city in this country. And in New York, Washington, LA, San Francisco. We will all make sure history never claws its way back.
ERNIE: What your father is trying to say is—
MARTIN: Ha! America created all of this.
LEO: Yeah, but they have every right to take their stand.
MARTIN: Every President since Truman has owned us. And it's not just them. Scott Morrison called to congratulate Bongbong!

ERNIE: Leo, I get people protesting. I understand. We do.
MARTIN: 'We' definitely do not.
ERNIE: I've got this.
LEO: You literally told me where BBM is staying.
MARTIN: Ernesto!
ERNIE: I thought it would stop him going to U.P.
MARTIN: How did you find out?!
ERNIE: Kuya Wally.
LEO: I already posted that it's happening. People will come.
ERNIE: Take it down.
MARTIN: Right now.
ERNIE: Give me your phone.
LEO: It has so many views.
MARTIN: That's not what this is about.
LEO: You tell me not to protest; you tell me not to go to U.P. Which I'm going to by the way. But the address is fine?
ERNIE: You can protest. Just don't go to the Philippines.
MARTIN: What?! No. Don't do any of it. No Philippines, no U.P, no more talking to kapatids. It's over. This doesn't work. We tried.
ERNIE: De, we can't forget that time no matter how hard we try.
LEO: Wait.
MARTIN: Every day I wish I could.
LEO: Forget what?
ERNIE: We loved that crowd.
LEO: Tay, you were there.
MARTIN: You remember every single face in that crowd, all of our friends.
LEO: What was it like? There would have been thousands of people there.
MARTIN: Try millions. Hanging off the streetlights, listening to the crowd. We watched with our jaws on the floor and our eyes getting wider as Enrile and Ramos … they'd mean nothing to you.
LEO: Juan Ponce Enrile and Fidel Ramos.
MARTIN: That's right!
LEO: The moment they walked through the crowd.
MARTIN: Like they had won the war.
LEO: Yeah, right before they had gone on TV.

MARTIN: They were rockstars! The titans you never thought you would see standing on your side.
ERNIE: Our hands were raw from clapping like thunder.
LEO: You were both there. At EDSA. Alright, I'm going to UP.
ERNIE: Maybe there is something else we can all talk about.
MARTIN: Don't even think about it.
ERNIE: Let me talk to him, Kuya.
MARTIN: You going to talk to him as his tito or his friend?!
LEO: I guess I'll start packing.
MARTIN: You don't know how to do this, Ernesto.
ERNIE: I know what to do.
LEO: Hello? Who's driving me to the airport?
ERNIE: You are on a watch list.
MARTIN: What?
LEO: Wait, actually?
MARTIN: Bakit. Why do they want him?
ERNIE: I should have told you earlier.
MARTIN: Where did you see his name?
ERNIE: I checked on him. I had to.
MARTIN: Where was his name?
LEO: Okay, so this watchlist, is it like a blacklist?
ERNIE: They have a photo of you.
LEO: Is it any good?
ERNIE: It's your photo and then your name: LEOPOLD CABAERO.
LEO: That ... that's incredible. Heaps of my friends have been put on watchlists.
MARTIN: Are you out of your mind?!
ERNIE: Don't be stupid Leo.
LEO: I can use this. People will listen to me if I tell them I'm on it.
MARTIN: How did this happen?
ERNIE: The video he did on extrajudicial killings. I thought maybe after that. It got viewed five hundred thousand times or something.
LEO: Seven hundred thousand times.
ERNIE: Even people at work knew about it! When he mentioned that he might be coming to the Philippines, I paid a friend of mine at the airport to look up his name.

LEO: Sley.
MARTIN: You got someone to hack into a / list?!
ERNIE: I had to do it.
MARTIN: What if they found out?
ERNIE: They fired me.
MARTIN: You told me you were laid off!
ERNIE: I'm glad I did it.
MARTIN: Ang tanga—tanga mo, Ernesto![20]
ERNIE: What if I didn't do it then? Hm?
LEO: I'm not going to be arrested the minute I get off the plane.
ERNIE: You will be.
MARTIN: You're not going anywhere.
LEO: People get put on and off watchlists all the time.
ERNIE: The law can be bent.
LEO: These lists are made to scare people.
MARTIN: Cancel that protest right now.
LEO: No.
MARTIN: Or you leave my house.
ERNIE: Kuya.
MARTIN: You're next. You didn't tell me any of this!
ERNIE: I hadn't really come up with a plan, but it was going to happen.
MARTIN: Mag-ama Talaga kayo!
LEO: I know what I'm doing.
ERNIE: You don't.
LEO: I know people who have vanished, okay? People who have not come back online for days.
ERNIE: It's not the same through your phone, De. They are usernames and emojis. These people were our friends.
MARTIN: Our real, breathing friends. Forty-three of them went missing. They were kids. We studied together through martial law. We were forced to do it by candlelight. Notes went around telling you, warning us who was next. Our lecturers targeted. Our friends, our lovers, our family—gone. One by one. We wear our living every single day.
LEO: But you won. EDSA was incredible.

---

20. You are so stupid, Ernesto.

ERNIE: I wish we won the night Marcos fled for Hawaii.

MARTIN: Marcos still had people controlling the waterboard, the railway, the airlines.

ERNIE: It took years for people to thaw.

MARTIN: Aquino may have won. But the sectors we wanted to work in were still controlled by people that thought we were no-good, loud-mouthed activists.

LEO: There were millions there.

MARTIN: But WE went to Malacañang. We foolishly scaled the gates to take it back.

ERNIE: That night in the palace changed who we were.

MARTIN: Ernie. Please.

ERNIE: He needs to know.

YOUNG ERNIE: KUYA! KUYA!

> YOUNG MARTIN *wanders through the courtyard of Malacañang.*

KUYA, I'M HERE.

YOUNG MARTIN: ERNIE, YOU MADE IT.

YOUNG ERNIE: KUYA, MOVE!

YOUNG MARTIN: COME DOWN HERE.

YOUNG ERNIE: MOVE! OUT OF THE WAY!

> YOUNG MARTIN *is caught in a fast-paced crowd and is knocked to the ground.*
>
> YOUNG ERNIE *fights through crowd to help his brother, lifts him from the floor and brings him to safety.*

SCENE 17: AUDIENCE

2022. May 14. 8 p.m. LEO *is in his room; he films a live reel.*

LEO: With demonstrations being held across the world, there will be protests you can attend. Here's where they are:

Okay for those in Gadigal, groups will be at the Philippine Consulate at Thirty-Three Wentworth Avenue.

Naarm folx, meet at Two-Five-Seven Collins Street.

And for our kapatids in Meanjin. We will meet tomorrow, at eight a.m., King George Square.

This rally is against ALL systems of a government that has been totally controlled by imperialism for literal centuries … and let's not forget the war machine.

Cute.

A combination of flame/heart reactions.

I have literally every reason to do this—

Sorry, we have literally every reason to do this now.

Like, even if you were born here. Or not. Or if your parents were born here.

This is my—

Sorry.

Our fight.

Don't listen to anyone else, if you want to show up. Show up.

Everyone should.

I think.

I don't live in the Philippines. I've grown up here. I was born there but I've never gone back.

I went to an all-boys private school; I have literal privilege. You can watch my video about that—link in my bio.

Tomorrow's rally in Meanjin against 'elected' President Bongbong Marcos, and the normalised cycle of dictatorship he represents … will not be going ahead tomorrow.

A flurry of 'question mark' reactions.

I know this is weird, but right now, I don't really have the capacity to do this.

    BUNSOYBBY *enters.*

BUNSOYBBY: @Bunsoybby! GURL STOP.
LEO: Oh my god, hi! Where have you been?!
BUNSOYBBY: I had to go under.
LEO: Oh my god!
BUNSOYBBY: It's fine. I started getting these really weird messages, and I had to.
LEO: Are you okay?
BUNSOYBBY: Gurl, I'm fine! What are you doing??!!
LEO: My dad and tito think I shouldn't go.

BUNSOYBBY: They don't have a say.
LEO: They were at EDSA, Malacañang, all of it.
BUNSOYBBY: Your content is literally all about harbouring intergenerational trauma.
LEO: I'm not doing it. I'm not protesting, I'm not organising, and I'm not / showing up.
BUNSOYBBY: 'I', 'I', 'I', 'I'! That's all I'm hearing! When did it become about you?
LEO: It's not.
BUNSOYBBY: Then you finish that live, you tell people it's still on and you get ready for tomorrow.
LEO: I mean I'm not really in the mood right now. I sort of found out my dad and my tito were at Malacañang and I need to process / it.
BUNSOYBBY: Oh my GOD. Get over it. You have all this reach, all this influence and you want to pull out now?!
LEO: It isn't my fight. I'm out.
BUNSOYBBY: So you wanna be the activist that cancelled a rally against BBM?! Do you think because you don't have 'capacity', others don't?!
LEO: Well, no.
BUNSOYBBY: These people. This system. This family. They are the reason your dad and your tito are like this. We've been talking since we were like thirteen and all you've said is your dad is cagey as fuck.
LEO: He is.
BUNSOYBBY: BECAUSE OF THE PAST THIRTY-SIX YEARS.
LEO: Okay. Okay I'll do it. I'll do it.
BUNSOYBBY: YES BITCH!
LEO: It's mine. It's all mine.
BUNSOYBBY: GURLLLL! YES!
LEO: I literally could protest right now.
BUNSOYBBY: Okay I think you need to go have fun.
LEO: Like, right now?
BUNSOYBBY: Yeah, first, like, process everything. Then protest tomorrow morning.
LEO: No, like, I should stay home and organise.
BUNSOYBBY: Or go out! Just wear that cute-ass T-shirt your uncle gave you.
LEO: Okay vibe. Where is that fucking shirt!

LEO *looks for the T-shirt.*
BUNSOYBBY: Have you found it?
LEO *continues to search.*
LEO: I'm not going out for long.
BUNSOYBBY: Just have fun!
LEO: I'm broke as fuck right now.
BUNSOYBBY: Oh my god same.

>*In his search around the apartment, which becomes more frantic,* LEO *finds the shirt.*
>
>*Eventually, he finds the money that* ERNIE *gave* MARTIN.

SCENE 18: LOOSE

2022. May 15. Midnight. A pumping queer space. It is totally fabulous.
LEO *dances in pure adulation and comfort.*
YOUNG MARTIN *and* YOUNG ERNIE *appear.*
LEO *begins to peak.*
It is part euphoric, part alarming.
The room spins.
LEO *shares the same space with* YOUNG ERNIE *and* YOUNG MARTIN *in celebration, and they run to the revolution as* MARTIN *and* ERNIE *enter, looking for* LEO.
ERNIE *winks to a few people.*

MARTIN: Ernesto!

>MARTIN *claps at him to focus at the task at hand.*
>
>MARTIN *freezes and tries to leave.*
>
>ERNIE *pulls him back in.*
>
>ERNIE *gestures to his phone.*

ERNIE: It says he's here!
MARTIN: What?!
ERNIE: HE'S IN HERE! Keep looking!

>*The brothers split, looking for* LEO.

The club becomes more vibrant, thumping loudly.

1986 and 2022 share space.

The rhythms of the dance floor and DJ make YOUNG ERNIE *think another stampede is coming.*

The club evolves into Malacañang Palace.

YOUNG ERNIE: HEY! HEY KUYA! UP HERE!
KUYA … KUYA … ! KUYA! KUYA!
Look up! KUYA MARTIN! LOOK UP!
Kuya! KUYA MOVE!
MOVE KUYA!
GET OUT OF THE WAY!

The rumbling grows, and soon the gates of the palace begin to edge forward.

YOUNG ERNIE *jumps down from the balcony, and at that exact moment,* YOUNG MARTIN *awakens out of delirium but is frozen in fear.* ERNIE *manages to push* YOUNG MARTIN *out of the way, just as the crowd moves quickly to seize the palace.*

He saves him.

The dust settles, as YOUNG ERNIE *cradles* YOUNG MARTIN.

YOUNG ERNIE *carries* YOUNG MARTIN *through the palace as a vision of the throne becomes evident.*

LEO *dances like crazy, and takes his shirt off, hurling it to the floor.*

YOUNG ERNIE *picks up* YOUNG MARTIN *and begins to ascend the thrones of Malacañang.*

Slowly, YOUNG MARTIN, YOUNG ERNIE *and* LEO *ascend to the thrones of Malacañang, as* MARTIN *and* ERNIE *enter the space.*

The music dies down, and YOUNG MARTIN, YOUNG ERNIE *and* LEO *are finally on the thrones of Malacañang.*

LEO *passes out.*

SCENE 19: TRUTH

2022. May 15. A hospital waiting room.
ERNIE *waits.*
MARTIN *enters.*

MARTIN: The nurse says he'll be fine.
ERNIE: He passed out, it's nothing. It's happened to me several times before and I'm okay!
MARTIN: He could have died!
ERNIE: Stop protecting him, Martin.
MARTIN: I know how to take care of him. I am his father!
ERNIE: When were you going to tell him? On your deathbed?
MARTIN: I never have to tell him.
ERNIE: Father of the year!
MARTIN: Go back to the Philippines, Ernest.
ERNIE: This is my home now.
MARTIN: You have no say here.
ERNIE: I had the biggest say the day he was born.
MARTIN: You gave up being his father.

Pause.

I knew the minute Ma called me to come to the hospital that he would be mine. I knew you wouldn't have the guts to ask me yourself.
ERNIE: Yes, thank god for you, Martin. Praise Saint Martin of the Railways.
MARTIN: You had no idea what you were doing.
ERNIE: Please, remind me.
MARTIN: You were so high.
ERNIE: Guilty!
MARTIN: When you knocked up that girl from Mindanao.
ERNIE: Uy! That was love.
MARTIN: Decades of living on the edge. Fucking everything that moved. When Ma said you got someone pregnant, I couldn't believe / it.
ERNIE: Yes, yes, bakla! The little gay brother! Come on! Let's all laugh together at how the little gay brother fell in love with a woman!

MARTIN: Are you done?
ERNIE: Continue.
MARTIN: You lived. You had fun. I haven't been intimate with anyone since I was a teenager.

> ERNIE *gasps dramatically.*

I haven't been completely alone!
There's this woman. She works at the station over. I tried calling her station a couple of times. We talked, we've flirted. I don't know if it's flirting.
ERNIE: Look, it probably isn't.
MARTIN: She's lovely though. You'd like her.
ERNIE: I can give you some tips. I was with a woman. Once.

> ERNIE *nudges* MARTIN.

MARTIN: I've had to decide between love and protection.
ERNIE: They're the same.
MARTIN: No. I brought him out here, I put him through the best school. I clothed him. I fed him.
ERNIE: On my dollar.
MARTIN: I wish it was on mine. I had dreams of being the best engineer in the world and because of one stupid night, I end up working at a train station.
ERNIE: I thought you loved it.
MARTIN: It was not my dream!
ERNIE: You're doing a great job with him. The best.
MARTIN: Thank you.
MARTIN: Dati napaka—close namin. So close when he was young.
ERNIE: The sporting years, yes. I remember the photos.

> ERNIE *shudders.*

MARTIN: But now I don't know how to talk to him.

> ERNIE *places his hand on* MARTIN*'s.*

ERNIE: I will talk to him.
MARTIN: No.
ERNIE: Jesus, Kuya you make it so / hard.
MARTIN: *We* will talk to him.
ERNIE: You've raised a genius, maybe he's figured it out by now.

MARTIN: He is, isn't he? It's the way he speaks.
ERNIE: Oh yeah.
MARTIN: It is beautiful.
ERNIE: No idea where he got it from.
　　He's very much your son.
MARTIN: And yours.
ERNIE: When he talks all that political stuff, doesn't it just make you feel like you're there? Like you could just burst?!
MARTIN: I love that boy.
ERNIE: And when he talks about Bongbong.
MARTIN: I know, it's great, isn't it?
ERNIE: You just want to hug him and swing him around and say:
MARTIN/ERNIE: Keep going!

They laugh.

ERNIE: I'm going to stay.

MARTIN accepts.

We saw the same thing, Kuya.
MARTIN: But we walked away different people.

SCENE 20: VOICE

2022. May 15. LEO *stands in Speakers' Corner of King George Square, Brisbane, with a microphone and speaker. Five-hundred people have gathered.*

ERNIE *and* MARTIN *enter.*

MARTIN *goes to leave.*

ERNIE *grabs* MARTIN*'s arm.*

ERNIE: Just watch.
MARTIN: He's not going to U.P.
ERNIE: Fuck no.
MARTIN: And we're going to Outback Steakhouse after this.

　　LEO *steps forward.*

LEO: We refuse to accept the results of the 2022 election!

　　Applause.

And hold serious concerns for the future of the principle democratics—sorry, democratic principles of the Filipino people.

MARTIN and ERNIE watch on, hopeful.

YOUNG MARTIN and YOUNG ERNIE run through King George Square.

They stop.

The older MARTIN and ERNIE acknowledge their younger selves.

YOUNG ERNIE runs through the square, as YOUNG MARTIN and MARTIN look at one another.

YOUNG MARTIN smiles at MARTIN, and gestures toward LEO with his head.

MARTIN looks at YOUNG MARTIN, as he runs past him, to join YOUNG ERNIE in their future.

LEO smiles at his family.

ERNIE walks toward the microphone and takes it from LEO.

MARTIN takes it from ERNIE.

LEO, MARTIN and ERNIE stand together, united.

MARTIN: Good morning. Magandang umaga sa in yong lahat.[21]

The square stops.

Listens.

THE END

---

21. Good morning to you all.

www.ingramcontent.com/pod-product-compliance
Lightning Source LLC
Chambersburg PA
CBHW040305170426
43194CB00022B/2905